Leo Strauss and the Recovery
of "Natural Philosophizing"

SUNY series in the Thought and Legacy of Leo Strauss
———————
Kenneth Hart Green, editor

Leo Strauss and the Recovery of "Natural Philosophizing"

Alberto Ghibellini

Published by State University of New York Press, Albany

© 2024 State University of New York

All rights reserved

Printed in the United States of America

No part of this book may be used or reproduced in any manner whatsoever without written permission. No part of this book may be stored in a retrieval system or transmitted in any form or by any means including electronic, electrostatic, magnetic tape, mechanical, photocopying, recording, or otherwise without the prior permission in writing of the publisher.

Links to third-party websites are provided as a convenience and for informational purposes only. They do not constitute an endorsement or an approval of any of the products, services, or opinions of the organization, companies, or individuals. SUNY Press bears no responsibility for the accuracy, legality, or content of a URL, the external website, or for that of subsequent websites.

For information, contact State University of New York Press, Albany, NY
www.sunypress.edu

Library of Congress Cataloging-in-Publication Data

Name: Ghibellini, Alberto, author.
Title: Leo Strauss and the recovery of "natural philosophizing" / Alberto Ghibellini.
Description: Albany : State University of New York Press, [2024] | Series: SUNY series in the Thought and Legacy of Leo Strauss | Includes bibliographical references and index.
Identifiers: ISBN 9781438498614 (hardcover : alk. paper) | ISBN 9781438498621 (ebook) | ISBN 9781438498607 (pbk. : alk. paper)
Further information is available at the Library of Congress.

Contents

Abbreviations		vii
Preface and Acknowledgments		xi
Introduction	"What Is Nature?" Leo Strauss and Socrates's Turn to *logoi*	1
Chapter I	Leo Strauss, Carl Schmitt, and the Search for the "Order of Human Things"	31
Chapter II	Ancient Liberalism vs. Modern Liberalism	49
Chapter III	The "Second Cave" and Historical Consciousness in the Correspondence of Leo Strauss and Gerhard Krüger	69
Chapter IV	Natural Right in Strauss and Krüger's Exchange	89
Chapter V	Strauss and the "Politicization of Philosophy"	105
Chapter VI	The "Pit beneath the Cave" and the Problem of Natural Right	141
Conclusion		183
Notes		189
Works Cited		237
Index of Names		247

Abbreviations

AAPL   Leo Strauss, *The Argument and the Action of Plato's* Laws (Chicago: University of Chicago Press, 1975)

CM   Leo Strauss, *The City and Man* (Chicago: University of Chicago Press, 1978)

EW   Leo Strauss, *The Early Writings (1921–1932)*, ed. Michael Zank (Albany, NY: State University of New York Press, 2002)

FPP   Peter Emberley and Barry Cooper, eds., *Faith and Political Philosophy: The Correspondence between Leo Strauss and Eric Voegelin, 1934–1964* (Columbia, MO: University of Missouri Press, 2004)

GN   Leo Strauss, "German Nihilism," *Interpretation. A Journal of Political Philosophy*, 26 (1999): 352–78

GS1   Leo Strauss, *Gesammelte Schriften, Band 1*, Dritte Auflage, hrsg. von Heinrich Meier (Stuttgart–Weimar: Verlag J. B. Metzler, 2008)

GS2   Leo Strauss, *Gesammelte Schriften, Band 2*, Zweite Auflage, hrsg. von Heinrich Meier (Stuttgart–Weimar: Verlag J. B. Metzler, 2013)

GS3   Leo Strauss, *Gesammelte Schriften, Band 3*, Zweite Auflage, hrsg. von Heinrich und Wiebke Meier (Stuttgart–Weimar: Verlag J. B. Metzler, 2008)

HCR   Leo Strauss, *Hobbes's Critique of Religion and Related Writings*, ed. Gabriel Bartlett and Svetozar Minkov (Chicago: University of Chicago Press, 2011)

HPP   Leo Strauss and Joseph Cropsey, eds., *History of Political Philosophy* (Chicago: Rand McNally, 1972)

JPCM   Leo Strauss, *Jewish Philosophy and the Crisis of Modernity*, ed. Kenneth Hart Green (Albany, NY: State University of New York Press, 1997)

LAM   Leo Strauss, *Liberalism Ancient and Modern* (Chicago: University of Chicago Press, 1995)

LIGPP   Leo Strauss, "The Living Issues of German Postwar Philosophy," in Heinrich Meier, *Leo Strauss and the Theologico-Political Problem* (Cambridge: Cambridge University Press, 2006), 115–39

NIPPP   Leo Strauss, "On a New Interpretation of Plato's Political Philosophy," *Social Research* XIII, no. 3 (1946): 326–67

NRH   Leo Strauss, *Natural Right and History* (Chicago: University of Chicago Press, 1953; 7th impression, 1971)

OMPT   Leo Strauss, "The Origin of Modern Political Thought," in TNRH, 163–206

OT   Leo Strauss, *On Tyranny. Including the Strauss-Kojève Correspondence*, Revised and Expanded Edition, ed. Victor Gourevitch and Michael S. Roth (Chicago: University of Chicago Press, 2000)

PAW   Leo Strauss, *Persecution and the Art of Writing* (Chicago: University of Chicago Press, 1988)

PL   Leo Strauss, *Philosophy and Law. Contributions to the Understanding of Maimonides and His Predecessors*, trans. Eve Adler (Albany, NY: State University of New York Press, 1995)

PPH   Leo Strauss, *The Political Philosophy of Hobbes. Its Basis and Its Genesis*, trans. Elsa M. Sinclair (Chicago: University of Chicago Press, 1963)

R   Martin D. Yaffe and Richard S. Ruderman, eds., *Reorientation: Leo Strauss in the 1930s* (New York: Palgrave Macmillan, 2014)

RCPR   Leo Strauss, *The Rebirth of Classical Political Rationalism*, ed. Thomas Pangle (Chicago: University of Chicago Press, 1989)

RR	Leo Strauss, "Reason and Revelation," in Heinrich Meier, *Leo Strauss and the Theologico-Political Problem* (Cambridge: Cambridge University Press, 2006), 141–80
SA	Leo Strauss, *Socrates and Aristophanes* (Chicago: University of Chicago Press, 1980)
SCR	Leo Strauss, *Spinoza's Critique of Religion*, trans. Elsa M. Sinclair (Chicago: University of Chicago Press, 1997)
SPPP	Leo Strauss, *Studies in Platonic Political Philosophy*, ed. Thomas Pangle (Chicago: University of Chicago Press, 1983)
TM	Leo Strauss, *Thoughts on Machiavelli* (Chicago: University of Chicago Press, 1978)
TNRH	J. A. Colen and Svetozar Minkov, eds., *Toward* Natural Right and History. *Lectures and Essays by Leo Strauss, 1937–1946* (Chicago: University of Chicago Press, 2018)
TWM	Leo Strauss, "The Three Waves of Modernity," in *An Introduction to Political Philosophy: Ten Essays by Leo Strauss*, ed. Hilail Gildin (Detroit, MI: Wayne State University Press, 1989), 81–98
WPP	Leo Strauss, *What Is Political Philosophy? And Other Studies* (Chicago: University of Chicago Press, 1988)
XS	Leo Strauss, *Xenophon's Socrates* (South Bend, IN: St. Augustin's Press, 1998)
XSD	Leo Strauss, *Xenophon's Socratic Discourse. An Interpretation of the* Oeconomicus (South Bend, IN: St. Augustin's Press, 1998)

Preface and Acknowledgments

Although broader in scope than originally planned, the present book is the outcome of a research project entitled "Leo Strauss on Natural Right" I started while visiting the Leo Strauss Center and the John U. Nef Committee on Social Thought at the University of Chicago in the fall of 2014. As the book's title shows, its main subject is now *natural philosophizing* rather than *natural right*. For reasons that should become clear in the next chapters, such a broadening of the book's main theme has become necessary in order to try to better understand the presuppositions of Strauss's philosophical (as distinct from a merely historical or antiquarian) interest in natural right. For closer inspection shows that the latter is only a piece of the puzzle of his whole thought, whose crux is nature understood as the cornerstone of genuine philosophizing.

This being the case, the task arises, first and foremost, to explain what *nature* means in Strauss's account. This is what the following introduction attempts to do by relying on both writings published by Strauss and some of his letters, notably to Karl Löwith, where this theme emerges as particularly prominent.

After such a preliminary explication, in the subsequent chapters Strauss's understanding of the question of nature is examined in depth and analyzed in different contexts. Chapter I draws from a paper I presented at the John Marshall Lecture and Seminar Series at Boston College, which was published in *History of Political Thought* (XL, no. 1 [spring 2019]: 138–57). It focuses on Strauss's "Notes on Carl Schmitt, *The Concept of the Political*," where Strauss's "change of orientation" found "its first expression," as he himself famously put it, and his distancing from "Hobbes's decisionism" (and from decisionism of any kind) emerges as clear and definitive. In this chapter, I argue that the cornerstones of such a distancing, and of Strauss's criticism of modern liberalism as a whole, are *nature* and *philosophy*, which he begins to see as indissolubly linked to Plato's approach.

Expanding on a paper I originally presented at the Philosophy Department of the University of Massachusetts, Boston, chapter II digs deeper into Strauss's criticism of modern liberalism and his attempt to unearth and revitalize an *ancient* version of it. Even in this case, the key role played by the concept of nature in that regard and its paramount importance for genuine philosophizing according to Strauss is underscored. Strauss's anti-modern stance is also duly emphasized and explained, even when it comes to dealing with some of his most controversial traits, such as his juvenile infatuation with Nietzsche and his ephemeral leanings towards Italian fascism.

Chapter III (which draws from a paper delivered at the Yale Political Theory Workshop and then published in *The Review of Metaphysics* [LXXIII, no. 2 (December 2019): 285–309]) explores the genesis, and tries to explain the meaning, of the "second, 'unnatural' cave," as Strauss called it, and its relationship with "historical consciousness." The setting of such exploration and attempt of explanation is represented by the correspondence between Strauss and Gerhard Krüger, where the discussion of the abovementioned topics emerges as particularly clear and revealing. Guided by Strauss's exchange with Krüger, but also relying on some writings by Strauss from the early 1930s, the chapter also emphasizes the link he establishes between the second cave, historicism, and biblical tradition, which prove to play a prominent role in negating the presuppositions lying at the basis of the "first, 'natural' cave" (the Platonic one) and of natural philosophizing more in general.

Previously published as a contribution to Susan Meld Shell (ed.), *The Strauss-Krüger Correspondence. Returning to Plato through Kant* (Cham, CH: Palgrave Macmillan, 2018, 181–98), chapter IV insists on the same correspondence to focus, this time, on the question of natural right. Besides revealing the difference of perspective characterizing the two authors— the ultimately Christian-believer influenced by Augustin (Krüger), the philosopher inspired by Plato (Strauss)—this chapter shows that Strauss's attempt to recover the quest for natural right, and for a standard more in general, is to be regarded as a distinctly rationalistic one that takes its inspiration from Socrates's second sailing.

Chapter V, whose main subject is Strauss's interpretation of what he described as the "politicization of philosophy," draws from a paper I delivered at the 2015 Annual Weissbourd Conference, *Theory & Practice*, which was held at the University of Chicago. In addition to underscoring the crucial role of the concept of nature in Strauss's interpretation of philosophy as an ultimately theoretical life, in this chapter, among other things, the influence of biblical revelation on both the crisis of that concept and the resulting politicization of philosophy is emphasized and explained. This leads to a critical reassessment of the presence in Strauss's thought of elements that can be ascribed to (a weak version of) the secularization theory—a theory Strauss distanced himself from since the mid-1940s despite having previously embraced it, at least to some degree.

Chapter VI, which brings the book to its conclusion, is the expanded version of the Ernest Fortin Memorial Lecture I delivered at Boston College in March of 2018 and draws on a paper I had previously presented, in June of 2015, at the Leo Strauss Center at the University of Chicago. Its main focus is the relation between the possibility of searching for natural right (and of revitalizing genuine philosophy as a whole) on the one hand, and the reattainment of the first, natural cave, with all this entails, on the other. By reviewing all the major writings, whether published or left unpublished by Strauss, where the question of the second, unnatural cave is dealt with, in this final chapter, as well as in the following conclusion, I aim to show that his philosophical approach is to be regarded as more decisively rationalistic, despite the *zetetic skepticism* it results in, than it is often conceded. I also suggest that the basis for such a rationalistic approach is the recovery of a concept of nature seen as a standard—a concept that becomes accessible again only once the Platonic (not by accident "natural") cave has been recovered by means of historical deconstruction.

As the just mentioned unpublished writings and previous reference to Strauss's letters show, in this book I by no means make use of Strauss's published books and essays only. The following introduction is just a first example of this tendency. Lest this choice of mine be criticized from the outset, not to say rejected, it is worth underscoring that Strauss himself, while interpreting the authors of the past, did not refrain from resorting to their private letters (if available) in order to better understand their sometimes publicly disguised or concealed thought.[1] This interpretive path is all the more reasonable in the case of heterodox thinkers who happened to be in quite an open conflict with the dominant views of their time. In light of Strauss's criticism of what he described as "modern liberalism," whose philosophical reach goes much beyond that of a mere political doctrine, it seems to me that he himself can be classified as one of those thinkers.[2] If so, an extensive use of Strauss's unpublished writings and, notably, private letters is to be regarded as an indispensable means to gain a better understanding of his genuine, deeper thought, especially if the views he puts forward in private are echoed in his published writings.

Having arrived at this point, I feel obliged (if by everything but a burdensome duty, to be sure) to thank all those who have helped me begin, carry on, and complete this book project. My first thought, not only for chronological reasons, goes to Nathan Tarcov who, as the director of the Leo Strauss Center at the University of Chicago, invited me as a visiting scholar for the 2014–2015 academic year and provided me, with the cooperation of the associate director Gayle McKeen and the then chair of the Committee on Social Thought Robert Pippin, with substantial support and precious advice during my stay in Chicago. Besides sharing his scholarship with generosity and showing genuine interest in my research, professor Tarcov was also instrumental in helping me receive financial support for it from the Earhart Foundation, whose then director of program Montgomery Brown I also wish to heartfully thank.

As I have underscored, most of the following chapters draw from papers I was invited to present at different venues, a few of which have already been published. While thanking the concerned editors and publishers for their kind permission to reprint the latter, I wish to express my gratitude to all those who invited me to share my research results and, thereby, stimulated me to put them into a more organic form. Following the order of the chapters, my warmest thanks go to Susan Meld Shell, Ajume Wingo, Steven Smith and Bryan Garsten, the Society of Fellows in the Liberal Arts at the University of Chicago, the Leo Strauss Center of the same university, and the Ernest Fortin Memorial Foundation in the person of Martha Rice Martini. With reference to my Fortin Lecture, I also wish to express my gratitude to Daniel Tanguay, who acted as my discussant providing me with insightful feedback.

My protracted stay in the US, and the further research I was thereby able to conduct, would not have been possible without the involvement of some scholars I am deeply indebted to: Harvey Mansfield, who invited me to join the Department of Government at Harvard University as a visiting scholar for the 2015–2016 and 2016–2017 academic years; Susan Meld Shell, who addressed me the same invitation on behalf of the Political Science Department at Boston College for the 2017–2018 academic year; and (last but not least) Bernhardt Trout, who hired me as a lecturer at the MIT Ethics, Engineering and Entrepreneurship Initiative for the whole three-year period, thereby enabling me to accept those invitations. Both professors Mansfield and Shell did not limit themselves to inviting me (the latter even to contribute a chapter to the above-mentioned book on the Strauss-Krüger correspondence she edited), but also supported my research by sharing their scholarship with me and reviewing some of the materials that have merged in this book. Professor Trout, on his part, always showed deep interest in my research and stimulated it in friendly talks and by actively attending the lectures I delivered during my stay in the Boston area.

On this occasion, I cannot forget my colleagues at MIT: Daniel Doneson, Rory Schacter, Derek Mess, Kathryn Sensen, and Peter Hansen. I am greatly indebted to the first two for the countless talks on Strauss and related matters we had after class and to the second, in particular, for his impeccable reviews of many of my papers.

Special thanks go to Svetozar Minkov, whose friendship and scholarship have always been most important to me and without whom I would not have been hired by MIT, which would have prevented me from extending my stay and research in the US. To put it simply, his support and advice turned out to be crucial at different stages of my book project and their effect has gone well beyond the latter's limits.

Warm thanks also go to Lynn Phalen for her always friendly, timely, and excellent reviews of most of the materials that now constitute this book. It is fair to say that without her help my task would have been much harder, not to say almost unbearable.

I also express my gratitude to all those who, either on the occasion of my lectures or in private exchanges, helped me develop my research and bring my book project to its completion. Besides those who, by their questions and comments at my talks, compelled me to deepen my understanding of the respective issues, I here wish to mention Giovanni Giorgini (to whom I am indebted for much more than only this), Nasser Behnegar, the late Robert Faulkner, Raimondo Cubeddu, Carlo Altini, Marco Menon, Charlotte Sieber-Gasser, Anna Schmidt, Clifford and Alexander Orwin, Ralph Lerner, Walter Lapini, Vincenzo Costa, Giulio De Ligio, Mauro Farnesi Camellone, Silvia Guslandi, Darren Nah, as well as the two anonymous readers at SUNY Press who reviewed my manuscript.

Finally, on a more personal note, I take the opportunity to publicly thank my family. During my long stays in the US the fatherly presence for my two children had to become merely virtual and even when we were together my research often so absorbed me that it was as if I were not entirely there. My wife, needless to say, had to bear the heaviest brunt of all this. Not only for this reason, I am deeply grateful and dedicate this book to her.

A.G.
Monterotondo di Gavi
August 2023

Introduction

"What Is Nature?"
Leo Strauss and Socrates's Turn to *logoi*

> Wir sind natürliche Wesen, die unter unnatürlichen Bedingungen leben und denken—wir müssen uns auf unser natürliches Wesen besinnen, um die unnatürlichen Bedingungen denkend aufzuheben.
>
> [We are natural beings who live and think under unnatural conditions—we must recall our natural being in order to remove the unnatural conditions by thought.]
>
> —GS3, 650[1]

Strauss's thought is characterized by a clear insistence on the concept of nature.[2] Not only in his magnum opus *Natural Right and History*, but also in most if not all of his other works, does nature, whether explicitly or implicitly, play a pivotal conceptual role, its occurrences being numerous.

This distinctive feature of Strauss's approach becomes easier to understand once due attention is devoted to the fact that, in his account, the discovery (and preservation) of the concept of nature amounts to a sine qua non for philosophy.[3] It seems no overstatement to claim that in Strauss's view, at least after his "change of orientation"[4] at the beginning of the 1930s, nature and philosophy stand or fall together. Such an assumption, as just observed, indeed helps the interpreter justify the many references to nature that are scattered throughout Strauss's opera given his attempt to revitalize philosophy against its historicistic reductio ad absurdum. It forces the same interpreter, on the other hand, to raise the question as to the meaning of nature in Strauss's philosophical perspective—a meaning that does not always emerge as entirely clear at first sight.

"What is nature?," hence, arises as one of the most urgent questions to ask if an adequate understanding of Strauss's thought, focused as it is on that very concept, is to be gained. Strauss himself, as we will see, explicitly raises this question at least once in his writings. Before analyzing his remarks in that instance, it is however worth explaining, to begin with, how and why such a question comes up in his philosophical path. A suitable manner to do so is to take into account some of the letters Strauss wrote to his lifelong friend Karl Löwith.[5] Despite ultimately diverging as to the interpretation of what nature (and therefore philosophy) means,[6] their whole correspondence remarkably shows the importance of such a question in Strauss's, as well as Löwith's account. For this reason, while referring the readers to their entire exchange in light of its overall significance and the various important matters it touches upon,[7] we will here comment, for the sake of our argument, on those letters where the question of nature arises as crucial.

I

The first is an early letter of December 30, 1932,[8] where Strauss comments on Löwith's essay *Kierkegaard und Nietzsche*,[9] which his friend had previously sent him along with another work of his on Karl Jaspers. The reason why Strauss finds the essay particularly interesting is that it shows him, once more, Löwith's remarkable "resoluteness [*Entschiedenheit*]" when it comes to raising "the question of the *nature* of the human being, of what is *universally* human [*die Frage nach der* Natur *des Menschen, nach dem* Allgemein-*Menschlichen*]."[10] This resoluteness, which Strauss evinces from the way Löwith frames his research question at the beginning of the essay, is however neglected, in his view, in its continuation. For despite beginning by asking, "What is the human being, and what has become of him? [*Was ist der Mensch, und was ist aus ihm geworden*]," which for Strauss should lead to interpret the answer to the first question as a "universal, *eternal* standard [*allgemeiner,* ewiger *Massstab*]" whereby the second question should be gauged, Löwith drops such a genuinely philosophical implication of his questioning. By contrast, he carries out his argument by affirming "the variability of the human nature [*die Wandelbarkeit . . . der menschlichen Natur*]."[11] In light of this apparent inconsistency, Strauss asks his friend: "What do you mean, thus, by your question concerning *the nature of the human being?*" "You understand 'nature' in opposition to unnaturality [*Unnatur*], i.e., to the unnaturality of Christianity," he adds, to observe that "this means that you too—not unlike Nietzsche—understand this concept only 'polemically and reactively.'"[12]

In fact, despite the similarity with Nietzsche, Löwith's exposure to Kierkegaard's existentialism (not to mention Heidegger's) makes his case even worse: "Admittedly, you now go beyond Nietzsche in that you also consider what is meant by 'existence,' so for you the question of human nature [*die Frage nach der Natur des Menschen*] turns into the question of the one human being in whom both 'life' and 'existence' lie [*die Frage nach dem einen Menschenwesen . . . in dem sowohl 'Leben' wie 'Existez' liegt*]." By doing so, Löwith "even widen[s] the polemic" according to Strauss. As a result, he does not "come to an unpolemical, 'pure and whole' question [*eine unpolemische, 'integre' Frage*],"[13] as Strauss, instead, aims to.

In Strauss's account, such an attainment is impossible as long as one follows Löwith who, in his essay, takes his bearings from "the extreme stage of the 19th century." By contrast, the only available path towards such an "unpolemical, 'pure and whole' question" is, in his view, the recovery of an original and genuine way of questioning:

> You yourself observe that it is always a matter of *rehabilitations* [*Rehabilitierungen*]: we want to repeat something lost, to unearth something buried. But what is lost is searched for again, is desired from what is presently actual [*Aber das Verlorene wird wiedergesucht, wird desideriert vom Gegenwärtig-Wirklichen her*]. Therefore, one affirms [*bejaht*] that which was negated by Hegel, and generally by modern philosophy [*das von Hegel, allgemein von der modernen Philosophie Negierte*], as it has been understood in that negation [*so wie es in dieser Negation verstanden worden ist*]: the original dimension [*die ursprüngliche Dimension*] is by no means achieved.[14]

The problem therefore arises how this "original dimension" can be recovered. In this regard, Strauss provides important indications in the continuation of his letter. After underscoring that for Löwith himself the possibility of an "unbiased knowledge [*unbefangene Erkenntnis*] of the human being" is in question, which however implies that such knowledge is currently unavailable for him as well, he observes:

Unbiasedness could not be in question for us if we were not "somehow" aware of it. What is to be done? It seems to me that we must follow, unconditionally follow, the feeble glimmer that the word "unbiasedness" gives us [*wir müssen dem schwachen Schimmer, den das Wort "Unbefangenheit" uns gibt, folgen*]; we must take wholly seriously the suspicion against our bias [*Befangenheit*]. The bias we mean consists in being trapped in the Christian tradition and in the polemic against this tradition [*Die Befangenheit, die wir meinen, ist die Befangenheit in der christlichen Tradition und in der Polemik gegen diese Tradition*]. From this circle of polemic and counter-polemic we can however get out only if we are guided by a positive, concrete *view* of nature [*positive, konkrete* Anschauung *von Natur*] that is not immediately construed, once again, in a polemical manner [*die nicht schon wieder gleich polemisch ausgelegt wird*]. Only pre-Christian, i.e., Greek philosophy fulfills this desideratum.[15]

Löwith, however, firmly rejects Strauss's approach: "There are no such things as an *immediate* being and an immediate view of man [*es gibt gar nicht ein* unmittelbares *Sein des Menschen und eine unmittelbare Anschauung vom Menschen*]."[16] In his account, "taking the 'view' of the Greeks [*die 'Anschauung' der Griechen*] for an absolute standard [*absoluter Massstab*] is unacceptable,"[17] and such an "entirely traditional" belief in the "unbiasedness of the *Greek* 'view' "[18] makes Strauss much more historically conditioned than him. The same goes for the attempt to gain a " 'whole and pure' knowledge [*'integres' Wissen*]" by recovering the Greeks that characterizes Strauss's perspective, whose quest for "integrity [*Integrität*]" he assumes to be motivated by an "extreme 'moral' prejudice [*höchst 'moralisches' Vorurteil*]."[19]

However exaggerated—if nothing else, Strauss was never an "extreme moralist," nor was he an "Orthodox Jew," as Löwith temporarily believed[20]—the latter's remarks about Strauss's "historicizing"[21] of his own philosophical path by promoting the ancient Greeks' "view" of nature to the role of an "absolute standard" prove to be by no means amiss. Strauss already concedes this in a letter he sent to his friend shortly afterwards where he hints at the legitimacy of doubts concerning his historical approach. In this letter, he begins by claiming that Nietzsche's immoralism ultimately amounts to a "*rediscovery* [wieder*entdeckung*] of the *original* ideal of humanity, of the ideal of manliness (courage),"[22] which, however,

Nietzsche does not limit himself to acknowledging, but polemically affirms to counteract its negation by "the Enlightenment"—as Strauss "prudently" contends against Nietzsche's own insistence on the role of Platonism, as well as Christianity, in that respect. Strauss then goes on to explain that, in his account, there is no need to stop at the "*antithesis* between courage and knowledge"[23] that stems from Nietzsche's polemical reinterpretation of philosophy against its traditional view: "Since I got to know Plato's *Laws*, it has become clear to me that this is *not* necessary, that if certain Platonic doctrines are remembered, *Nietzsche's* questions, and thus *our* questions, arise more easily, clearly and originally."[24] Having added that subsequent observations concerning medieval philosophy have also convinced him of the opportunity to "make an attempt" with Plato, Strauss finally points out: "The abstract historical doubts are known to me, but I believe that at the end they will come up differently from the beginning. Long story short: I must see if I 'get through' it. Once I have made my emendation of Nietzsche by means of my interpretation of Hobbes plausible to you, my 'Platonizing' will no longer appear to you as 'romantic' as it now does."[25]

Strauss's attempt to recover a "positive, concrete *view* of nature" through Plato by "historicizing" his own philosophical approach emerges in greater clarity—even when it comes to laying bare its presuppositions— in a *post scriptum* he added to a subsequent letter dated June 23, 1935.[26] Commenting on *Philosophy and Law*, whose subject Löwith openly admits to be unfamiliar with, he had written to Strauss:

> As foreign as that is to me, I nonetheless admire the single-minded energy and tenacity with which you, in everything you think and do, through a masterful use of polemical alternatives, press your fundamental thought, with compact and strict consistency, to the point where the problem proves to be unsolvable, and as solvable only through transformation of the systematic question into historical analysis; thereby you (like Krüger) presuppose that one can render the modern—Enlightenment—presuppositions inoperable by historical deconstruction [*historische Destruktion*]—which *I* do not believe—*unless* this historical deconstruction is merely a theoretical method of presentation, while in reality the tradition of philosophizing under this tradition's religious "law" [*die Tradition des Philosophierens unter deren religiösem "Gesetz"*] (= revelation) is still alive in you yourself; this not in the vague,

intellectual-historical sense of a *so-called* living tradition, but in the special and determined sense of a still-being-at-home [*Nochzuhausesein*] in orthodox Judaism.[27]

To these remarks (which, apart from the hint at Strauss's alleged religious belief, prove to be quite insightful), Strauss first replies with a summary of Löwith's argument, which reinterprets the religious undertones of his friend's interpretation in a distinctly philosophical perspective: "You contest whether it is possible to bring the systematic question over into historical analysis, *unless* 'this historical deconstruction is merely an historical method of presentation, while in reality' the *old* way of thinking is still alive in the analyst."[28] Then, he adds straightforwardly:

> This I willingly concede; but I believe you too must concede that this condition is fulfilled with all of us, because all of us indeed—are men, and do not live and breathe and also perform a few other, "higher" functions differently than our—not however "animal-like"—ancestors. We are natural beings [*natürliche Wesen*] who live and think under unnatural conditions [*unnatürliche Bedingungen*]—we must recall our natural being in order to remove the unnatural conditions by thought [*wir müssen uns auf unser natürliches Wesen besinnen, um die unnatürlichen Bedingungen denkend aufzuheben*].[29]

Strauss's conclusion of his *post scriptum* is also quite revealing regarding his attempt to rediscover, by way of historical deconstruction, a truly original philosophical perspective. In his letter, Löwith had declared his intention to overcome modern nihilism by attempting a recovery of the "Stoic—Epicurean—Skeptic—Cynic"[30] schools of thought. Exhorting his friend to be more radical in his approach, Strauss first replies: "But these late-ancient philosophies—even the Skeptics—are much too *dogmatic* for you, especially, to be able to stay with them, and not to have to return to the ancestor of them all, Socrates, who was *no* dogmatic."[31] Then, he points out: "The so-called Platonism is only a flight from Plato's problems"—a comment hinting at his reinterpretation of the Platonic Socrates as a "zetetic sceptic" that will become a key feature of his mature interpretation.[32]

The fact remains, at any rate, that the recovery of Plato's problems by means of a *"historische Destruktion"* that, unlike Heidegger's, aims to unearth the conditions for a genuinely ahistorical, natural philosophizing, is indicated by Strauss as the only possible way out of modern nihilism.[33] For this reason, he indeed willingly borrows Löwith's description of Nietzsche's philosophical goal as a "repetition of the ancients at the peak of modernity."[34] In doing so, however, he also distances himself from Nietzsche due to the polemical character of his account, as we have already underscored.[35] Regardless of Löwith's perplexity concerning the legitimacy of his effort,[36] Strauss's return to the ancients—notably to their "positive, concrete *view* of nature"—aims to be an unbiased, detached recognition (*Anerkennung*) rather than a polemical and historically conditioned affirmation (*Bejahung*).[37]

In their correspondence, Strauss's departure from Nietzsche's "repetition of antiquity at the peak of modernity" comes up, for example, in a late letter of April 2, 1962. In it, taking up Löwith's terms again, he distinguishes Nietzsche's "repetition"—which "constitutes an insoluble difficulty" due to its entanglement in modern presuppositions as is shown by the contradiction between eternal return and freedom—from an "unqualified return to the principles of antiquity," which arguably comes closer to his own unpolemical approach.[38] As Strauss famously wrote in the almost coeval introduction to *The City and Man*: "Only we living today can possibly find a solution to the problems of today. But an adequate understanding of the *principles* as elaborated by the classics may be the indispensable starting point for an adequate analysis, to be achieved by us, of present-day society in its peculiar character, and for the wise application, to be achieved by us, of these *principles* to our task."[39]

The main issue in this regard, thus, boils down to the meaning of those *principles*. By referring to Strauss's letter of December 30, 1932, we have already emphasized that what he aims towards, in order to come, unlike Löwith, to an "unpolemical, 'pure and whole' question," is a "positive, concrete *view* of nature that is not immediately construed, once again, in a polemical manner."[40] Strauss resumes this key issue in a letter to Löwith of August 15, 1946. Among the various relevant questions he touches upon in it,[41] he once again addresses the problem of nature and its understanding, this time in connection with the opposition between "philosophy and history."[42]

After reading Strauss's review essay on John Wild's book *Plato's Theory of Man*,[43] Löwith had expressed his bewilderment at Strauss's "historicizing" approach to a genuinely philosophical thinking: "Is your differentiation of historical epochs . . . according to their proximity to truth and its form not still, precisely, a historical reflection, so that your tendency to an in principle de-historicization of the question of truth is still, indeed, a modern approach and you can reach your goal without historical 'deconstruction' just as little as Heidegger?"[44]

Replying to this question, Strauss does not only distance himself from Heidegger's *Destruktion* due to its complete replacement of nature by historicity, as we have already emphasized. Moving from an appraisal of what he and Löwith share regarding the question of historicity, he also observes:

> We agree that today we need historical reflection—only I assert that this is neither a progress nor a fate to submit to with resignation, but is an unavoidable means for the overcoming of modernity. One cannot overcome modernity with modern means, but only insofar as we also are still *natural beings with natural understanding* [natürliche Wesen mit natürlichem Verstand]; but the way of thought of natural understanding [*die Denkmittel des natürlichen Verstandes*] has been lost to us, and simple people [*einfache Leute*] such as myself and those like me are not able to regain it through their own resources: we attempt to *learn* from the ancients.[45]

The emphasis on simplicity, despite Löwith's irony and persistent doubts about the possibility to retrieve an ahistorical paradigm of nature along with its natural understanding,[46] proves to be no mere rhetorical device. As Strauss points out in a letter of August 20, 1946:

> It is astounding that we (although up to a certain point we understand one another very well) above and beyond that understand one another so little—it is astounding considering the importance of the points at which we understand one another. Where do our ways part? I really think that you on the decisive point are not *simple, simple-minded* [einfach, simpel] enough, while I believe that I am. You do not take the simple sense [*einfacher Sinn*] of philosophy literally enough: philosophy is the attempt to replace opinions about the whole with genuine knowledge of the whole. For you, philosophy is nothing but the self-understanding or self-interpretation of man, and, that means, naturally of historically conditioned man, if not of the individual. That is, speaking Platonically, you reduce philosophy to description of the interior decoration of the respective cave,

of the cave (= historical existence) which then can no longer be seen *as* a cave. You remain bogged down in idealism-historicism. And you interpret the history of philosophy in such a way that it confirms the unavoidability of historical relativity, or of the rule of prejudices, asserted by you. You identify philosophy as such with "Weltanschauung"; you therefore make philosophy radically depend on the respective "culture."⁴⁷

Strauss could hardly have uttered clearer, weightier, and more explicit remarks. In the following chapters, we will try to explain their meaning in greater detail, notably when it comes to the Platonic cave as distinct from a second, unnatural cave.⁴⁸ Here we must limit ourselves to asking: how can we be so "simple [*einfach*]" as to take the original meaning of philosophy literally enough and—we should add—achieve a "positive, concrete *view* [Anschauung] of nature that is not immediately construed, once again, in a polemical manner"?⁴⁹ In other words, what can we "attempt to *learn* from the ancients" for that purpose? If we stick to Strauss's letter to Löwith of August 20, 1946, we can find an answer that, as we will see by referring to some of his published books, proves to be of crucial importance.

Later in this letter Strauss takes up the question of nature again, this time under the heading "return to the natural view [*Rückkehr zur natürlichen Ansicht*]."⁵⁰ In his previous letter of August 18, 1946, Löwith had argued that historicity is too inherent to humanity to allow for a meaningful search for a natural paradigm. In addition, he had pointed out that grasping such a paradigm in natural phenomena is ultimately impossible.⁵¹

By referring, in particular, to the second objection, Strauss observes: "You confuse the Greek man-in-the-street, and as far as I am concerned also the Greek poet, for the Greek *philosopher*. (It does not make things better that Nietzsche often—not always: *On the Genealogy of Morals*, 'What Is the Meaning of Ascetic Ideals?'—made the same mistake)."⁵² "Plato and Aristotle," Strauss continues borrowing some of the words Löwith had used in his letter, "never believed that 'stars, heaven, sea, earth, generation, birth, and death give' them 'natural answers to their unnatural questions.'" Then, he concludes his comments on this matter with the following remark, whose significance will become clearer in the next paragraphs: "Plato 'flees,' as is well known, from these 'things' (πράγματα) into the λόγοι, because the πράγματα give no answer *directly*, but are mute riddles."⁵³

II

With this reference to Socrates's famous turn from the direct experience of natural phenomena to the *logoi* (discourses) that are made about them—namely, to his *deuteros plous* or "second sailing"[54]—Strauss's correspondence with Löwith concerning the question of nature, apart from some further sporadic references to it, is virtually finished. We are therefore left with the impression that, if a genuine path towards a "positive, concrete *view* of nature [*positive, konkrete* Anschauung *von Natur*]" is to be found, and therewith an "unpolemical, 'pure and whole' question" is to be restored, there must be a link between the discourses or *logoi* on the one hand, and nature or *physis* on the other. Although arguably implicit in the concept of "*view* [Anschauung] of nature,"[55] this link is never made explicit in the correspondence. Nonetheless, there are some published works of Strauss's where it is clearly underscored.

An example to consider first, also for chronological reasons, is Strauss's book *The Political Philosophy of Hobbes. Its Basis and Its Genesis*. As is well known, even if Strauss had already completed its original German manuscript in 1935, the book was published for the first time in English in 1936 and only about three decades later in German.[56] For our purpose, the eighth and final chapter of this book turns out to be of the utmost importance, since it is there that Strauss establishes an insightful comparison between the new science of politics introduced by Hobbes and the "old" one represented by Plato and Aristotle.

It is also worth observing that in Strauss's view this conflation of Plato and Aristotle, at least from such an "epistemological" standpoint, can be misleading. For Strauss convincingly explains that in his search for exactness Hobbes ends up agreeing with Plato against Aristotle and his view of political science as valid only *pachylos kai typo*, "roughly and in outline."[57] Despite this agreement concerning the need for exactness, which leads him to replace Aristotle with Plato as "the best of the ancient philosophers" in his mature assessment, Hobbes however departs from Plato's rationalism because the latter becomes untenable if one starts, as Hobbes does, from the premises of the "impotence of reason [*Ohnmacht der Vernunft*]" and the "wrongness of opinions as such [*prinzipielle Verkehrtheit der Meinung als solcher*]."[58] Hobbes therefore (partially inspired by Descartes in this regard[59]) inaugurates a new kind of rationalism that is centered on the passions and that, if judged from the perspective of Platonic rationalism, can well be described as "irrational" and ultimately regarded as a form of "sophistry" due to its ruling out of any transcendent objective standard.[60]

Hobbes, then, ends up rejecting both Plato and Aristotle and thus seeks a new paradigm of exact political science. It is worth insisting, however, on the reason why in his maturity—namely when, by way of his turn to Euclid, he was searching for a new method in order for political science to be exact and wholly implementable—he developed a penchant for Plato as "the best of the ancient philosophers." In Strauss's view, this reason consists in Hobbes's claim that Plato's political and moral philosophy is a "critique" of opinions along with the passions they rest on, unlike Aristotle's, which ultimately amounts to a mere "description" of those passions.[61] For Aristotle, according to Hobbes as Strauss interprets him, remains under the spell of what is ordinarily said about things—in the given case about moral and political phenomena—unlike Plato who takes his bearings from "ideas" that are considered to be beyond opinions and, therewith, truly and literally "paradoxical." This paradoxical character, this going against and beyond the opinions, the passions, as well as sensuality, is what Hobbes feels to have in common with Plato, irrespective of his deeper critique, and rejection, of the latter's sort of rationalism.[62]

This interpretation, which for Strauss is Hobbes's ultimate interpretation, does not stand, however, the test of an "unbiased [*unbefangen*] study of the sources"[63]—at least not completely. At closer inspection, Plato proves to take his bearings from what the people say about the things—their *speeches*—even more decidedly than Aristotle, who in this regard is only following in his footsteps. For Plato, as he shows in the *Phaedo* by having Socrates recall his turn to the *logoi* when he began his "second sailing," rejects as insufficient the "cause-effect" explanations sought by *physiologoi* like Anaxagoras and "takes refuge," instead, in human speech:

> Against this explanation of nature by the physiologists there is not only the objection that it is an insufficient explanation or no explanation at all; physics of the type of the Anaxagorean, "Epimethean" physics, which as such takes—whether expressly and intentionally or implicitly and unintentionally is of no importance—not the ordering power of reason, but disorder and irrationality as the principle of nature, necessarily leads to the destruction of all certain and independent standards, to finding everything in man's world very well as it is, and to subjection to "what the Athenians *believe.*" Confronted with this

absurd conclusion, Plato does not without further ado oppose to materialistic-mechanistic physics a spiritualist-teleological physics, but keeps to what can be understood without any far-fetched "tragic" apparatus, to what the "Athenians" *say*.[64]

What the Athenians, or rather, speaking more generally, human beings say is, however, contradictory. This means that if speech is to be the true starting point for any genuine explanation of nature, the art of right argumentation or dialectics becomes paramount. In an entirely meaningful fashion, therefore, does Strauss define *dialectics* as "the art of truth-revealing discussion [*die Kunst des die Wahrheit offenbar machenden Mit-einander-Sprechens*]" that, by showing which of two *endoxa* or "authoritative opinions" must be rejected, and which kept as granting rational coherence, reveals the "paradoxical" truth that—these are Strauss's precise words—is "hidden [*verborgen*]" in what humans say in their mutually contradictory speeches.[65] Moreover, by pointing to a pure pattern of what is being discussed by way of abstraction, dialectics is the path towards "ideas." This, as Strauss explains, comes out most clearly when one speaks of good and virtue. What is meant when people say that they seek good or virtue is that they wish these latter in their purity, "unalloyed" with any evil or vice. By their speech, and "in speech" only, people thus fathom their pure pattern or idea, which essentially transcends what can be found "in deed":

> The virtue which is not found in the works of men is found in speech alone, in the divinatory, "supposing" and "founding" knowledge incorporated in speech. Speech alone, and not the always equivocal deeds, originally reveals to man the standard by which he can order his actions and test himself, takes his bearings in life and nature, in a way completely undistorted and, in principle, independent of the possibility of realization. This is the reason for Plato's "escape" into speech, and for the theory thereby given of the transcendence of ideas; only by means of speech does man know of the transcendence of virtue.[66]

Plato, hence, on the one hand, contrary to what Hobbes maintains, sticks to the words and to speech as much as, or even more than Aristotle does (who, after all, tried to weaken the close connection Plato had established between words and true being[67]). On the other hand, Strauss points out that Hobbes's view regarding the difference between the two ancient philosophers is vindicated by the dialectical and therefore "paradoxical" character of Plato's approach: pointing to speech in its contradictoriness, Plato seeks to go beyond what is commonly said or believed—namely, the *endoxa* qua *endoxa*—thereby expressing that need for exactness that Hobbes is eager to underscore and resume.

The exactness as Hobbes understands it and the exactness as Plato understands it are, however, quite different. Strauss explains that the latter amounts to the "undistorted reliability of the standards"[68]—of those standards that, as we have seen in the wake of his comment, are available in speech and are disclosed to humans by way of dialectics only. The former, by contrast, stems from Hobbes's un-Platonic (and more generally un-Greek) interest in applicability.[69] It is this interest that leads him from Plato as an "anti-Aristotelian" example of exactness in political philosophy to Euclid as the embodiment of methodological rigor. Euclid here stands for the "resolutive-compositive" method Hobbes takes from Galilei. Thanks to this adoption, his aim as a political scientist becomes not so much to know the essence of the state and raise the "most urgent question," "the truly primary question" of its aim,[70] as to break down the state into its most basic components and rebuild it so that it can properly function by granting peace and security to its members.[71] What the "resolutive" phase arrives at is indeed "human nature," the natural selfishness and vanity of human beings that can never be forgotten if a stable and well-functioning political mechanism is to be built at the end of the process. But this "nature," unlike the Platonic one that amounts to a standard or paradigm, is conceived of as only the "matter" constituting human beings, i.e., "what falls to man's share before all education."[72]

The exactness Hobbes seeks is, thus, the exactness by which the new political scientists must deal with their most basic matter—namely, the passions characteristic of humans qua humans—if they want to fulfill their new task: guaranteeing peace at all costs due to the irresistible character of fear of violent death.[73] The novelty of this task is shown by the fact that, as Strauss emphatically points out, Plato never ceased to raise the question of the aim of the state along with the correlative question of the essence of virtue.[74] What Plato looks for by way of his political philosophy, as we have observed, is exactness understood as the "undistorted reliability of the standards," irrespective of their applicability. "The 'resolutive-compositive' method," Strauss maintains, "thus presupposes nothing less than a systematic renunciation of the question of what is good and fitting." Then, with words that do not seem to suit the role of a mere commentator, he adds:

> Convinced of the absolutely typical character [*schlechthinnige Vorbildlichkeit*] of mathematical method, according to which one proceeds from self-evident axioms to evident conclusions, "to the end," Hobbes fails to realize [*verkennt*] that in the "beginning," in the "evident" presuppositions whether of mathematics or of politics, the real problem [*das eigentliche Problem*], the task of "dialectics," is hidden [*verborgen*]. "Dialectics" is the discussion and testing of what men *say* of the just and the unjust, of virtue and vice. Hobbes considers superfluous, even dangerous, to take as one's point of departure what men say about justice and so forth: "the names of Virtues, and Vices . . . can never be true grounds of any ratiocination." That one can base no reflection on how men usually apply the terms virtues and vices, is not a datum [*Feststellung*] which Hobbes would be justified in pitting against the tradition founded by Socrates-Plato, for the Socratic-Platonic reform of philosophy [*Wendung*] rests precisely on the perception of the unreliability and contradictoriness of ordinary speech [*die Einsicht in die Unzuverlässigkeit, in die Widersprüchlichkeit der gewöhnlichen Rede*]. But it does not follow from this perception that one is to consider "not the words but the things." For to give up orientation by speech [*Orientierung an der Rede*] means giving up the only possible orientation, which is originally at the disposal of men [*die einzig mögliche Orientierung, die dem Menschen ursprünglich zu Gebote steht*] and therewith giving up the discovery of the standard which is presupposed in any orientation [*der in aller Orientierung vorausgesetzte Massstab*], and even giving up the search for the standard [*die Frage nach dem Massstab*].[75]

Not nature understood as *matter*, hence, must be sought if even the mere search for the standard—which Strauss, with all his might, tried to revitalize throughout his philosophic life—is not to be relinquished. In the wake of the Platonic Socrates, a different meaning of nature as *essence* or *idea* must be looked for with the mind's eye (by way of dialectics) in its stead. Strauss makes this clear while explaining Hobbes's faulty perspective:

"He [Hobbes] begins his political philosophy not with the question as to the essence of virtue, or with the question (which to a certain extent is equivalent) as to the *'nature' of man in the sense of the 'idea' of man [die Frage nach der 'Natur' des Menschen als nach der Idee des Menschen]*, but with the question as to the 'nature' of man in the sense of that which falls to all men before education [*die Frage nach der 'Natur' des Menschen als nach dem, was allen Menschen vor aller Erziehung zukommt*]."[76] Due to this defect, which deprives Hobbes of the possibility to raise the question of the standard, he even ends up in a fundamental incoherence. For under those conditions Hobbes cannot fully justify his view of the properly constituted state—namely, the state that grants security and peace to everybody starting from each and everyone's natural "right" to everything—if not at the price of an exception to his resolutive-compositive method, which in itself would not allow for such ultimately moral evaluations. Hobbes's political philosophy, however morally indulgent compared with Plato's, is not, after all, a form of pure naturalism like Spinoza's, as Strauss insightfully underscores.[77]

In any event, what is important for us to underscore is that besides nature understood as matter according to the Hobbesian, modern sense (irrespective of Hobbes's inconsistences), there is, at least, another meaning of nature. This meaning is the Platonic one, which proves to be of the utmost importance for Strauss in view of its ability to open up the path towards the standard—even to the mere search thereof. This second and more important meaning is—it is worth repeating—nature in the sense of idea or essence.

Although not explicitly mentioned, we can find an echo of this Platonic perspective at the end of chapter VIII of *The Political Philosophy of Hobbes* we are currently commenting on. In that context, Strauss discusses the primacy of "internal policy" that distinguishes classical political philosophy from its modern counterpart, which is instead mostly concerned with foreign policy. The reason why Plato and Aristotle agree on that primacy—Strauss informs us—is that in both authors' view, regardless of their differences, "what lends to a thing its being, its peculiar essence, what limits it—that essence is what we mean when we speak, e.g., of a horse as a horse—takes precedence over all other reasons for the thing in question, and particularly over all external conditions."[78] This assumption allows them to favor matters of internal order and justice over those concerning war and defense, which are at most regarded as by-products of the first.

Another relevant instance of such an "essentialist" approach occurs shortly afterwards when Strauss compares, once again, the "paradoxical" character of Plato's and Hobbes's political philosophies. "The antithesis between classical and modern political philosophy," he begins to observe, "more accurately between Platonic political philosophy and that of Hobbes, reduced to principle, is that the former orientates itself by speech [*sich an der Rede orientiert*] and the latter from the outset refuses to do so."[79] "This refusal arises originally from insight into the problematic nature of ordinary speech [*Fragwürdigkeit der gewöhnlichen Rede*], that is, of popular valuations ['*vulgäre' Wertschätzungen*], which one may with a certain justification call natural valuations [*natürliche Wertschätzungen*]," Strauss adds by making reference, in an attached note, to his close friend Jacob Klein and thereby, arguably, to Husserl's concept of "natürliche Einstellung" (natural attitude).[80] Then, he observes:

> This insight leads Hobbes, just as did Plato, first to the ideal [*Desiderat*] of an exact political science. But while Plato goes back to the truth hidden in the natural valuations and therefore seeks to teach nothing new and unheard-of, but to recall what is known to all but not understood [*das von allen Gewusste aber nicht Verstandene*], Hobbes, rejecting the natural valuations in principle, goes beyond them, goes forward to a new *a priori* political philosophy, which is of the future and freely projected [*eine neue, zukünftige, frei zu entwerfende, "apriorische" Politik*]. Measured by Aristotle's classical explanation of natural morals, Platonic moral philosophy is paradoxical, as is Hobbes's. But whereas the paradoxical nature of Platonic moral philosophy is as irreversible as the "cave" existence of men bound to the body, Hobbes's moral philosophy is destined sooner or later to change from paradox to an accepted part of public opinion.[81]

The paradoxical character of Plato's approach, then, amounts to "the paradox of the unpretentious old and eternal [*Paradoxie des unscheinbaren Alten, Ewigen*],"[82] of the "undistorted reliability of the standards" that can never be found, in their purity, "in deed" but only "in speech," as we have seen before. The paradoxical character of Hobbes's approach, by contrast, consists in "the paradox of the surprising new, unheard-of venture [*Paradoxie des überraschenden Neuen, des unerhörten Wagnisses*]"[83] that, if eventually successful, becomes the backbone of a new worldview. This intrinsically relativistic trait of Hobbes's approach is duly underscored by Strauss when, shortly afterwards, he observes that "whereas Plato retraces natural morals [*natürliche Moral*] and the orientation [*Orientierung*] provided by them to their origin [*Ursprung*], Hobbes must attempt in sovereignty [*wahrhaft souverän*], and without this orientation, to discover the principle of morals," thereby traveling "the path which leads to formal ethics and finally to relativist scepticism."[84]

Such a radical shift concerning morals becomes clear, for instance, in the case of courage, which we have already dealt with while commenting on Strauss's correspondence with Löwith (recall Strauss's comments on Nietzsche's "*re*discovery of the original ideal of humanity," which is however "polemically" affirmed by him to counteract its negation by "the Enlightenment"). Resorting to some of the terms he had used in his exchange,[85] Strauss now explains that "Plato does not question the virtue-character of courage, to which speech bears witness, but simply opposes the over-estimation [*Überschätzung*] of courage which underlies the popular opinion [*vulgäre Meinung*] about courage."[86] By contrast "Hobbes, because he renounced all orientation by speech [*kraft seines Verzichtes auf die Orientierung an der Rede*], goes so far as systematically to deny the virtue-character of courage."[87] The consequence to this denial, here as in Strauss's letter, could not be more decidedly underscored: "And just as disdain of speech [*Verachtung der Rede*] finally leads to relativist scepticism, the negation of courage leads to the controversial position [*polemische Position*] of courage which becomes more and more acute on the way from Rousseau by Hegel to Nietzsche and is completed by the reabsorption of wisdom by courage, in the view that the ideal is not the object of wisdom [*Gegenstand der Einsicht*], but the hazardous venture of the will [*Wagnis des Willens*]."[88]

Strauss concludes his remarks, in this connection, by observing that Hobbes's skepticism leads him not to abandon the question of the standard altogether—as we have already noted—but to raise it only surreptitiously and improperly, as one can see by comparing his perspective with Plato's. For, due to his "disdain of speech," Hobbes must find his bearings only in what he regards as "necessary" (the irresistible passion of fear of violent death and the natural "right" resulting from it) and not also in what is "dialectically" fathomed as "good" or virtuous starting from the *endoxa*. This exclusive reliance on necessity is for Strauss the result of Hobbes's "denial of the existence of a natural law, that is, of a natural standard [*natürlicher Massstab*]."[89] In its turn, such a denial is "the result of relinquishing orientation by speech,"[90] as Strauss prudently limits himself to "asserting [*behaupten*]"[91] despite having previously shown, as has been emphasized, that this is his own view (no matter how "tentative") not only as a commentator.

III

At the beginning of this introduction, we pointed out that at least in one instance Strauss explicitly raises the fundamental philosophical question, "What is nature?" Bearing in mind what has been observed so far, it is now time to focus on this context.

The question occurs in the introduction Strauss wrote for the *History of Political Philosophy* he edited with Joseph Cropsey in 1963.[92] After pointing out that political philosophy presupposes philosophy, which in turn presupposes the discovery of "nature" as its "primary theme," Strauss asks: "What is nature?" Then, to begin to answer this question, he recalls the story of Odysseus, Hermes, and the herb called *moly*, which Homer tells in the tenth book of the *Odyssey*.[93] There—Strauss informs us—we can find the first occurrence ever in Greek (and the only one in Homer) of the word *physis*, an occurrence that, despite being in an epic poem, "gives us a most important hint to what the Greek philosophers understood by 'nature.'"[94]

In the Homeric context Strauss refers to, the "nature of the herb," which is not made but only known by the gods, amounts to "its looks and its power." "'Nature' means here," Strauss continues, "the character of a thing or of a kind of thing, the way in which a thing or a kind of thing looks and acts, and the thing, or the kind of thing, is taken not to have been made by gods or men."[95] Shortly afterwards, coming to a more straightforwardly philosophical context, he adds: "It seems that the Greek word for nature (*physis*) means primarily 'growth' and therefore also that into which a thing grows, the term of the growth, the character a thing has when its growth is completed, when it can do what only the fully grown thing of the kind in question can do or do well."[96] These observations allow him to note that there are things "by nature" and things "by convention" (which do not grow because they are made), and that among the former some are "'by nature' without having 'grown' and even without having come into being in any way."[97] These are, of course, the "first things, out of which or through which all other natural things have come into being," like, for instance, Democritus's atoms.[98]

Having reached this point, and having underscored that nature had to be discovered, as is shown by the fact that the Hebrew Bible has no equivalent word for *physis*, its closest concepts being "way" or "custom," Strauss points out that "the discovery of nature led to the splitting up of 'way' and 'custom' into 'nature' (*physis*) on the one hand and 'convention' or 'law' (*nomos*) on the other," a distinction that "implies that the natural is prior to the conventional."[99]

Here is where political philosophy comes in, and therewith Socrates as its founder.[100] For the splitting up of way and custom into *physis* and *nomos* necessarily leads to the question as to whether the law, or more generally what is regarded to be right, is by nature or by convention: "The precise question therefore concerns the relation of what is by nature good for man, on the one hand, to justice or right on the other. The simple alternative is this: all right is conventional or there is some natural right."[101]

Strauss informs us that apparently "Socrates was induced to turn away from the study of the divine or natural things"—i.e., "the first things" we have previously mentioned in his footsteps—"by his piety."[102] In light of the distinction between esoteric and exoteric teaching that became increasingly relevant in Strauss's approach since the end of the 1930s,[103] this information would lead us, to begin with, to grow suspicious towards Socrates's turn to the "human things" and his pursuing of his investigations "by means of conversations," as Strauss explains shortly afterwards. We are also told, however, that even the "pious" Socrates was compelled to raise, in his conversations, the question "of nature"—which essentially exceeds the limits of piety—and that he raised that question by asking "'what is . . . ?' regarding everything," thereby originating "a new kind of the study of the natural things."[104] This being the case, Strauss's description of Socrates's dialectical procedure, which, as will immediately become clear, follows along the lines of his previous discussion of the same matter in *The Political Philosophy of Hobbes*, can be received with less hesitation.

We have already observed that "Socrates pursued his investigations by means of conversations." Strauss now explains that "this means he started from generally held opinions," the most authoritative among which are "those sanctioned by the city and its laws, by the most solemn convention."[105] Due to the fact that opinions, including the most authoritative ones, the *endoxa*, contradict one another, it "becomes necessary to transcend the whole sphere of the generally held opinions, or of opinion as such, in the direction of knowledge":

Since even the most authoritative opinions are only opinions, even Socrates was compelled to go the way from convention or law to nature, to ascend from law to nature. But now it appears more clearly than ever before that opinion, convention, or law, contains truth, or is not arbitrary, or is in a sense natural. One may say that the law, the human law, thus proves to point to a divine or natural law as its origin. This implies, however, that the human law, precisely because it is not identical with the divine or natural law, is not unqualifiedly true or just: only natural right, justice itself, the "idea" or "form" of justice, is unqualifiedly just.[106]

In light of what we have already observed while dealing with *The Political Philosophy of Hobbes*, we cannot help but notice some important similarities to this presentation and vocabulary. The first similarity consists in the view that opinion contains truth. As has been previously underscored, in his 1936 book Strauss speaks of "truth hidden [*verborgen*] in what [men] say" or "truth hidden [*verborgen*] in the natural valuations [*natürliche Wertschätzungen*]."[107] Even the "in a sense" only "natural" character of opinion reflects what Strauss maintains in his previous book, where he, by way of Klein, refers to "popular valuations ['*vulgäre*' *Wertschätzungen*], which one may *with a certain justification call natural* valuations [natürliche Wertschätzungen]."[108] Analogous considerations can be made regarding the second half of the quotation above. For the themes Strauss touches upon in it find an almost exact correspondence in his previous remarks about the "natural law" or "natural standard" denied by Hobbes[109] (unlike Plato who "retraces natural morals and the orientation provided by them to their origin [*Ursprung*]"[110]) and in the view—which Strauss also puts forward in his 1936 book—that it is "speech alone," by grasping the "essence" or "idea," that "originally reveals to man the standard by which he can order his actions,"[111] and which, therefore, is unqualifiedly just.

It is, however, what Strauss adds in the following paragraph that should now catch our attention, notably because he there reiterates, and expands on, his previous remarks concerning the meaning of nature as idea or essence. He begins by pointing out that to understand why Socrates is regarded as the founder of political philosophy one must consider "the character of the questions with which he dealt in his conversations."[112] Socrates, Strauss continues, "raised the question 'What is . . . ?' regarding everything," as we have already underscored to show the "impious" stance of his investigation. Then, he explains:

> This question is meant to bring to light the nature of the kind of thing in question, that is, the form or the character of the thing. Socrates presupposed that knowledge of the whole is, above all, knowledge of the character, the form, the "essential" character of every part of the whole, as distinguished from knowledge of that out of which or through which the whole may have come into being. If the whole consists of essentially different parts, it is at least possible that the political things (or the human things) are essentially different from the nonpolitical things—that the political things form a class by themselves and therefore can be studied by themselves. Socrates, it seems, took the primary meaning of "nature" more seriously than any of his predecessors: he realized that "nature" is primarily "form" or "idea." If this is true, he did not simply turn away from the study of the natural things, but originated a new kind of the study of the natural things—a kind of study in which, for example, the nature or idea of justice, or natural right, and surely the nature of the human soul or man, is more important than, for example, the nature of the sun.[113]

Nature, hence, is "primarily 'form' or 'idea.'" It is only by way of an investigation on this kind of nature, which presupposes an "orientation by speech," that the knowledge of the whole that is available to human beings can apparently be achieved. In this perspective, knowing means to genuinely understand, by way of dialectics, what is already, to some extent, "naturally" given in the opinions.[114] Once again, without explicitly mentioning it, Strauss points to Socrates's "second sailing." What he adds, in this case, is an explanation of the fact that, if there is what he sometimes refers to as "noetic heterogeneity,"[115] political philosophy can become the "first philosophy" because it is through the part political philosophy focuses on, namely "the city and man," that the whole can be accessed best by humans.[116] This, in turn, shows that, rather than being an essentially "pious" investigation, political philosophy as Socrates understood it—and as Strauss seems to understand it—is just a new type of investigation on "the natural things," its true distinctive character being "the orientation by speech" as the *only* available path towards raising the question of the standard.[117]

Although through the opposite route (from idea to nature rather than the other way round), the view that nature is primarily form or idea is again brought up by Strauss in the chapter on Plato he also wrote for *History of Political Philosophy*.[118] In this context, while commenting on the doctrine of the ideas as expounded in Plato's *Republic*, Strauss deals with the question of the possibility of the good city. In doing so, to begin with he follows along the lines of his previous treatment in the introduction and, therewith, of his presentation in *The Political Philosophy of Hobbes*. Even now we are told that the "effort to discover what justice is . . . [is] a quest for 'justice itself' as a 'pattern,'" which implies that "the just man and the just city will not be perfectly just but will indeed approximate justice itself with particular closedness; only justice itself is perfectly just."[119]

This being the case, always reconstructing Socrates's view as is presented in the *Republic*, Strauss observes that "justice itself is not 'possible' in the sense that it is capable of coming into being, because it 'is' always without being capable of undergoing any change whatever. Justice is an 'idea' or 'form,' one of many 'ideas.'"[120] Until now, nothing (substantially) new has been added compared with the previous presentations. The novelty is, however, in what follows. For here Strauss, but only summarizing Plato's theory of the ideas as is described in the *Republic*, gives the whole argument a distinctly metaphysical twist by pointing out that "ideas are the only things which strictly speaking 'are,' i.e., are without any admixture of nonbeing, because they are beyond all becoming . . . Since the ideas are the only things which are beyond all change, they are in a sense the cause of all change and all changeable things."[121] This means, Strauss goes on, that ideas "are self-subsisting beings which subsist always," to conclude his summary with a mention of the Platonic notion of the "idea of the good" regarded as above, and the cause of, the other ideas.

As one might expect, Strauss immediately casts doubt on such a metaphysical view of the ideas as "self-subsisting" beings: "The doctrine of ideas which Socrates expounds to Glaukon is very hard to understand; to begin with it is utterly incredible, not to say that it appears to be fantastic."[122] It soon becomes clear, however, that in Strauss's view this "substantialist" interpretation of the ideas is ultimately meant by Socrates as a replacement for the belief in the self-subsisting gods characterizing both of his interlocutors in that circumstance: Glaukon and Adeimantos.¹²³ Arguing from a more philosophical perspective, on the other hand, Strauss observes:

> No one has ever succeeded in giving a satisfactory or clear account of this doctrine of ideas. It is possible, however, to define rather precisely the central difficulty. "Idea" means primarily the looks or shape of a thing; it means then a kind or class of things which are united by the fact that they all possess the same "looks," i.e., the same character and power, or the same "nature"; therewith it means the class-character or the nature of the things belonging to the class in question: the "idea" of a thing is that which we mean by trying to find out the "what" or the "nature" of a thing or a class of things.¹²⁴

As is also shown by the fact that right at the end of this quotation Strauss adds a parenthetical reference to the introduction, it is quite clear that in this more philosophical account of the question of the ideas Strauss is ultimately reiterating what he has previously observed, the major difference being that here he explains the concept of idea by way of nature and not vice versa. The end result is, however, identical: idea and nature mean, primarily, the same.¹²⁵ Strauss concludes his philosophical account by explaining that the view of the self-subsistent character of the ideas can be somewhat explained by referring to the self-subsistence of mathematical objects and, "above all," of the purity or perfection of justice and similar things, which always transcend "everything which men can ever achieve."¹²⁶ While Strauss finds "obviously reasonable"¹²⁷ to share such a view, we have already underscored that any extension of it beyond these limits, following its exposition in the *Republic*, would ultimately be mythical in his account.

IV

We have now reached a point where we can review our findings concerning the question, "what is nature?" and the different meanings the term *nature* has in Strauss's account. A first, obvious meaning is *physis* understood as the *physiologoi* understand it, namely, as the "first elements," which cause all other things. In light of what we have observed so far, it is fair to say that this is not Strauss's pivotal meaning when it comes to raising the question above.

There is, then, a second meaning of nature as matter that shows a close kinship with the first. We have seen this second meaning implied, particularly, with reference to Hobbes when he, by resorting to the "resolutive-compositive" method, breaks down the individual psyche into its constitutive and basic elements. These basic elements—which, as such, can be regarded as the nature of human beings understood as their matter preceding any refinement or education—turn out to be, in Hobbes's case, the passions of vanity and fear of violent death, on which he consequently founds his artificial political system with a view to its applicability. Though a relevant element not only in Hobbes's perspective, but also in Strauss's interpretation thereof, again in this case one can hardly claim that this is Strauss's crucial meaning when it comes to his own philosophical perspective.

A third important meaning—in this case more of the adjective *natural* than of the noun *nature*—is that by means of which, following Klein and, thereby, possibly Husserl, Strauss describes (but "with a certain justification" only) the "popular valuations" or "common opinions." The reason why the latter can be referred to as natural, however qualifiedly, is that qua common opinions they are the starting point from which only what is truly and genuinely nature can be grasped in Strauss's dialectical approach. It is only by taking our bearings from speech, following the example of "Socrates-Plato" and, therewith, rejecting Hobbes's "disdain" of it, that we can avoid radical skepticism and even just search for a standard according to Strauss, as he lays bare in *The Political Philosophy of Hobbes*.

This being the case, Strauss's genuine answer to the philosophical question, "what is nature?"—an answer that will have to be borne in mind in the next chapters—is, "primarily," "idea." It is arguably in this essentialist sense only that the concept of nature, along with the resulting search for a standard or *Massstab* that so decisively characterizes his philosophical approach, can become entirely consistent. From this perspective, nature as idea or essence (or the other way round) is the answer to the question, "what is?," which dialectics pursue starting from the opinions in their contradictoriness and taking its orientation by speech.

If need be, additional proof of the reliability of this assumption can be found in Strauss's "golden sentence," as Seth Bernadete used to call it: "The problem inherent in the surface of things, and *only* in the surface of things, is the heart of things."[128] As will be argued in greater detail later, the meaning of this sentence is by no means easy to grasp, and a case can be made for the view that it has also to do with the so-called second, unnatural cave.[129] The fact that Strauss connects it with the exhortation to not despise the surface represented by "common opinion"—in the given case about Machiavelli as a "teacher of evil"—if one seeks to truly understand his thought (and more in general the "heart of things"), should however be regarded as a preliminary indication that, by pronouncing that sentence, he also wanted to reaffirm the need for the "orientation by speech" as the only possible path towards the standard, even towards the mere question thereof.[130]

This indication becomes even clearer if one considers, in the same breath, what Strauss had already observed in *Natural Right and History* regarding Socrates's change of approach and his turn to the *logoi*:

> In present day parlance one can describe the change in question as a return to "common sense." That to which the question "What is?" points is the *eidos* of a thing, the shape or form or character or "idea" of a thing. It is no accident that the term *eidos* signifies primarily that which is visible to all without any particular effort or what one may call the "surface" of the things. Socrates started not from what is first in itself or first by nature but from what is first for us, from what comes to sight first, from the phenomena. But the being of things, their What, comes first to sight, not in what we see of them, but in what is said about them or in opinions about them. Accordingly, Socrates started in his understanding of the natures of things from the opinions about their natures. For every opinion is based on some awareness, on some perception with the mind's eye, of something. Socrates implied that disregarding the opinions about the natures of things would amount to abandoning the most important access to reality which we have, or the most important vestiges of the truth which are within our reach. He implied that "universal doubt" of all opinions would lead us, not into the heart of the truth, but into a void. Philosophy consists, therefore, in the ascent from opinions to knowledge or to the truth, in an ascent that may be said to be guided by opinions. It is this ascent which Socrates had primarily in mind when he called philosophy "dialectics."[131]

There is, moreover, another reason why it appears meaningful to take the essentialist account of nature as idea that we have described above (with all that this entails) as indicative of Strauss's own philosophical approach. Strauss is broadly, and justly, known for his defense of the philosophic life. Although he seems to refrain from openly embracing, in his own name, an axiological account of its justification,[132] the philosophic life turns out to be entirely meaningful if, in the terms of Strauss's *zetetic* skepticism, at least "fundamental and permanent problems" are available for human rational inquiry. Strauss often relates the justification of philosophy to the rejection of the challenge represented by revelation.[133] But we have also observed that, for instance in *The Political Philosophy of Hobbes* where he compares Plato's "orientation by speech" with Hobbes's "denial" of it (which leads the latter to *radical* skepticism), Strauss ends up embracing a view according to which such an orientation is what makes not only the discovery of a standard, but also its mere search (its mere "question") possible and meaningful. Now, the orientation by speech is precisely what lies at the basis of Socratic dialectics and the conception of nature as idea we have previously defined as "essentialist." Is such a conception, at least in the weak sense that it is the only one that can truly enable even the mere "search for the standard," not what Strauss ultimately needs in order to make his investigation of the "fundamental and *permanent* problems" wholly meaningful?[134] Would an elenctic justification of philosophy faced by the challenge of revelation truly suffice for this purpose?[135] Arguably, the answer to this second question could be positive if, and only if, such a refutation eo ipso implied the restoration of the orientation by speech, by "appearance and opinion," which characterizes philosophy in the Platonic, natural cave.[136] Such a view, however, would already rest on a positive answer to the first question as well, since the conditions enjoyed by philosophy in the first, natural cave are precisely those that allow it to start from "appearance and opinion" (as distinct from the "prejudices" deriving from its encounter with the Biblical tradition) and, thereby, to orient itself by speech once again.

These observations lead us to take into consideration a fifth and—as far as I can see—last meaning of nature or natural in Strauss's account. In this sense, natural designates the ancient Greeks' philosophical approach as distinct from any such approach following philosophy's encounter with the Bible, which resulted in its entanglement with the latter. We have seen this meaning intended, to a certain extent, in Strauss's correspondence with Löwith when the two friends discuss the role of Christianity—but it would perhaps be better to refer to the biblical tradition as a whole[137]—in triggering the crisis of philosophy. In this perspective, as Strauss implicitly maintains in a letter of December 30, 1932, we have already insisted on, Greek philosophy embodies the natural approach in that it alone can grant the conditions that are needed in order for genuine philosophizing to arise against its "denaturalization [*Denaturalisierung*]" caused by Christianity (as Löwith puts it).[138] Now, a crucial role regarding this denaturalization is played by the biblical concept of creation out of nothing, which clashes against the concept of an eternal and immutable nature (not only in the physiological sense)[139] as is confirmed by the absence of the term (and concept) of nature in the Hebrew Bible—a fact Strauss often emphasizes. This conceptual antithesis, if not by way of direct secularization, at least due to a polemical stance towards the destabilizing effect of divine omnipotence or unfathomability on any effort to achieve a stable and reliable knowledge, affects modern philosophy and science as well.[140] This fact is reflected, for instance, in the shift from mere "appearance and opinion"— the starting point for Greek philosophy—to "prejudice," which, as we have observed, is a historical concept characterizing modern philosophy in its fight against the kingdom of darkness. It is not accidental, in this regard, that "appearance and opinion" are considered by Strauss as the basis from which philosophy begins its journey in the "first, 'natural' cave" as distinct from the "second, 'unnatural' cave, into which we have fallen less because of the tradition itself, than because of the tradition of the polemics against the tradition."[141] Nor is it accidental, as we will see, that Strauss defines natural philosophizing the kind of philosophizing (ultimately consisting in the Greek philosophical approach) that is re-enabled by the historical deconstruction of the presuppositions lying at the basis of the second, unnatural cave.

Finally, a last word on the historico-philosophical background of Strauss's attempt to recover the Socratic-Platonic dialectical approach. While commenting on his correspondence with Löwith, we have already pointed out that Strauss, trying to recover the Greek approach he regarded as the natural approach, was under the influence not only of Nietzsche, but also of twentieth-century phenomenology.[142]

Despite assuming a polemical posture, which Strauss openly rejects and stigmatizes, Nietzsche turns out to be a key inspiration for Strauss's own philosophical attempt in that Nietzsche wished to carry out a "repetition of antiquity at the peak of modernity"—not to mention the fact that, in Strauss's view, Nietzsche's "deepest concern," irrespective of all his ambiguities and shortcomings, was with a "philosophy" seen as "the sake of *natural* men, of men capable and willing to live 'under the sky,' of men who do not need the shelter of the cave, of *any* cave."[143]

Regarding the influence of twentieth-century phenomenology, on the other hand, the picture appears to be more nuanced. To put it in a nutshell, Husserl's influence can be detected, as we have underscored, both in his effort to seek "a new beginning, *integre et ab integro*" (which matches Strauss's own attempt to re-enable "an unpolemical, 'pure and whole' question [*eine unpolemische, 'integre' Frage*]"[144]) and in his concept of "natürliche Einstellung,"[145] which Strauss arguably took on by way of Klein. In addition, despite acknowledging some limits in Husserl's approach overall, Strauss himself underscores his crucial role in enabling an effective "critique of modern science in the light of genuine science, that is to say, Platonic-Aristotelian [science]."[146]

Husserl is then praised by Strauss for having paved the way for Heidegger's phenomenological reading of Aristotle, a reading Strauss regarded as a decisive achievement, albeit as a first step only.[147] Of course, Heidegger's influence on Strauss, whether as a source of inspiration or a polemical target, can hardly be underestimated. Previously, we have insisted on the historical deconstruction (*Destruktion*) whereby Strauss tries to rediscover or revitalize the natural philosophizing of the ancient Greeks, of "Socrates-Plato" in particular. Although other authors have influenced Strauss's attempt to recover the classics (besides Nietzsche, he also explicitly mentions Werner Jaeger and Schiller[148]), the role of Heidegger's *Destruktion* in that regard proves to be crucial.[149]

As Strauss himself points out in a letter to Löwith we have already referred to,[150] however, his employment of such a Heideggerian tool turns out to have quite a different, even opposite goal. While Heidegger "historicizes" his ontological account, thereby wholly replacing nature by history, Strauss attempts a recovery of, precisely, "nature" by "historicizing" philosophy as a "desperate remedy for a desperate situation."[151] More generally put, even if not only twentieth-century phenomenology, but also Nietzsche appears to have facilitated or even, to some extent, enabled Strauss's own attempt to revitalize the Greek "natural philosophizing," his original and genuine contribution—by no means a negligible one— seems to be his effort to simply "*learn* from Plato and Aristotle" and to recover, in particular, the "orientation by speech" characteristic of Socratic dialectics.[152] If so, any organic attempt to trace Strauss's thought back to its historico-philosophical sources—a task that exceeds the limits of the present work—ought to show, case by case, not only the influence on, but also the originality of Strauss's own philosophical perspective.[153] Arguably, this is one of the major tasks of future scholarship on Strauss.

Chapter I

Leo Strauss, Carl Schmitt, and the Search for the "Order of Human Things"

Man does not happen to be an innocent animal.

—PPH, 14

The "Notes on Carl Schmitt, *The Concept of the Political*"[1] have a prominent position in Strauss's works. The only essay Strauss published four times, he underlined its importance by referring to it as the "first expression" of a "change of orientation" he underwent in the early 1930s, which radically affected his approach and led him towards the rediscovery of the esotericism of earlier philosophy.[2]

In order to adequately understand Strauss's project, it is therefore important to identify the fundamental elements of this change of orientation. We must search for terms or concepts in his thought (or new interpretations of them) that surface for the first time in his appraisal of Schmitt's *The Concept of the Political* and that, in the years following, would become the distinctive traits of his position, explicitly or implicitly. My contention is that the two best candidates for that role are *nature* and *philosophy*.

In Strauss's mature view, these two concepts are interrelated. Nature, understood as the opposite of convention, is the foundation of philosophy as distinct from faith. It is surely no accident that, in *Natural Right and History*, Strauss points out that the Old Testament, the document that embodies the spirit of Jerusalem, does not know nature.³ The discovery of nature is the starting point of Athens. Philosophy needs nature as its sine qua non. Without the concept of nature as distinct from convention, one can have at best a kind of thought that imitates or resembles philosophy, but cannot be it. One can have "pseudo-philosophies," as Strauss puts it in *Persecution and the Art of Writing*, probably making reference to historicism but perhaps, before it, also to those threads that, intermingling with biblical faith and its idea of God's omnipotence and inscrutability, would lead to historicism.⁴

First expression does not mean that the new approach must be already fully developed. The first expression of a change of orientation can consist in new insights only in draft form. One would seek too much if one expected to find an absolutely clear and detailed perspective. It is therefore understandable that Strauss's view of nature and philosophy—as can be found in a nutshell in his "Notes"—shows the traits of what is still provisional and merely (but firmly) believed, of what still presents difficulties or obscurities that only later will be overcome. Nonetheless, his insights seem to be clear and precise enough to allow us to say that they indicate the right interpretive path. As I explain in the following sections, Strauss's mention of two different views of nature as "exemplary order" and "disorder to be eliminated," as well as his emphasis on the necessity to know that the political is "real" and "inescapable," his reference to Plato regarding "the question of what is right," and his subordination of the justification of the political to the ability to raise this quintessentially philosophical question, constitutes the act of birth, at least in his writings, of a new approach. This approach later crystallizes in the reopening of the "Quarrel of the Ancients and the Moderns" and in Strauss's attempt to recover the horizon of the former so as to help us solve the problems of the latter (our problems).⁵

I

What Strauss finds remarkable in *The Concept of the Political* is that Schmitt, in this essay, provides the outline of an understanding of the question of *the political* that opposes the typically modern liberal one. According to the liberal understanding, the political is nothing but one of the independent domains of "culture," one of the "provinces" of an "autonomous," "sovereign creation . . . of the human spirit [*Geist*]."⁶ As such—as something not given "by nature," but established by human convention and contrivance—the political, as well as the state, can be "negated." For this reason, according to Schmitt, modernity, dominated by a "liberal" mindset, can be considered as an age of "neutralization" and "depoliticization," in which all the conflicts and oppositions that characterize the political domain have come to be seen in principle as resolvable.

To this liberal view, Schmitt wants to oppose the "position [*Position*]" of the political.[7] He begins by showing that the political cannot be properly understood as one among other domains of culture, like the moral, the aesthetic, the economic, etc. Since the fundamental opposition on which the political rests as its own criterion is that between "friend and enemy [*Freund und Feind*]"[8]—one that implies the "real possibility of the *physical killing*"—the political represents the domain in which the "most extreme possibility," namely that of life or death, may occur.[9] This fact makes it much more than a "relatively independent domain" alongside others. It makes the political the *fundamental* domain. In the words of Strauss: "The political is the 'authoritative.' It is in this sense that we are to understand the remark that the political is 'not equivalent and analogous' to the moral, the aesthetic, the economic, etc."[10]

According to Strauss, Schmitt—at least implicitly—addresses the question of the *genus* of the political. Although Schmitt refrains from providing an "exhaustive definition" of this concept (which would have forced him to explicitly deal with the question of its genus, along with that of its specific criterion or difference), his criticism of the liberal view is already deep enough to undermine the "philosophy of culture" on which the dominant answer to that question was based. Schmitt's criticism, underscoring the "fundamental" and "authoritative" character of the political, is in fact sufficient to make it understood that the political cannot be adequately seen as the mere creation of an independent and sovereign human mind. The political is instead, in Schmitt's parlance, "destiny," or, in Strauss's terms, something that transcends what is established by convention and appears to be given by nature.[11]

Consequently, after having traced Schmitt's criticism back to the question of the genus of the political and highlighted its implicit rebuttal of the liberal answer, Strauss departs from his (till then) strict comment on Schmitt's essay in order to introduce on his own the concept of nature as the possible alternative answer. No matter how absolutized culture may have become within the liberal understanding and its characteristic "philosophy of culture," according to Strauss one should never forget that "'culture' always presupposes something that is cultivated: culture is always the *culture of nature* [Kultur der Natur]."[12] If this is so, culture as the autonomous creation of the human mind becomes an inconsistent concept that can no longer be considered as the genus of the political.

What culture understood as the sovereign creation of the human mind loses, nature gains. Nature—in the case of the political, human nature—becomes the concept that must be scrutinized if one really wants to understand the political and culture itself. Strauss, thus, swiftly points out that there are two senses in which nature—and therewith culture as *culture of nature*—can be understood: "This expression [culture of nature] means, primarily [*ursprünglich*], that culture develops the natural predisposition; it is careful nurture of nature [*sorgfältige Pflege der Natur*]—whether of the soil or of the human spirit makes no difference; it thus *obeys* [*gehorcht*] the orders [*Anweisungen*] that nature itself gives."[13]

According to this classical interpretation of culture, it is then in nature itself, and not in one's will, that one can find an objective measure or standard.[14] Indeed, nature itself gives "orders" or "indications" (*Anweisungen*), and culture, consequently understood as *cultura animi*, cannot but follow these orders or indications by carefully nurturing nature and developing the natural disposition.[15]

Besides this classical view, however, Strauss sets down another conception of nature that represents the typically early modern interpretation. According to this conception, culture of nature means not so much nurture of nature, as "*conquering* nature through obedience to nature [*durch Gehorsam gegenüber der Natur die Natur* besiegen]."[16] In this context, Strauss quotes Bacon's *parendo vincere* as an example of the latter view. But it is obvious that Hobbes, who not by accident becomes the central figure of his "Notes," could also have served equally well as an example of this interpretation. At any rate, Strauss goes on to state that, according to the modern view, "culture is not so much the faithful nurture of nature [*treue Pflege der Natur*] as a harsh and cunning fight *against* nature [*harter und listiger Kampf* wider *die Natur*]."[17] And highlighting a distinction that pertains to nothing less than the core of the quarrel between ancients and (early) moderns, he explains that "whether culture is understood as the nurture of nature or as a fight with nature depends on how nature is understood: as exemplary order [*vorbildliche Ordnung*] or as disorder to be eliminated [*zu beseitigende Unordnung*]."[18]

I have added *early* to moderns because that opposition seems to mostly apply to the ancients versus the modern theorists of natural law.

Not accidentally, in referring again to the liberal philosophy of culture, Strauss feels the need to add that "'culture' is to such an extent culture of nature that culture can be understood as a sovereign creation of the spirit only if the nature being cultivated has been presupposed to be the opposite of spirit, and been *forgotten*."[19] Unlike early modern natural law theory, which at least starts from the "state of nature," the philosophy of culture that informs later liberalism forgets nature altogether, so that culture can fully become a "sovereign creation" and a "pure product" of the human mind.[20]

This clearly is not the case of Hobbes who, in the attempt to lay down the foundations of liberalism in a world still unshaped by the liberal mindset and its characteristic philosophy of culture, starts from the "natural social relations of men, that is the way in which man—prior to all culture—behaves toward other men."[21] For this reason, despite his polemic against Aristotle's conception of the human being as by nature a political animal,[22] Hobbes is *the* author whom both Strauss and Schmitt feel the need to return to in order to "strike at [*treffen*] the root of liberalism in Hobbes's explicit negation of the state of nature."[23]

In negating the *status naturalis*, however, Hobbes interprets the *status civilis* in accordance with the modern concept of culture that nature is "disorder to be eliminated." In Hobbes's polemical description, the state of nature becomes a state of war, nay of war of everyone against everyone—if not actual, at least potential—and as such it proves to be in need of being negated by an act of the sovereign will of human beings. For this reason, although Hobbes is still aware of the fundamental role of nature, he is rightly the philosopher of civilization, so much so that he can even be considered the founder of the essentially "unpolitical" liberalism that Schmitt so strongly opposes. It is in Hobbes, in fact, that the idea of negating the state of nature as a state of unbearable disorder and conflict by way of civilization finds its first mature form.

Contrary to what Schmitt thinks, therefore, Hobbes is "*the* antipolitical thinker," once political is understood precisely in Schmitt's sense.[24] Like Hobbes, Schmitt sees the political as a condition characterized if not by actual conflict, at least by its "real possibility" (though to be sure in Schmitt's view this latent state of war pertains primarily to human groups instead of individuals).[25] This means that Schmitt's concept of the political corresponds to Hobbes's state of nature. However, unlike Hobbes who in his polemic against Aristotle describes that state as in itself "impossible" precisely in order to negate it[26] (therewith giving rise to the ideal of civilization as an unpolitical "partnership in consumption and production"), Schmitt wants to achieve the position of the political by showing its reality, that is its undeniable, natural character. In Strauss's words:

> ... the political that Schmitt brings to bear as fundamental is the "state of nature" that underlies every culture; Schmitt restores the Hobbesian concept of the state of nature to a place of honor ... Therewith the question about the genus within which the specific difference of the political is to be stipulated has also been answered: the political is a *status* of man; indeed, the political is *the* status as the "natural," the fundamental and extreme, status of man.[27]

At least from Strauss's standpoint, the gist of Schmitt's argument consists in the search for the "order of human things" seen in an eternal, "natural" perspective. Strauss, however, not only lays bare this implicit line of thought. He also shows that, precisely in light of Schmitt's presuppositions, his attempt to achieve the position of the political—to show that the political is "real [*wirklich*]," "to know *what is*," i.e., to know the "basic characteristic of human life"[28]—turns out to be inconsistent. This is due to the fact that, although Schmitt apparently seeks after the "pure and whole knowledge" of the political, and therewith of the "order of human things"—which is only possible, as he himself points out, by way of a return to "undamaged, noncorrupt nature [*unversehrte, nicht korrupte Natur*]"—he instead approaches the question of the political polemically and from a perspective that ultimately remains entangled in the liberal view he wanted to oppose.[29]

Schmitt's recognition of the political in opposition to its liberal negation is thus only the surface of his argument. Its core, as we shall now see, proves instead to be his "battle of decision [*Entscheidungskampf*]" against the ideal of civilization and the "spirit of technicity" that informs its final stage, a battle of decision that forces Schmitt surreptitiously to replace such a position of the political with its "affirmation" (*Bejahung*) or "espousal" (*Eintreten*) out of a purely moral concern.

II

Strauss devotes the third and longest part of his "Notes" to the explanation of both Schmitt's entanglement in the liberal perspective and real intention, an explanation that culminates in the astonishing remark that Schmitt's conception is a form of "liberalism with the opposite polarity [*Liberalismus mit umgekehrtem Vorzeichen*]."[30] An extensive comment on this part is beyond the scope of this work. It is however important to lay down the fundamental elements that cause Schmitt to remain entrapped in liberalism and to embark on the "battle of decision" referred to above.

Regarding his entrapment, what ultimately emerges as decisive is Schmitt's acceptance of the view that "all ideals are private and thus nonobligatory [*unverbindlich*],"[31] whose corollary is that man's evil has to be interpreted in an amoral, innocent sense: as *naturae potentia* instead of as *humana impotentia*.[32] This is not only Spinoza's explicit conception, as Strauss underscores, but also Hobbes's ultimate presupposition, no matter how inconsistent and removed from Spinoza's naturalism his perspective may be.[33] Since Hobbes starts from the modern view of nature as disorder to be eliminated instead of exemplary order—while also denying any revealed source of morality[34]—he is driven to assert that the "fundamental political fact [is] natural right as the justified *claim* of the individual," as well as to conceive "of obligation as a subsequent restriction upon that claim" ultimately caused by a state of "inescapable necessity," that is by the "impossibility" of the state of nature understood as disorder, as war of everyone against everyone.[35]

Now, while trying to achieve the position of the political instead of its liberal or anarchistic negation, Schmitt accepts—even admires[36]—this amoral view of human dangerousness, and therewith of the "transprivate obligation" that characterizes the political as "inescapable necessity."[37] Due to the same presupposition, however, he is also forced to admit the possibility that this necessity may not in reality be so "inescapable": "Once one understands man's evil as the innocent 'evil' of the beast, but of a beast that can become astute through injury and thus can be educated, the limits one sets for education finally become a matter of mere '*supposition*'—whether very narrow limits, as set by Hobbes himself, who therefore became an adherent of absolute monarchy; or broader limits such as those of liberalism; or whether one imagines education as capable of just about everything, as anarchism does."[38] Misunderstanding Hobbes, in other words, Schmitt uncritically accepts what links Hobbes, no matter how absolutist his conclusions may be, to liberalism and even to anarchism: the idea that human nature is malleable, that man is first and foremost a free being who can be indefinitely educated, even to the point of losing his dangerousness, and therewith his need for dominion and politics understood in Schmitt's sense.

This is why Schmitt can only believe, but not *know*, that man will always be dangerous and therewith that the political will always be necessary. Instead of the actually "antipolitical" Hobbes and his view of man's evil as amoral and innocent, Schmitt would have had to endorse the opposite view that evil is the violation of a "primary obligation [*primäre Verpflichtung*]" in order to secure the nonpolemical position of the political he apparently seeks.[39] Having failed to do so, he cannot but admit the potential final victory of civilization, of the movement, originated by Hobbes, that strives for the depoliticization and neutralization of the world, to the end that a globalized rational society, seen as a "partnership in production and consumption," be eventually established. Against this nightmare scenario for him, resembling Nietzsche's last man,[40] Schmitt puts forward a resolute affirmation and espousal of the "endangered" political. He does so because he considers a world exclusively based on production and consumption to be the definitive sacrifice of everything serious, while he sees the endangered political, with its reference to the possibility of physical killing, as the last bulwark of seriousness.[41] No matter how apparently neutral and morally detached, his appraisal of the political is thus not so much a purely positive one—the mere position or recognition of the political in its reality—as it is a moral affirmation prompted by the endangered character of the political within his evolutive perspective.

This same perspective constitutes the reason why another argument of Schmitt's against the liberal negation of the political cannot be considered as definitive. At the end of section IV of *The Concept of the Political*, Schmitt tries to show that any attempt to eliminate the political can be successful only if it is capable of becoming political precisely in his sense, that is "sufficiently strong to group men according to friend and enemy" and "to drive the pacifists into a war against the nonpacifists, in a war against war."[42] In light of the fact that, as Strauss underlines, one cannot expect humanity to become more humane after having undergone such a final global war between pacifists and nonpacifists, in which the enemy would be seen as an "inhuman monster" who must be not so much fended off, as definitively destroyed, Schmitt concludes that nothing, even the attempt to negate the political, "can escape [the] logical conclusion of the political,"[43] which is the grouping into friends and enemies. Therefore, as Strauss summarizes Schmitt's position, "if man . . . gets entangled in contradictions when he attempts to eliminate the political, that attempt is ultimately possible only through dishonesty."[44] In Schmitt's own words: "To curse war as the murder of men, and then to demand that—so that there will 'never again be war'—they wage war and kill and allow themselves to be killed in war, is a manifest fraud."[45]

Now, let us leave aside the observation that by denouncing fraud, unless he is arguing rhetorically, Schmitt rules out the possibility of resorting to it—instead of or in addition to force—precisely as an indispensable political tool.[46] Let us underscore instead that his argument regarding the inescapability of the political turns out to be valid only if war is the only way to negate the political or, as Strauss puts it, "as long as there is just one political opposition, even just as a possibility."[47] The situation changes, however, if one attempts to negate the political by way of education. In this case, even that single political opposition between pacifism and nonpacifism could disappear. This is why Strauss, after reaffirming that from Schmitt's perspective the necessity of the political, along with the dangerousness of man on which it is based, can only be "supposed or believed in, not genuinely known,"[48] claims that Schmitt's "line of argument presupposes that the opposition between pacifists and nonpacifists does not disappear. The inescapability of the political thus exists only conditionally; ultimately, the political remains threatened."[49]

For this reason, Schmitt is eventually forced to affirm (*bejahen*), not merely recognize (*anerkennen*), the political. Strauss thus raises the question whether this affirmation occurs on a political level—as it should according to Schmitt, for whom all spiritual concepts are polemical and grow out of the political situation of the present—or on a moral level. According to Strauss, there is no doubt that the right answer to describe Schmitt's real position is the latter. To affirm politically, that is "existentially," the dangerousness of an enemy is in fact meaningless, for that would be to affirm the dangerousness of one's own enemy in a "dire emergency [*Ernstfall*]" and therewith to will to be put in jeopardy and possibly destroyed. No matter how morally neutral Schmitt tries to appear in his treatment of the political, his affirmation of it rests therefore on moral grounds.[50]

In Strauss's view, these grounds are however not those embodied by the opposition between pacifist internationalism and bellicose nationalism.[51] Schmitt does not affirm war for war's sake or embrace a purely warlike morality. Closer inspection shows that the ultimate ground on which Schmitt affirms the political out of moral reasons is the opposition between authoritarian and anarchistic theories.[52] Schmitt in fact arrives at his affirmation of the political, as distinct from its mere position or recognition, by raising the question of who would eventually rule in a fully pacified and reconciled global state. The question of the political, which boils down to the question of "man's dangerousness or undangerousness," is thus tantamount to the question "whether the government of men over men is, or will be, necessary or superfluous."[53]

Accordingly, for Strauss Schmitt's affirmation of the political for moral reasons is ultimately the affirmation of a need of dominion. As a need, which is a deficiency, the dangerousness of man cannot however be affirmed, that is wished for: "Man's dangerousness, revealed as a need of dominion, can appropriately be understood only as moral baseness [*moralische Schlechtigkeit*]. As such, it must indeed be recognized, but it cannot be affirmed [*Als solche muss sie zwar anerkannt, kann sie aber nicht bejaht werden*]."[54]

Strauss makes this significant remark after referring to Schmitt's *Political Theology*.[55] Quoting from this book, he expressly states that "the task therefore arises—for purposes of the radical critique of liberalism that Schmitt strives for—of nullifying the view of human evil as animal and thus innocent evil, and to return to the view of human evil as moral baseness; only in this way can Schmitt remain in harmony with himself if indeed 'the core of the political idea' is 'the *morally* demanding decision.' "[56] However, that Strauss, by saying so, is not merely restituting Schmitt's argument is not only shown by the objective form of his remark about moral baseness: "As such, it *must indeed be* recognized, but it cannot be affirmed" (my emphasis). It is also confirmed by what he reiterates, about four years later, in *The Political Philosophy of Hobbes*, where he plainly states that Hobbes "is no better able than any other to make us forget that man does not happen to be an innocent animal."[57] In the "Notes," Strauss is thus also arguing in his own name. For purposes of the radical critique of liberalism that he, no less than Schmitt, strives for, the task arises to return to the view of human evil as moral baseness. This being the case, how should one interpret such a moral baseness, which needs to be recognized if one wants to achieve the position of the political as distinct from its affirmation or espousal?

In light of Strauss's remark about Schmitt's *Political Theology* and its emphasis on the "*morally* demanding decision," it seems that Schmitt's position, to remain consistent, should be seen as essentially informed by moral-theological motives. In a context where decision is considered as the only possible source of any measure or standard, only reference to God's will allows one to establish such a moral baseness. On the other hand, Strauss clearly aims to gain a natural, truly philosophical understanding of the political and the order of human things, as we have already emphasized while commenting on paragraph 10 of his "Notes."[58] In his case, only human reason can try to ascertain that standard and therefore recognize man's moral baseness as failure to meet it. What Strauss shares with Schmitt is the need for a radical critique of liberalism and the attempt to gain a horizon beyond it. But the primary obligation that is, or should be, at the basis of their respective attempts emerges (thanks to Strauss's critique of Schmitt) as quite different, not to say opposite: nature understood as exemplary order or standard in Strauss's case; a morality ultimately based on theological concerns in Schmitt's.[59]

Seen as a need of dominion, man's dangerousness, and therewith the political, cannot thus be affirmed, i.e., wished for. Strauss consequently advances another, more consistent explanation as an attempt to unearth Schmitt's most profound intention. The true, no matter how concealed, reason why Schmitt affirms (*bejahen*: to say yes to) the political is that this affirmation is a means to say no to the opposite ideal of civilization, first envisioned by Hobbes, as a global partnership in production and consumption, in which entertainment will finally be guaranteed at the expense of everything demanding seriousness and sacrifice. Out of the disgust Schmitt harbors for this outcome, he affirms the political—that is Hobbes's state of nature as a state of at least potential war—as the serious par excellence precisely where liberalism and anarchism agree to negate it.[60] As we have seen, this however does not mean that his stance is a typically bellicose nationalism. On the contrary, Schmitt affirms the political as a *status belli* because in this manner one can relinquish "the security of the *status quo*" represented by liberalism and its tendency towards a global partnership in production and consumption. His affirmation of the political as such—and therewith of the state of nature—is therefore only instrumental, nothing more than his "first word" against liberalism and its civilization.[61] His "last word" is instead "the order of human things," which can arise again, " 'out of the power of a pure and whole knowledge,' " only by returning "from the 'comfort and ease of the existing status quo' to the 'cultural or social nothing,' to the 'secret, humble beginning,' 'to undamaged, noncorrupt nature [*unversehrte, nicht korrupte Natur*].' "[62]

In light of Schmitt's still liberal presuppositions—according to which "all ideals are private and thus nonobligatory" and nature is unable to set a standard since it is seen as "disorder to be eliminated"—his affirmation of the political can however only mean "the affirmation of fighting as such, wholly irrespective of *what* is being fought *for*," as "he who affirms the political as such comports himself *neutrally* toward all groupings into friends and enemies."⁶³ This ultimately means that Schmitt and his liberal counterparts share the idea of "something that is beyond all decision [*ein Jenseits aller Entscheidung*]."⁶⁴ In light of this idea, every decision is made, as it were, in a void. Only human will, whether public or private, can fill that void by its "sovereign" act and thereby attempt to turn natural disorder into an artificial order. As a consequence, culture, understood as the "sovereign creation of the human spirit," comes to the fore, while nature is compelled to recede from view to the point that it is finally forgotten.

Nor is this all: the same void operates in the background of what Strauss, in the wake of Schmitt, defines as "depoliticization."⁶⁵ In Strauss's interpretation, Schmitt's definition of the modern age as depoliticized does not mean that the political is less present or real today than in previous ages. It rather means that the still effective grouping into friends and enemies now revolves around a central domain that, as a tendency, leads towards the neutralization of the political, that is towards a ground on which agreement and peace—agreement and peace "at all costs," as Strauss puts it—can finally be reached. This central domain is technology: "In comparison to theological, metaphysical, moral, and even economic questions, which one can quarrel about forever, purely technical problems entail something refreshingly objective; they allow of solutions that are clear."⁶⁶ Therefore, as Strauss had previously remarked: ". . . if one seeks agreement at all costs, there is no other path than to abandon entirely the question of what is right and to concern oneself solely with the means. It thus becomes intelligible that modern Europe, once it had started out—in order to avoid the quarrel over the right faith—in search of a neutral ground as such, finally arrived at faith in technology."⁶⁷

Faith then seems to emerge as the fundamental concept, also with regard to the question of what is right (*die Frage nach dem Richtigen*). But here again, as previously in paragraph 10 on the different understandings of nature,⁶⁸ Strauss gives the whole argument a philosophical twist. Unlike Schmitt, who already as a legal theorist (and not only as a political-theologian) starts from tradition, if not from faith or belief,⁶⁹ Strauss proves to interpret the question of what is right as truly philosophical. He does so in a twofold manner: First, by making reference to Plato when he states that "in principle . . . it is always possible to reach agreement regarding the means to an end that is already fixed, whereas there is always quarreling over the ends themselves: we are always quarreling with each other and with ourselves only over the just and the good [*das Gerechte und das*

Gute] (Plato, *Euthyphro* 7B-D and *Phaedrus* 263A)."[70] Second, at the end of the same paragraph, by restating his point in the following manner:

> Agreement at all costs is possible only as agreement at the cost of the meaning of human life; for agreement at all costs is possible only if man has relinquished asking the question of what is right; and if man relinquishes that question, he relinquishes being a man. But if he seriously asks the question of what is right, the quarrel will be ignited . . . the life-and-death quarrel [*der Streit auf Leben und Tod*]: the political—the grouping of humanity into friends and enemies—owes its legitimation to the seriousness of the question of what is right.[71]

Unlike Schmitt—or better, in accordance with his x-ray interpretation of Schmitt as not only polemically opposed to liberalism, but also aimed at the question of the "order of human things"—Strauss thus focuses on the substantial question of what is right. He does so to such an extent that he apparently comes to see in this question a legitimate ground for the distinction of human beings into different groups that fight one another. Strauss himself, however, explains that this still warlike (no matter how philosophical) justification of the political is not to be taken as his last word, but as an ad hominem argument.

In a 1932 letter, upon reading Strauss's "Notes," Krüger asks him the following: "Do I understand your reference to Plato and therewith your own intention correctly if I think that what is of concern to you is the 'political' dialectic of the totalities which fight one another over the right? But how would one avoid the Schmittian neutral affirmation [*Bejahung*] of all that is 'meant seriously [*Ernstgemeint*]'? How can there be a decisive concretization of the search for the right without a 'profession of faith'?"[72] To these challenging questions, which point to the core of Strauss's thought as distinct from both any decisionistic affirmation of the political and any blind, purely fideistic approach to the question of what is right, Strauss responds:

> I *believe* [*glaube*] there is ultimately only *one* opposition, the opposition between "left" and "right," between "freedom" and "authority," or, to put it in more honest ancient terms, between ἡδύ [delight, pleasure] and ἀγαθόν [good] . . . The "profession

of faith" [*Glaubensbekenntnis*] you demand seems to me to lie in the δουναι και δεξασθαι [*sic*; "to give and receive," meaning "reason" (λόγον)] as such, in modern parlance, in "probity" [*Redlichkeit*]: the struggle between "left" and "right" is the struggle between utopian dizziness [*Schwindel*] and sobriety.[73]

To these remarks, which already show the extent to which one has to interpret Strauss's perspective as genuinely philosophical,[74] he adds the following, almost definitive comment: "What one reads on page 746f," meaning the paragraph about Plato and the quarrel over the right that seemingly justifies the grouping of humanity into friends and enemies, "applies thus only ad hominem. Compared to agreement at all costs, quarrel [*Streit*] is truer; but the last word can only be peace, that is agreement in the truth [*Verständigung in der Wahrheit*]. That this rational agreement [*Verständigung der Vernunft*] is possible—*firmiter credo* [I firmly believe]."[75]

Once more, Strauss's last word proves to be genuinely philosophical. Although still in the form of opinion or belief ("ich *glaube*" at the beginning of the quotation, "*firmiter credo*" at its end), his attempt is to recover a perspective from which "agreement in *the truth*"—which can be reached only if one fully recognizes the role of philosophical *reason*—can be seen as possible once again. From the point of view of the question of what is right that is at stake here, as well as of the question of the political that flows from it, that attempt seems to imply that nature must be seen, in some way, as "exemplary order."[76] Otherwise, if one continues to start from nature conceived as "disorder to be eliminated," or even worse, if one "forgets nature altogether," the quarrel that question ignites can only be settled by an act of a sovereign will—by a decision. Whether it is human or divine makes no difference from the philosophical point of view.

This is why Strauss cannot ultimately side with Schmitt in his battle of decision (*Entscheidungskampf*) against the "spirit of technicity" and the "mass faith that inspires an antireligious, this-worldly activism."[77] Although he too searches for "the order of human things" and an answer to the question of what is right that differs from the answer characteristic of modern civilization, his "horizon beyond liberalism" is not, like Schmitt's, that embodied by "the opposite spirit and faith, which, as it seems, still has no name."[78] Whether under this allusive description one can see traditional faith or, as this faith's tool, the nihilistic destruction of modern civilization,[79] Strauss still thinks that "agreement in the truth," "rational agreement," is the "last word," no matter how much "quarrel" may be truer compared to the agreement at all costs envisioned in modern liberal neutralization and depoliticization.[80]

Strauss's own intention is therefore "unpolemical." Although the political, with its polemical essence, remains a fundamental feature of human nature, the peace of reason and philosophical inquiry are his authentic goal. Schmitt's "liberalism with the opposite polarity" is therefore entirely insufficient. To decisionism of a Hobbesian cast, which is substantiated in a philosophy that interprets culture as a sovereign creation of the human mind, one cannot, on an exclusively polemical basis, respond *Yes* where the liberal tradition responded *No*. Nor can one blindly side with faith and accept, as a "Christian Epimetheus," any means that seems to lead back to an original order, no matter how destructive and inhuman this means may be.[81] In order truly to acquire a "horizon beyond liberalism,"[82] and beyond the "decisionism" that constitutes its foundation, one must propose again a "natural philosophizing,"[83] following the example of the classics, according to which nature itself ceases to be "disorder to be eliminated" and becomes "exemplary order" once again.[84] Strauss is indeed convinced that the "poet-philosopher" Horace was right to say *naturam expellas furca, tamen usque recurret*.[85] For this reason, when Schmitt, in a 1934 essay, moves away from "Hobbes's decisionism" and declares himself in favor of "thinking in terms of order [*Ordnungsdenken*]," he will see this move as an answer—to be sure a tacit one—to the critique he elaborated in his "Notes."[86] In this objectivist perspective, one can find traits not so dissimilar from what, in Strauss's mature reflection, will become classic natural right.[87] And only in this objectivist perspective can the political, understood as a domain whose genus is human nature, be non-polemically recognized as real: "For a pure and whole knowledge is never, unless by accident, polemical; and a pure and whole knowledge cannot be gained 'from concrete political existence,' from the situation of the age, but only by means of a return to the origin, to 'undamaged, noncorrupt *nature*.'"[88]

III

My contention is thus that nature as exemplary order, along with the natural philosophizing that can be consequently envisioned, represent the two pillars of Strauss's change of orientation. As far as his "Notes" are concerned, at least one major objection can be advanced. In paragraph 20, after Strauss has introduced that concept of nature and raised the question of the genus of the political, as well as that of its real and permanent character resulting from man's dangerousness, he himself voices this objection as follows: "The train of thought just recounted is in all probability not Schmitt's last word, *and it is certainly not the most profound thing* [das tiefste Wort] *that he has to say.*"[89] There follows Strauss's x-ray critique of Schmitt's polemical affirmation of the political out of moral reasons, as distinct from its mere, unpolemical recognition.

Now, how are we to interpret the part of Strauss's statement I have italicized, particularly the idea that the train of thought previously recounted is not the most profound thing Schmitt has to say? Put in this manner, this statement may indeed sound like an actual distancing from the previous philosophical interpretation of the question of the political, also on Strauss's part.

This, however, turns out not to be the case once we consider again what Strauss writes, over the same period, to Krüger. In a letter from December 27, 1932 (only four months after sending his "Notes" to Krüger), he expands on the meaning of depth (*Tiefe*) from a perspective he regarded as truly philosophical. Admittedly, the context of the letter does not concern Schmitt in particular, nor the question of the political. But what Strauss writes there, in that instance about philosophy and the concept of a standard (*Massstab*) in general, can arguably be projected onto his interpretation of Schmitt's most profound position as well. Taking issue with historicism and its idea that there is neither an eternal truth nor a stable, permanent nature to rely on, Strauss in fact questions the assumption that what is deeper or more profound (*tiefer*) is, by the same token, philosophically more radical (*radikaler*). "Is depth identical with radicality?"—he significantly asks Krüger—"Is it not perhaps the case that 'depth' is not *actually* radical?" And to explain this striking remark, he goes on to say that "depth has its home in introspection. The latter presupposes a standard [*Massstab*]. The question of the standard is the radical question. I find that the moderns have neglected this radical question to the extent that they have promoted introspection."[90]

Unfortunately, an extensive treatment of this relevant topic is beyond the scope of this chapter.[91] In conclusion, it remains, however, important to point out that the *Massstab* (measure or standard), whose question Strauss considers as more radical than depth and introspection, proves to be strictly related, also in his correspondence with Krüger, to the understanding of nature as exemplary order and to the philosophy that flows from it. As Strauss puts it in a previous letter to Krüger from

November 17, 1932: ". . . I believe in a '*natural*' basis *and* view antiquity to be exemplary [*massgeblich*]. I am inclined to assume—until there is evidence to the contrary—that antiquity (more precisely: Socrates-Plato) is exemplary *precisely because* it philosophized *naturally*, i.e., originally inquired into the order that is *natural* for human beings."[92] Unlike Schmitt who, starting from the "modern" Hobbes, neglects the question of the standard (of primary obligations) and is therefore polemically driven to "affirm" the political out of his "profound" disgust for a world without "seriousness" and the political itself, Strauss tries to stick to the example of the natural philosophizing of the ancients, who unpolemically inquired into the exemplary "order that is *natural* for human beings." While Schmitt, in other words, goes deeper into introspection, thereby losing his bearings about the political, Strauss insists on the radical question of the *Massstab*, which for him is that "nature as exemplary order" that makes "philosophy" possible again.

Chapter II

Ancient Liberalism vs. Modern Liberalism

> Liberal education is the necessary endeavor to found an aristocracy within democratic mass society.
>
> —LAM, 5

Strauss's political philosophy has increasingly become the object of thorough and unbiased studies in recent years. Apart from some quite polemic but often not equally informed works,[1] many scholars have felt the need to devote their time and energy to his thought, based on the assumption of the "enduring importance" of Strauss among twentieth-century philosophers.[2] At the basis of such a growing interest lies, at least, one shared conviction: that Strauss is an author worth being accurately read, studied, and interpreted, despite the complexity of his thought when it comes to going beneath a surface apparently plain and clear.

If the attempt is made to find other common views in Strauss scholarship, however, one is forced to recognize—as indirect proof of the complexity, perhaps even of the ambiguity of Strauss's thought—that the outcomes of those interpretive efforts show a rather high degree of variety. Admittedly this is very common with all great authors, whose richness and complexity hardly lead the interpreters to shared, let alone univocal conclusions. In the case of Strauss, however, the differences among the readings are so noteworthy, that he has gained a reputation as a hotly debated, not to say controversial political philosopher. Just to mention the most common interpretations of his political views: on the one hand, there are those who maintain he can be assimilated to the ancient philosophers (whom, not accidentally, Strauss greatly admired) also with reference to their depreciation of democracy and individual liberty, which were ultimately regarded as forms of anarchy and license.[3] More or less adumbrated in the writings of these scholars is the idea that Strauss, too, advocated some form of authoritarian regime, as long as the latter proves to be favorable to philosophy and beneficial to the governed (at least in the sense that it is capable of gaining enough consent from them not to be overthrown). On the other hand stand those who consider Strauss, despite his apparent criticism of modern liberalism and mass democracy, a true friend of liberal democracy, at least in essence.[4] In this perspective, he has even been compared, for instance, to such a liberal thinker as Alexis de Tocqueville, who, while criticizing modern mass democracy for its conformism, leveling, and tendency to promote the prosaic aspects of human life, fully recognized its right, inevitability, and advantages.[5]

As one can easily see, at issue among these different interpretations is, notably, Strauss's view of liberalism. On this specific theme, his thought is particularly engaging, since it is characterized by the presence of two quite different versions of liberalism: modern liberalism, of course—that represented by such authors as Locke, Kant, Constant, and Tocqueville—but also what Strauss himself defines as "ancient liberalism," namely, a form of "rational liberalism"—to keep using his words[6]—that finds its archetype in the political philosophy of such authors as Plato and Aristotle.[7] Undoubtedly, this is one of the most important questions to address if one wants to wholly grasp Strauss's attitude towards modernity and, as a result, his political philosophy as a whole, characterized as it is by the rediscovery of the ancients. What really is ancient liberalism? What are the main differences between it and modern liberalism? Despite their differences, are they compatible or does one represent the substantial negation, the antithesis, of the other?

The present chapter is mainly devoted to the attempt to answer these questions. To this end, in the following paragraphs an explanation of what is to be understood, in Strauss's terms, by modern and ancient liberalism is outlined. I will provide this explanation, to begin with, by means of a comparison with one of the most important texts of the modern liberal tradition: Benjamin Constant's speech "The Liberty of the Ancients Compared with That of the Moderns."[8] Admittedly, this reference is not justified by a real presence of Constant in Strauss's writings. Unlike his contemporary Schmitt, who called the Swiss-French author "the initiator of the whole liberal spirit of the nineteenth century,"[9] Strauss—as far as I know—never quotes Constant. Nonetheless, there are still good reasons to follow this path: not only the beauty, clarity, and exemplarity for modern liberalism of Constant's speech, but also the similarity of the terms the two authors adopt despite the substantial difference between them with respect to their conception of the liberty, or liberalism, of the ancients, as we will now see.

I

In his widely known 1819 speech "The Liberty of the Ancients Compared with That of the Moderns," Constant underscores that modern liberty—namely, that on which the tradition of modern liberalism rests—is to be understood as the independence (non-impediment, self-determination) of the individual private sphere from the possible encroachment by collective power. "Our freedom," he points out, "must consist of the peaceful enjoyment of private independence [*Notre liberté . . . doit se composer de la jouissance paisible de l'indépendance privée*]"—a private independence that, as Constant makes clear earlier in his lecture, entails the enjoyment of some fundamental individual rights, including the right to be subject to the laws only, to express one's opinion, to dispose of one's property (and even to misuse it), to come and go without permission, and to associate with other individuals for whatever purpose.[10] In other words, by "liberty of the moderns" Constant means what we have become accustomed to calling, in Isaiah Berlin's footsteps, "freedom from" or "negative liberty." According to the latter, in Berlin's words, "no power, but only rights, can be regarded as absolute," and "there are frontiers, not artificially drawn, within which men should be inviolable."[11]

In opposition to this conception stands Constant's "liberty of the ancients" (which, despite the name, presents traits he also detected in such modern authors as Rousseau and Mably). This liberty consists in the "active and constant participation in collective power."[12] It is thus a kind of democratic (or at least republican) autonomy, according to which citizens take part directly, and not only through representatives, in public decisions and in the formulation of the laws that will rule them, without preventively questioning the limits of state power.[13]

If we now turn to Strauss, it does not seem improper to say, roughly speaking, that his conception of modern liberalism does not differ too much from Constant's. Although with a critical intent, Strauss once famously implied that modern liberalism—whose true founder, in his view, was Hobbes—is "that political doctrine which regards as the fundamental political fact the rights, as distinguished from the duties, of man and which identifies the function of the state with the protection or the safeguarding of those rights."[14] In another context, this time dealing with religion and the "Jewish problem" in particular, he points out that "liberalism stands and falls by the distinction between state and society or by the recognition of a private sphere, protected by the law but impervious to the law, with the understanding that, above all, religion as particular religion belongs to the private sphere."[15]

When it comes to Strauss's conception of ancient liberalism, on the other hand, we cannot but notice that the similarity between his and Constant's view becomes much less conspicuous. Strauss's ancient liberalism—irrespective of whether he truly advocated its recovery or not—has indeed little in common with the "democratic" perspective Constant ascribes to the liberty of the ancients. Although Strauss himself underscores the link between modern republicanism and the mixed regime of the classics,[16] his view of ancient liberalism is characterized by a distinctly aristocratic penchant that is at odds not only—as one may expect—with the fundamental tenets of modern liberal individualism, but also with a conception like that of Rousseau and his ancient precursors as Constant describes it.

In order to have proof of this, it may be useful to consider "What Is Liberal Education?," a 1959 essay by Strauss that opens the collection *Liberalism Ancient and Modern*. In this essay Strauss starts from the analysis of the possible uses of the term *culture*, pointing out that in a first and basic meaning this term should be considered as a *singulare tantum*:

> Liberal education is education in culture or toward culture. The finished product of a liberal education is a cultured human being. "Culture" (*cultura*) means primarily agriculture: the cultivation of the soil and its products, taking care of the soil, improving the soil in accordance with its nature. "Culture" means derivatively and today chiefly the cultivation of the mind, the taking care and improving of the native faculties of the mind in accordance with the nature of the mind. Just as the soil needs cultivators of the soil, the mind needs teachers.[17]

If liberal education consists in such a *cultura animi* (cultivation of the mind), which can be metaphorically compared to a *cultura agri* (cultivation of the soil) meant as the care and improvement of the soil in accordance with its nature, it is clear that the adjective *liberal* (as the context insisting on education already suggests) is also used by Strauss in a traditional meaning that is quite far from the one the adjective takes in the corpus of modern liberalism. The liberal education Strauss addresses in his essay, as everyone familiar with this expression can easily understand, is not, at least primarily, an education to the basic principles of liberal individualism and artificialism—with what these entail in terms of individual rights and ethical pluralism. On the contrary, it is an education inspired by the classical ideal of the free man, of the magnanimous and liberal man according, for instance, to the Aristotelian definition of *megalopsychia* and *eleutheriotes*.[18] In other words, it is an education to virtue interpreted as the excellence or perfection, as the *areté*, that man can achieve by fulfilling his nature.[19]

Precisely this connection to the concept of nature provides us with a clear indication of what Strauss has in mind and of the extent to which his use of such terms as *liberal* and *culture* pursues an aim that is quite remote from the modern liberal tradition. Nature, as is here understood, is identified with the *physis* that, at the very beginning of the philosophic tradition, was opposed to *nomos* or "convention."[20] It is the kind of *physis* into which philosophy inquired in order to find a standard that is not merely man-made, conventional, and therewith contingent.[21] To educate liberally, in this perspective, means to probe the paradigm represented by human nature—the nature of a human being considered in his or her excellence and perfection—in order to come as close as possible to it. It means, in other words, to aim at a kind of rationalism that is not only formal (a means-end calculation), but also substantial or axiological (engaged in the attempt to discern the highest human ends). Faced with such a paradigm, with a *physis* by whose contemplation human beings can divine a hierarchy of their ends or ways of life,[22] it is clear that the neutral soil that put the cultivator in the condition of choosing freely the kind of cultivation to pursue becomes instead a soil with a given vocation. As a result, it is also clear that the ancient liberalism that Strauss describes does not aim at recognizing de jure any legitimacy to that pluralism of individual and cultural purposes that modern liberalism acknowledges in the moral sphere, once it has established suitable legal limits. From this perspective, the only type of pluralism that Strauss's ancient liberalism admits—if one can still speak of pluralism—is that which, de facto, one has to recognize when faced with unfit and inadequate types of cultivation.[23]

The rational liberalism that Strauss outlines is, therefore, deeply rooted in the conceptions of those ancient philosophers whom he often refers to: not only Aristotle, as we have already underscored, but also Xenophon, with his *kalos te kagathos aner* (the perfect gentleman who conforms his behavior to a certain paradigm of virtue[24]), and in particular Plato who, in book VIII of the *Republic*, speaks of *akairos eleutheria* (inappropriate liberty) with reference to the pluralistic tendency of democracy, and who thinks that the individuals should be left free only after their psyches have been placed under the control of the *logos* through adequate education.[25]

On this matter, only a caveat needs to be added: Strauss apparently establishes a peculiar relationship between—to put it in Aristotelian terms—the "ethical" and the "dianoetic virtues" according to which the latter, as ends in themselves, are not wholly dependent from the prescriptions of the former. From a truly philosophical standpoint, ethical virtues are for Strauss only means conducive, first, to the exercise of philosophy itself and, second, to the preservation of the order in the political sphere (of which the philosopher, qua philosopher, is not a part). As Strauss once put it, the philosopher is like a "jockey": he or she must be self-restrained and ethically virtuous in order to be fit and win the race (namely, to devote him- or herself to the philosophic life). But what truly matters to him or her is only the latter goal, and not the means that are subservient to it.[26] As Strauss observes in this regard: "Philosophy is as such transpolitical, transreligious, and transmoral, but the city is and ought to be moral and religious."[27]

II

Highlighting the substantial or axiological rationalism that characterizes Strauss's conception of ancient liberalism, we have referred to the concept of nature, *physis*, as that which is defined in opposition to convention, *nomos*. This reference brings us to consider another work of Strauss's that is fundamental in order to understand his critical posture towards modern liberalism: *Natural Right and History*.

From a superficial reading, this book may seem a criticism, developed from a standpoint that endorses some kind of natural law doctrine, of the relativism that for Strauss lies at the core of both Heideggerian radical historicism and Weberian value-free social science. As has been emphasized, Strauss even begins his book by quoting the world-famous passage of the US Declaration of Independence where the following "self-evident truths" are enshrined: "that all men are created equal, that they are endowed by their Creator with certain unalienable Rights, that among these are Life, Liberty, and the pursuit of Happiness" (or better, as Strauss soon explains while interpreting the modern liberal perspective, the pursuit of their own conception of happiness and the good).[28] If we pay attention to Strauss's precise lexicon, in particular to his varied use of the term *right*, however, we realize that he in fact underscores a substantial gap in the tradition appealing to natural law in contrast to legal positivism and historicism. Proof thereof is that in *Natural Right and History*, as we will see in greater details in chapter VI, the very term *right* does not always designate the right in a subjective sense, namely, the *facultas agendi* of the individual. Often, and notably when Strauss refers to the classical tradition, right means instead "what is right or just," seen therefore in an objective perspective (and this in light of a paradigm of reason that, as we have seen before, is understood not only in terms of formal coherence or means-end calculation, but also as a sieve aiming to distinguish between ends worthy of a human being qua human being and not). Strauss obtains such an effect by using right as a *singulare tantum* (a term used only in the singular) every time he refers to the classics, to Plato and Aristotle in particular. Following this lexical use, the expression "natural right" comes to mean, above all, "what is by nature right or just" from an ethico-political perspective, and not, at least at first, the natural right in the legal, subjective sense.

In doing so, Strauss paves the way for a harsh criticism of the modern view of natural law. This view is interpreted by him as ultimately leading to the relativism of legal positivism, in that both approaches reject the "objective" stance on natural right characteristic of the classics. Beginning from Hobbes's contractarianism, and continuing with Locke and the liberal tradition proper, modern thinkers start in fact to interpret the right in an individualistic perspective—as a pre-political right that political society, viewed as an artificial mechanism made on purpose by individuals through a pact, has the task to protect.[29]

As a consequence of this mechanistic conception—which takes hold not only in the philosophico-political sphere, but also in the scientific one (consider, e.g., Galilean natural science)[30]—the axiological rationalism that characterized the inquiry on natural right of the classics is definitely set aside. One no longer searches, in short, for what the right end for a human being qua human being is—one no longer seeks, in the practical realm, a standard capable of leading at least some human beings towards *the* best way of life[31]—but one claims the liberty, nay "the right,"[32] to pursue his or her own conception of happiness (his or her idiosyncratic sort of best life), assuming a perspective where the norm—moral and legal—depends on subjective preferences and not vice versa.[33] The modern perspective, in other words, is indeed a natural law doctrine, but in a sense that has little in common with the classical perspective, which saw the human being as a *physei politikon zoon* (by nature a political animal) with a *telos* (end) given by nature (at least in terms of a best life to pursue), and with a *physei dikaion* (natural right) that was regarded as a standard, no matter how hard to achieve.[34] From a moral and political standpoint, for Strauss this means that modernity, from the very beginning and not only after its turn towards positivism and historicism, abandons a substantial kind of rationalism to embrace a rationalism that is only formal and, as a result, ultimately conducive to relativism.[35]

In Strauss's view, this change of perspective does not occur without serious "side effects." Abandoning the classics' emphasis on a paradigm of human excellence—of virtue interpreted as *areté*—modernity brings about a lowering of the moral and political aims. It is no longer a question of approaching a standard of excellence for the human being, even at the price of legitimating the harshest differences.[36] What now matters the most is, rather, ensuring security (along with the affluence it fosters) for all those who have artificially created political society by means of a pact.[37] In this regard, increasing the available material goods and enforcing suitable laws are viewed as by far the most effective tools. As a result, modernity embraces a "political hedonism"[38]—as Strauss puts it—that is regarded as capable of solving the political predicaments by purely economic and legal means, thereby abandoning the classics' emphasis on education, on the formation of character, viewed, of course, in a moral perspective as well. Peculiar to modernity is, thus, a conception that Strauss sees epitomized by Kant when, in *Toward Perpetual Peace*, he claims that "establishing a state, as difficult as it may sound, is a problem that can be solved even for a nation of devils (if only they possess understanding)" and if it is possible to "arrange a constitution for them."[39] For a constitution, in this sense, is a legal and institutional system that is regarded as capable of making the selfish intentions of the individuals, in themselves conflicting, reconcilable and even useful from the public perspective, provided the individuals are sufficiently enlightened.

Following the example of the classics, Strauss contests that such a society of devils can endure. In his view, aside from legal, institutional, and economic arrangements, great attention ought to be paid to the individuals' moral education, according to either a liberal model (in the classical sense) for the few, or a religious one for the many.[40] In this regard, it is also important to stress, as anticipated above, that for Strauss the same liberal education (that is to say, the education to virtue classically interpreted as *areté*) divides in two according to the distinction between gentlemen and philosophers: while the former are supposed to consider the moral paradigms as ends in themselves, the latter, being devoted to the theoretical life, critically analyze those paradigms and come to regard them mainly as useful means in the political sphere—of which, qua philosophers, they are not a part.[41]

This differentiation notwithstanding, it is only by way of moral education that for Strauss the "liberty of the moderns" can be balanced with a tension towards an ethico-political order able to prevent a lapse into relativism.[42] Just like Plato with respect to ancient democracy, Strauss sees the liberty characterizing modern liberalism and, even more so, modern mass democracy, if not properly mitigated, as an *akairos eleutheria*: a form of license (literally, of "inappropriate liberty") that leads political society to degenerate into anarchy and, from there, to expose itself to the risk of vulgar tyranny. In such a pessimistic analysis, Strauss not only drew inspiration from the teaching of the classics, but he could also see in the tragic epilogue of the Weimar Republic, in which he spent his youth, an important historical warning.[43] The "inappropriate liberty" of the moderns, with its rejection of classical rationalism, its almost exclusive insistence on the legal and economic side of political life, and the merely residual importance it attributes to the role of education, leads for him to a moral relativism and a political hedonism that pave the way for a nihilistic revolution, as is shown, most clearly, by the rise of Nazism in 1930s Germany.

III

In light of what we have observed so far, it is fair to say that the ancient liberalism Strauss describes is not only far from the "democratic" conception Constant presents as the liberty of the ancients, but also at odds, as one would have expected, with the view characteristic of modern liberalism. Unlike what has been claimed, relying on isolated quotations, by some of his students, Strauss can hardly be considered a true friend of liberal democracy.[44] From a political standpoint, as distinct from the philosophical one,[45] he can at most be regarded as an ally of that regime against twentieth-century totalitarianisms[46] (and it seems to me needless to insist on the difference between a real endorsement and a pragmatic alliance). Having said that, I find it equally misleading to concede to an interpretation of Strauss's political views that goes so far as to consider him not so much a conservative, or even "reactionary"[47] critic of modern liberalism, as nothing less than a supporter of a radical form of authoritarianism that would take inspiration, despite the reticence in openly recognizing it, from Nietzsche's nihilism.[48] According to this interpretation, the true source of Strauss's political thought would have to be found not in such classical authors as Plato, Xenophon, and Aristotle, but rather in a philosopher of the "third wave of modernity" like Nietzsche, that very Nietzsche whom Strauss himself defines "the stepgrandfather of fascism."[49]

To prove that this interpretation is exaggerated, it may be useful to take into account "German Nihilism,"[50] a 1941 lecture where, with clearly autobiographical accents, Strauss addresses the question of the essence and roots of that intellectual movement. According to Strauss, German nihilism, which he sees as comprising Nazism as its most vulgar and extreme form, is characterized, first and foremost, by a will of negation ("nihilism" from *velle nihil*, to want the nothing, the annihilation).[51] This will of negation, however, is by no means complete—of self-destruction as well—but it seeks the negation of something specific: Western civilization. In this context, moreover, it is worth noting that Strauss employs the term *civilization* to designate a particular kind of culture, namely, culture interpreted as a *singulare tantum* according to the meaning we have previously described. Civilization, therefore, is ultimately the culture or cultivation of reason.[52] It is the cultivation of the mind that leads to the flourishing of the *civis* ("citizen," from which the term *civilization* precisely comes), the capable and virtuous human being in the classical sense who reaches his or her peak by the full development of the moral and intellectual faculties—of the ethical and dianoetic virtues, to borrow again from Aristotle.[53]

In Strauss's view, German nihilism, including Nazism, opposes that view notably because it starts from the modern conception of civilization.[54] Unlike its ancient counterpart, the modern conception, as we have observed, is characterized by an interpretation of morality that rests on the interests and "rights" of the individual, that is to say, on a perspective that put the emphasis on private usefulness, leading to a conception of morality that Strauss defines as "mercenary."[55] Against this conception, German nihilism insists on the fundamental distinction, in the moral realm, between *utile* and *honestum*, between an approach that regards the moral rules as means to an end and an approach that, by contrast, sees them as ends in themselves.[56] Moreover, insisting on the difference between useful and honest, for Strauss German nihilism proves to be akin to militarism—likewise deeply rooted in the German tradition—because it too understands the most unselfish virtue, the farthest from a "mercenary" conception of morality, as courage in war: the courage of the soldiers who go so far as to sacrifice their lives for the fatherland if need be.[57]

Nazism takes then this conception to paroxysm, in addition interpreting it in a vulgar and inhuman manner. Unlike German nihilism and militarism as such, it moves indeed from a protest of a moral kind, but only in order to seek power and empire by any means (and therewith immorally).[58] In addition, interpreting oppression and cruelty as true expressions (no matter how beastly and inhuman) of the vital forces of the community, it even derives a "disinterested pleasure from the aspect of those qualities which enable nations to conquer," as well as a "genuine pleasure from the aspect of the strong and ruthless who subjugate, exploit, and torture the weak and helpless," as Strauss bluntly points out.[59]

Now, despite this beastly and inhuman outcome embodied by Nazism (and we should not forget that Strauss himself, as a Jew, could directly sense what we are describing with words[60]), in his interpretation German nihilism as a whole shows, all the same, a trait of loftiness, which consists in its revolt against the "political hedonism" that characterizes modernity since Hobbes and Locke.[61] In this revolt, however, in opposing a mercenary conception of morality, for Strauss German nihilism—taking inspiration from such authors as Fichte, Schelling, Hegel, and then, above all, Nietzsche—goes too far in aspiring to a strictly "non-utilitarian" conception of virtue (hence its kinship with militarism, of which German nihilism is a "radicalized form").[62] While in classical rationalism the end to which the whole moral and political framework tends, despite all its restrictions, is in any case the *eudaimonia* (the happiness of the human being in his or her full flourishing, and so, if not what is implied in the US Declaration of Independence, namely, the happiness as each understands it, nonetheless a positive and worldly end), in German nihilism, as a polemic reaction to the modern "mercenary" conception, the emphasis is mostly put on, as it were, negative aspects: self-sacrifice, self-denial, and above all, as we have seen, a radical depreciation of the individual sphere that, while going against common sense, combines well with the celebration of military courage and the supreme sacrifice in battle.[63]

Due to this exaggeration in reacting to modern political hedonism, to say nothing of the risks of vulgar and inhuman degeneration represented by Nazism, for Strauss German nihilism, no matter how lofty, is to be rejected as an only "negative" answer. By contrast, in spite of all its difficulty, he saw in the attempt to revitalize classical rationalism—namely, what we have previously described, following in his footsteps, as ancient liberalism—a wiser and more promising path.[64]

Faced with the harsh reality of the then raging Anglo-German war and its implications from a geopolitical perspective, in "German Nihilism" this attempt takes the shape of a recovery of the Roman imperial tradition by way of a quotation from Virgil's *Aeneid*. In this respect, having underscored that "in defending modern civilization against German nihilism, the English are defending the eternal principles of civilization," Strauss observes:

> No one can tell what will be the outcome of this war. But this much is clear beyond any doubt: by choosing Hitler for their leader in the crucial moment, in which the question of who is to exercise military rule became the order of the day, the Germans ceased to have any *rightful* claim to be more than a provincial nation; it is the English, and not the Germans, who *deserve* to be, and to *remain*, an *imperial* nation: for only the English, and not the Germans, have understood that in order to *deserve* to exercise imperial rule, *regere imperio populos*, one must have learned for a very long time to spare the vanquished and to crush the arrogant: *parcere subjectis et debellare superbos*.[65]

This eloquent statement concerning the higher right of the English to imperial rule (which, incidentally, despite all its civilizing intention, seems to leave little room for such democratic principles as national self-determination)[66] is prepared by Strauss through a qualified criticism of Nietzsche's indictment of British thought. However right Nietzsche may have been in denouncing the shortcomings of such thinkers as Bacon, Hobbes, Locke, and Hume,[67] Strauss acknowledges that, from a political standpoint, their lack of philosophical radicality "proved to be a blessing to English life."[68] For, unlike the Germans with their "contempt for commonsense and the aims of human life, as they are visualized by commonsense," the English "almost always had the very un-German prudence and moderation not to throw out the baby with the bath, i.e., the prudence to conceive of the modern ideals as a reasonable adaptation of the old and eternal ideal of decency, of rule of law, and of that liberty which is not license, to changed circumstances."[69]

In Strauss's account, in addition, such a "muddling through" concerning philosophical questions—which, no matter how disputable in principle, has allowed the English to realize a practically viable synthesis of the premodern and the modern view of civilization—has the merit of handing down the premodern ideal better than in any other case. As he explains, "Whatever may be wrong with the peculiarly modern ideal: the very Englishmen who originated it, were at the same time versed in the classical tradition, and the English always kept in store a substantial amount of the necessary counterpoison. While the English originated the modern ideal—the pre-modern ideal, the classical ideal of humanity, was no where better preserved than in Oxford and Cambridge."[70]

In 1941, when Strauss delivered "German Nihilism," he thus credited the English for having a sufficient dose of that counterpoison, which he later identified with "liberal education."[71] As further proof of this, at that time he could still notice a clear expression of magnanimity and moral greatness in certain figures belonging to their tradition. A case in point is Winston Churchill who, from 1940, rose as a symbol of the resolute, if necessary deadly, fight against Nazism.[72] In the aftermath of the Second World War, however, Strauss's interpretation arguably became gloomier. At least starting from the early 1950s, when he published *Natural Right and History*, the strength of Western liberal democracies seemed to him considerably weakened. As he observed in that book, they combined the tendency towards political hedonism and a legal and mechanistic view of the state with the adoption of the most thorny aspect of the German philosophical tradition, defeated on the battle field but victorious on the intellectual one: a radical relativism that, from the moral perspective, for Strauss characterizes both Heideggerian historicism and Weberian value-free social science. Given such a condition, modern liberalism, having embraced historicism or legal positivism as a result of the intellectual victory of Germany, not only no longer believed in the "self-evident" truths enshrined in the US Declaration of Independence, thereby relinquishing any gleam of the natural law teaching; it also began to lose faith in its own principles, among which tolerance:

When liberals became impatient of the absolute limits to diversity or individuality that are imposed even by the most liberal version of natural right, they had to make a choice between natural right and the uninhibited cultivation of individuality. They chose the latter. Once this step was taken, tolerance appeared as one value or ideal among many, and not intrinsically superior to its opposite. In other words, intolerance appeared as a value equal in dignity to tolerance . . . Liberal relativism has its roots in the natural right tradition of tolerance or in the notion that everyone has a natural right to the pursuit of happiness as he understands happiness; but in itself it is a seminary of intolerance.[73]

Already in the aftermath of the Second World War, in short, Strauss saw also in the Anglo-American world some of the intellectual shortcomings he had seen in the Weimar Republic before 1933.[74] Moral relativism and a lack of confidence in their own principles put liberal institutions in a condition of weakness and crisis.[75] This condition, needless to say, was for Strauss wholly inadequate to contrast the adversaries of Western rationalism, both at home—due to an excessive tolerance of what happens in the private sphere (a tolerance that put those adversaries in the ideal condition for making new proselytes)—and abroad.[76] As a result, he defined this form of modern liberalism as "perverted" and recommended to "true liberals," in its stead, a recovery of the "quality, excellence or virtue" characterizing the classical approach.[77]

IV

The view that Strauss, already in the early 1940s, was attempting the recovery of classical liberalism, and of the Roman imperial tradition more specifically, as a way to counterbalance the shortcomings of modern liberalism, has however been hotly contested. The reason for this is that "German Nihilism" is not the only place where Strauss quotes Virgil's dictum *parcere subjectis et debellare superbos*. The latter already occurs in a 1933 letter Strauss wrote to Löwith, which has by now become quite (in)famous. This is due to the fact that in this letter Strauss indeed observes: "I am reading Caesar's *Commentaries* with deep understanding, and I think of Virgil's *Tu regere imperio . . . parcere subjectis et debellare superbos*."[78] Unlike in

"German Nihilism," however, he appears to interpret such a reference as hardly compatible with an even qualified acceptance of the principles of modern liberalism. Right before the quote from Virgil's *Aeneid* and the reference to Caesar's *Commentaries*, Strauss in fact writes to his Jewish compatriot Löwith: "The fact that the new right-wing Germany does not tolerate us says nothing against the principles of the right. To the contrary: only from the principles of the right, that is from fascist, authoritarian and *imperial* principles, is it possible with decency, that is, without the laughable and despicable appeal to the *droits imprescriptibles de l'homme* to protest against the shabby abomination [*das meskine Unwesen*]."[79]

Retrospectively, the authoritarian and emphatically imperial inspiration of Strauss's protest against Nazi Germany appears steady. What, however, clearly differs from the later "German Nihilism" is his explicit reference to fascism, as well as, quite consistently, his disdainful dismissal of any attempt to carry out such a protest by appealing to the "imprescriptible human rights" enshrined in modern liberalism.

Now, as we will see in greater detail later,[80] although sympathizing, to some extent, for Italian fascism and its leader Mussolini till, possibly, the mid-1930s (to wit, till Italy started to build an alliance with Nazi Germany),[81] Strauss began soon to realize that his association of more traditional authoritarian and imperial principles with those epitomized by that "ultra-modern" ideology had been inadequate. In this respect, he may well have been urged by Löwith's rejoinder that "there is *a lot* to say against the principles of the right if they do not *in fact* tolerate the spirit of science and of German Judaism—and you know that I by no means defend the intellectual freedom characteristic of liberalism and human rights. Moreover, fascism is definitely a *democratic* excrescence."[82] At any rate, it is worth noting that in a letter Strauss wrote to Krüger shortly afterwards, which, of course, cannot help but touch upon the dire political situation of 1933 Germany, he laments: "There could have been a decent, just, *imperial* solution"—in which remark the omission of any reference to fascism is likely due to his meanwhile improved assessment of that political movement.[83]

Although Strauss soon distanced himself from such ultra-modern solutions as fascism, as well as from its "stepgrandfather" Nietzsche,[84] his posture towards the predicament of modern liberalism, in Germany and elsewhere, remained distinctly conservative, not to say "reactionary." Above, we have already described his attempt—not only in *Liberalism Ancient and Modern* but also, *mutatis mutandis*, in "German Nihilism"—to make room, within the liberal tradition, for the revitalization of an ancient pattern of liberalism with a distinctly aristocratic penchant. At the basis of this penchant ultimately lies the idea of a natural hierarchy among human beings that no artificial intervention on society will ever be able to eliminate.[85] This idea, while capable of being juxtaposed to modern liberalism and even democracy, as we will now see, clearly is at odds with the principle of human equality that ultimately pervades political modernity.[86] This is the reason why, in my view, Strauss can hardly be regarded as a "genuine" friend of liberal democracy, as distinct from an ally for pragmatic reasons. As has been correctly emphasized (although with a different aim in mind), Strauss's endorsement of liberal democracy is philosophical rather than political:

> While we are not permitted to remain silent on the dangers to which democracy exposes itself as well as human excellence, we cannot forget the obvious fact that by giving freedom to all, democracy also gives freedom to those who care for human excellence. No one prevents us from cultivating our garden or from setting up outposts which may come to be regarded by many citizens as salutary to the republic and as deserving of giving to it its tone.[87]

By arguing this way Strauss was ultimately reiterating what, in his view, Plato thought of democracy. The latter is indeed a defective political regime, but by way of its comparison to Hesiod's divine race of the heroes—Strauss maintains—Plato implied that, from the standpoint of philosophy with its "selfish and class interest," democracy is the "only regime other than the best in which the philosopher can lead his peculiar way of life without being disturbed."[88] Leaving aside the intriguing question of what this best regime is where "the philosopher can lead his peculiar way of life without being disturbed" (which makes it impossible that this regime is Plato's *kallipolis*, where the philosopher-king would have to rule),[89] what is here important to emphasize is that Strauss's endorsement of democracy, as much as Plato's according to his reading, is philosophical rather than political. In this perspective, democracy is choiceworthy not as such, as a political regime, but for the sake of philosophy, since under that political regime, precisely like under the best (whichever this may be), philosophers are "left alone" and they are "allowed to live the life of the blessed on earth by devoting themselves to investigation of the most important subjects."⁹⁰

Politically and morally speaking, by contrast, aristocracy seems to be a much better choice in Strauss's view, at least in principle. As he plainly puts it in a 1946 letter to Löwith, "In any case, I assert that the πόλις—as it has been *interpreted* by Plato and Aristotle, a *surveyable, urban*, morally serious (σπουδαία) society, based on agricultural economy, in which the *gentry* rule [*herrscht*]—is *morally-politically* the most reasonable and most pleasing."⁹¹ Of course, this does not mean that, as a philosopher, Strauss would choose to live under such an ideal polis. "Do not forget," he is quick to add, in perfect keeping with what we have just observed, "that Plato and Aristotle preferred democratic Athens as a place of residence to the εὐνομούμεναι πόλεις [*well-ordered cities*]: for philosophers moral-political considerations are necessarily secondary."⁹²

However ill-suited for genuine philosophy,⁹³ the closed society dominated by a landed and morally conservative "urban patriciate" is then, in Strauss's account, the best *political* arrangement.⁹⁴ The "open society" becomes good, to a certain degree, from the perspective of philosophy only. At this juncture we can fathom the full scope of the insurmountable tension that for Strauss characterizes the relationship between politics and philosophy. "Philosophy transcends the city, and the worth of the city depends ultimately on its openness, or deference, to philosophy. Yet," he explains, "the city cannot fulfill its function if it is not closed to philosophy as well as open to it; the city is necessarily the cave."⁹⁵

Such an insurmountable tension and the essential limits of politics also surface in Strauss's correspondence with Löwith. In a letter that antedates the one just mentioned by a few days only, Strauss writes to his friend:

> I *really* believe, although to you this apparently appears fantastic, that the perfect political order, as Plato and Aristotle have sketched it, *is* the perfect political order. Or do you believe in the world-state? If it is true that genuine unity is only possible through knowledge of the truth or through the search for the truth, then there is a genuine unity of all men only on the basis of the popularized final *teaching* of philosophy (and naturally this does not exist) or if all men were philosophers (not Ph.D.s, etc.)—which likewise is not the case. Therefore, there can only be closed societies, that is, states. But if that is so, then one can

show from political considerations that the small city-state is in principle superior to the large state or to the territorial-feudal state. I know very well that *today* it cannot be restored (but we live precisely today in the *extremely* unfavorable situation; the situation between Alexander the Great and the Italian πόλεις of the thirteenth to fifteenth centuries was considerably more favorable); but the famous atomic bombs—not to mention at all cities with a million inhabitants, gadgets, funeral homes, "ideologies"—show that the contemporary solution, that is, the completely modern solution, is *contra naturam*.[96]

I have deemed it opportune to quote such a long paragraph because in it we can find summarized and explained some of the major points Strauss raises in the essays we have focused on above. The open society, as "German Nihilism" shows, is to be rejected notably because its ultimate goal is the "universal and homogeneous state," which, besides being hostile to philosophy, constitutes the demise of any moral and political greatness.[97] As such, it must be opposed not only from a political, but also from a philosophical standpoint.[98] As its more politically viable alternative, an aristocratic regime, like the one outlined by Plato and Aristotle, proves to be the best choice. If so, liberal and constitutional democracy, which is the closest approximation to that alternative available in our time,[99] is indeed choiceworthy according to Strauss, but only after its democratic and modern liberal features are adequately tempered. This is, precisely, the task of liberal education "here and now." As Strauss puts it:

> Liberal education is the counterpoison to mass culture, to the corroding effects of mass culture, to its inherent tendency to produce nothing but "specialist without spirit or vision and voluptuaries without heart." Liberal education is the ladder by which we try to ascend from mass democracy to democracy as originally meant. Liberal education is the necessary endeavor to found an aristocracy within democratic mass society. Liberal education reminds those members of a mass democracy who have ears to hear, of human greatness.[100]

This is the utmost one should hope for while living in an "*extremely unfavourable* situation."[101] The fact remains, however, that the natural inequality of human beings, as well as the unbridgeable "gulf separating 'the wise' and 'the vulgar,' "[102] cannot but require some sort of aristocracy, which is the best political order whether "open or disguised."[103] As Strauss observes in conclusion to the letter to Löwith we have quoted above, notably after pointing out that "the completely modern solution is *contra naturam*": "Whoever concedes that Horace did not speak nonsense when he said 'Naturam furca expelles, tamen usque recurret [expel nature with a hayfork, but it always returns],' concedes thereby precisely the legitimacy *in principle* of Platonic-Aristotelian politics. Details can be disputed, although I myself might actually agree with everything that Plato and Aristotle demand (but that I tell only you)."[104]

The danger of the "universal philistinism and creeping conformism" that mass democracy entails must then be counteracted, no matter how cautious one need be due to the limits characterizing even the allegedly "absolute tolerance" preached by modern liberalism.[105] For that tolerance, perverted by the abandonment of any standard, "turns into ferocious hatred of those who have stated most clearly and most forcefully that there are unchangeable standards founded in the nature of man and the nature of things."[106] Arguably, this is why in his published writings, unlike in his private communications, Strauss limits himself to exhorting today's "true liberals" to "counteract the perverted liberalism which"—forgetting "quality, excellence, and virtue"—"contends 'that just to live, securely and happily, and protected but otherwise unregulated, is man's simple but supreme goal.'"[107] Not to recall Strauss's qualified (philosophical) acceptance of liberal democracy, the US where he lived and taught was not, after all, one of those "extremely liberal" societies "in which men can attack in writings accessible to all both the established social or political order and the beliefs on which it is based."[108]

Chapter III

The "Second Cave" and Historical Consciousness in the Correspondence of Leo Strauss and Gerhard Krüger

"The problem inherent in the surface of things, and only in the surface of things, is the heart of things." This famous quotation from Strauss, taken from *Thoughts on Machiavelli*,[1] has never ceased to puzzle his interpreters.[2] As is well known, it occurs in the context of a preliminary appraisal of Machiavelli, particularly of the "simple opinion" according to which he allegedly was a "teacher of evil," the destroyer of a sound and established morality. In that context, Strauss urges the reader not to despise that simple opinion, since, despite all its superficiality, it appears to him to be not only "wholesome"—likely meaning "politically sound"—but also the only available access to "the core of Machiavelli's *thought*."[3]

The surface, meant as a starting point for the analysis, turns out to be central from the philosophical point of view: the problem inherent "only" in the surface of things is the heart of things. It thus seems that, to be truly able to philosophize, one needs first to reemerge from the deep abysses that have opened up over centuries of more or less genuine philosophical thinking. For this is the question: is this deeper and deeper thinking truly philosophical?

According to its original Greek meaning, after all, to philosophize means to go upwards, to try to reach the light of the sun, as Plato puts it in the allegory of the cave. The basic stratum enabling this ascent is that constituted by opinions, like the simple one regarding Machiavelli just referred to. If, instead of trying to leave the cave by moving upwards and towards the sun, we dig deeper in the cave because we "take for granted or otherwise despise the obvious and the surface"[4] that are available in opinions, we end up preventing ourselves from any true understanding. Instead of better discerning things as they are, we will eventually find ourselves in a "pit beneath the cave" or in a "second, 'unnatural' cave," as Strauss puts it,[5] in which the very attempt to gain any philosophical knowledge becomes meaningless, not to say ludicrous: something belonging to a definitively buried naive past, to a stage of human thinking that had better be defined as an "old time philosophy."[6]

Now, all these rather "untimely" themes, among many others, find punctual and admirably clear treatment in Strauss and Krüger's correspondence.[7] At first, both Strauss and Krüger appear to be engaged in an attempt to recover a more traditional type of philosophy, based on such concepts as eternal truth and objective measure or standard (*Massstab*). They both do so by trying to return to the origin of philosophical thinking, in particular, by attempting to unearth the presuppositions of Plato's thought and approach. However, we will see that they end up disagreeing profoundly on this very matter, due to their different intellectual backgrounds: unbelieving and mediated by the medieval Islamic and Judaic tradition in his approach to Plato in Strauss's case; believing and mediated by Augustine's thought in Krüger's. Nonetheless, no matter how much this difference of perspectives leads the two authors to border incommunicability regarding their ultimate positions—a problem demonstrated by two draft letters apparently never sent by Strauss—the same difference, as it unfolds in the correspondence, makes their exchange an invaluable document for the interpretation of Strauss's and Krüger's respective intentions, as well as an uncommonly perspicuous path to fully grasp Strauss's "intrepidity of thought, grandeur of vision, and graceful subtlety of speech" in his published works.[8]

I

The debate between Strauss and Krüger on the second cave and historical consciousness begins with some remarks by Strauss about what he regarded as their common view of the crisis of present-day philosophy and the necessity to recover, as an attempt to solve this crisis, a more traditional perspective, which Strauss sees as particularly exemplified by Plato. Although Strauss notices some reservations in Krüger's stance towards this matter from the very beginning,[9] he praises his friend's approach to Plato as superior to the typical neo-Kantian one, which he considers defective: "Instead of understanding Plato by way of Kant—as the neo-Kantians do—[you] conversely allow Plato to put Kant, and especially us, in question."[10]

In Strauss's view, Krüger's original approach equates his position with that of Julius Ebbinghaus, whose *On the Progress of Metaphysics* Strauss would comment on shortly afterwards in a brief but very deep review.[11] What Strauss sees as common in the two authors, as well as between them and himself, is their opposition to a "philosophical" perspective that accepts and even welcomes the "anarchy of systems" as the last word, since it considers this anarchy not so much as a starting point for philosophy but as the final and insurmountable outcome of its more than two-thousand-year-old investigation. Just like Krüger, who allows Plato to place modernity into question, "Ebbinghaus renounces *all* modern objections by abandoning *the* modern prejudice, namely, the prejudice that *the* truth has not already been found in the past."[12]

According to Strauss, both Krüger and Ebbinghaus help us go against what he had previously defined, in a then unpublished essay, as "conspectivism."[13] From the Latin *conspectio*, like the Greek *synopsis* meaning "overview" or "summary," conspectivism is that view, or better "literary genre," according to which, given the present anarchy of the systems and assuming its unsurmountable character, "the dialectical combination of the keywords and catchwords of present-day philosophy"[14] is what remains available to us. The assumption behind that approach, as Strauss clearly points out in the almost coeval lecture "Religious Situation of the Present," is that "since everything human is historical, there is not *the* question, but always only the question of the *present*."[15] Everything human, including philosophy, would then be "historically conditioned," and this would lead to the meaninglessness of every attempt to philosophize in a more naive, genuine perspective. Strauss even grows poetic, and rather Nietzschean in style, in representing this situation by a prosopopoeia of the Present in "Religious Situation of the Present":

> Stop! You unsuspecting ones! Do you not know that the inexhaustible earth brings forth new generations year after year, which, barely having reached maturity, are all destined to charge with all the fire of youth directly at the truth, at *the*

truth? This has now been happening for thousands of years. For thousands of years the attempt has been made, and time and again it has failed. At one time, later generations did not let themselves be confused by the failure of earlier ones; full of delusion they said to themselves, if they failed—perhaps they approached the issue the wrong way; let's just begin from the beginning; let's begin completely from the beginning. And they began from the beginning, and they also failed. The unhappy ones did not know—what I, the Present, the powerful goddess know—that they *had* to fail. They had to fail since they were seeking *the* truth. For there is not *the one eternal* truth, but each age has *its* truth.[16]

According to Strauss, however, this standpoint is, as it were, not historicist enough. For the historicist perspective embodied in the prosopopoeia of the Present would have to raise the question of its own historicity to be fully consistent, as he will famously reiterate in *Natural Right and History*.[17] This is precisely what Strauss does in a letter to Krüger dated November 16, 1931. There, he plainly states that "if historical consciousness isn't a carriage that one can stop whenever one pleases, then one arrives at a historical destruction [*Destruktion*] of historical consciousness. The latter proves to be historically conditioned and limited to a particular situation; it is nothing other than the attempt, untransparent to itself [*der sich selbst undurchsichtige Versuch*] to win *back* [wieder*zugewinnen*] the ancient freedom of philosophizing: the battle against prejudices is the primordial form [*Urform*] of historical consciousness."[18] The letter significantly goes on, and ultimately ends, with a reference to an enclosed review, presumably the previously mentioned one of Ebbinghaus published the same year. But what should catch our attention here are the terms *destruction* and *prejudices* (*Destruktion* and *Vorurteile*).

Destruktion, in fact, is certainly translatable with *destruction*. However, a more explicit and philosophically pregnant equivalent in the given context (as has been held in the introduction) would be *deconstruction*. By saying that one arrives at the historical deconstruction of historical consciousness, Strauss is implying that he himself is employing the tools characteristic of historicism, notably in its Heideggerian form. He is doing so, nonetheless, with an opposite objective. What Strauss aims at is not so much the indictment of the whole metaphysical and rationalistic tradition. He rather seeks its rehabilitation (at least of its original, naive approach) through the destabilization of that indictment's foundation, which is the concept of a historical consciousness that unreflectively considers itself as the last word—as the final, even benevolent judgment of the Present on the entire preceding philosophical tradition.[19]

The attempt to follow this Heideggerian approach, after turning it upside down, is well-documented in the much later "An Unspoken Prologue to a Public Lecture at St. John's College,"[20] which proves that we are dealing with no passing insight. It will be seen how the correspondence with Krüger as well as the review of Ebbinghaus are quite generous in that regard. First, however, let us consider the other key reference in the previous quote from Strauss, namely "prejudices [*Vorurteile*]," since this reference will lead us to deal with the topic of the so-called second cave in which not only the genuine meaning of Strauss's critique of historical consciousness, but also the role played by Heidegger in that respect become fully perspicuous.

In mentioning the "battle against prejudices" and the attempt to "win *back* the ancient freedom of philosophizing" in his letter of November 16, 1931, Strauss could not fail to think of his recent lecture "Religious Situation of the Present" and "Review of Julius Ebbinghaus, *On the Progress of Metaphysics*," in which the topic of the second cave is addressed. A striking terminological similarity can be noticed above all in the lecture. There, after putting the prosopopoeia of the Present on stage and carrying out a critique of conspectivism that culminates in the reassertion of the "necessity of the naivety of questioning," Strauss quotes Maimonides as saying that compared to the "*natural* difficulties of philosophizing" of Plato's time, as represented in the allegory of the cave, in his time there is a new, additional reason that accounts for "the differences of opinion in philosophy, and therefore for the difficulty of philosophy simply."[21] This additional reason that "did not exist" among the Greeks—addressed by Maimonides in the quoted passage from the *Guide of the Perplexed* at first in terms of *habituation* and *schooling*, but later on with the more explicit "habituation to *writings* in which they [the multitude] firmly believe"—turns out to be biblical revelation.[22] Consequently, this time in his own name, Strauss concludes: "Let us sum up: by the fact that a tradition resting on revelation has entered the world of philosophy, the difficulty of philosophizing is fundamentally augmented, the freedom of philosophizing fundamentally limited." And then, again referring to Maimonides, he goes on to say that "in RMbM's [Maimonides's] remark, the struggle of the entire last 3 centuries, the struggle of the Enlightenment, is in a sense sketched, outlined: in order to render possible philosophy in its natural difficulty, the artificial difficulty of philosophizing has to be eliminated; there has to be a struggle against *prejudices* [Vorurteile]. In this, modern philosophy is fundamentally different from Greek philosophy: the latter struggles only against appearance and opinion; modern philosophy's struggle begins prior to that against prejudices."[23]

Unlike appearance and opinion, prejudices are therefore engendered by revelation, i.e., as Strauss puts it in a 1932 letter to Krüger, by a "νομος-tradition" or "a tradition of obedience" where "beliefs" are seen as deriving from an absolutely authoritative source, making the "'tradition' of questioning," which is philosophy, not only more difficult but also less free and more precarious.[24] Yet this is not the only insight we can get from "Religious Situation of the Present." The link between prejudices and historical consciousness, which we have briefly seen in the November 16, 1931, letter to Krüger, is also more broadly explained in this lecture. As we have seen, in the letter Strauss refers to "the battle against prejudices" as the "primordial form [*Urform*] of historical consciousness." In "Religious Situation of the Present" he had already dwelled on this interpretation, observing that the "entanglement" of modern philosophy in the tradition of obedience triggered by the emergence of revelation in the world of philosophy "is further intensified by a *theory* that *legitimizes* this entanglement."[25] Unlike the Enlightenment that "was wholly convinced that history was accidental, that the victorious party was not in the right just because it happened to be victorious, in the nineteenth century the belief that world history is the world's court of judgment becomes dominant."[26] And once this belief becomes accepted, it evidently takes no great effort to move from the philosophy of history of a Hegelian mold, alluded to here, to the recognition of the absolute authority of the present that is at the basis of present-day philosophy and its historical consciousness.

According to Strauss, this ever-deeper entanglement is ultimately the reason why we cannot simply ask and try to answer the questions of the ancients, starting from the one *pos bioteon* (how should one live? what is the best way of life?). In his view, we now need a longer detour in order to first free ourselves from the layers of prejudices that the "νομος-tradition" engendered by revelation, as well as the revolt against that tradition, have laid down on us. In "Religious Situation of the Present," once again recalling the allegory of the cave, Strauss clearly voices this need: ". . . we cannot answer immediately as we are; for we know that we are deeply entangled in a tradition; we are yet much further down than Plato's cave dwellers. We must raise ourselves to the *origin* of the tradition, to the level of *natural ignorance*."²⁷ It is, however, in his "Review of Julius Ebbinghaus, *On the Progress of Metaphysics*," where Strauss is most explicit regarding the relationship of this upward movement of disentanglement with a reinterpretation of the deconstructive approach of Heideggerian historicism. In this review essay, where he praises Ebbinghaus for abandoning "*the* modern prejudice . . . that *the* truth has not already been found in the past," Strauss contrasts our condition with that of the cave dwellers in Plato's allegory: "Today we find ourselves in a second, much deeper cave than the lucky ignorant persons Socrates dealt with."²⁸ In addition, he gives us a hint of what one needs in order to regain a condition of "natural ignorance," as well as an indication of his own philosophical agenda: "We need history first of all in order to *ascend* to the cave from which Socrates can lead us to light; we need a propaedeutic, which the Greeks did not need, namely, learning through reading [*lesendes Lernen*]. It is the merit of Ebbinghaus's writing that it has called attention, with fitting forcefulness, to this desideratum of all present-day philosophy."²⁹

All these observations—which clearly relate Strauss's distinctive hermeneutical approach, learning through reading the old books, to the metaphor of the second cave, making that historical approach a mere propaedeutic to the reactivation of an essentially unhistorical philosophy— are echoed and further explained in the Strauss-Krüger correspondence. The first instance of this can be found in a letter of October 15, 1931, in which Strauss proves to be convinced, at that time, that Krüger shares his views regarding the second cave. Anticipating the imminent publication of his review of Ebbinghaus to his friend, he enthusiastically comments: "I have now discovered a fourth man who shares our opinion concerning the present as a second cave: Ebbinghaus. His talk 'On the Progress of Metaphysics' contains several quite excellent formulations."³⁰

However, the conviction soon fades away. After reading a manuscript on Hobbes by Strauss that has so far remained unpublished, in a letter dated November 13, 1932, Krüger criticizes Strauss's approach, as shown in a critique of Dilthey he conducted in that manuscript, by claiming: "You too don't really start from a 'natural' basis when you begin from the situation of the falling-away [*Abfall*] from revelation. It is not clear to me how you understand antiquity to be exemplary here."³¹ To this remark, addressing the core of Strauss's position about the possibility to regain the first, natural cave, on November 17, 1932, Strauss replies: "Of course the difference between you and me lies deeper. You touch upon this in your comment about my Dilthey-critique . . . It is a matter of 'historicity.' You see a contradiction in the fact that I believe in a *'natural'* basis *and* view antiquity to be exemplary [*massgeblich*]."³² To substantiate these remarks, he significantly goes on:

> I am inclined to assume—until there is evidence to the contrary—that antiquity (more precisely: Socrates-Plato) is exemplary *precisely because* it philosophized *naturally*, i.e., originally inquired into the order that is *natural* for human beings. That this possibility was uncovered in Greece and only there is a matter of indifference as long as it is understood that Socrates-Plato's question and answer are the natural question and the natural answer: *by* philosophizing, Socrates is *already* no longer a Greek, but a human being.³³

And after having expanded on philosophy's historical inception amidst the decay of the Greek polis, he concludes: "In this sense, philosophy has *always* been and has remained unhistorical."³⁴

Then Strauss more pointedly comes to the question of the second cave. "That *we, today*, cannot get by without history," he argues, "is a question external to philosophy," its true reason being that "we . . . have been pushed into a second cave and today no longer even have the *means* to philosophize naturally."³⁵ This is due not only, as we have underscored, to "the absurd intermixing of a νομος-tradition with a philosophical tradition, i.e., of biblical revelation with Greek philosophy, of a tradition of obedience with a 'tradition' of questioning (which, as a tradition, is no longer a questioning)," but also to "the struggle against the tradition of revelation, undertaken in a manner of speaking in the dark."³⁶ Strauss elaborates on the meaning of these latter remarks in the continuation of the letter, where he describes modern philosophy since the seventeenth century as committed to fighting against tradition in order to "recover the Greek freedom of philosophizing" and "find *again* . . . an original, *natural* basis." In his view, however, by doing so modern philosophy, "from its inception until Heidegger (*including* the latter), . . . understood itself to be progress and progressive" and therewith remains "unradical" in that "it thinks it can presume that the fundamental questions have already been answered, and can therefore 'progress.' " This eventually leads to the "neglect of the Socratic question that Nietzsche later denounced," and to that of "ontology that Heidegger uncovered."³⁷

II

Nietzsche as the "*last* Enlightener" had already been evoked in "Religious Situation of the Present."[38] In this lecture, Strauss had also explained, albeit slightly differently, the process of opposition—but at the same time further entanglement—characterizing modern philosophy in its struggle against the "obedience tradition" engendered by revelation. In that context, his emphasis was not so much on the progressive character of modern philosophy, as on its ability, at least at its inception with the Enlightenment, to achieve a mere "freedom of *answering* but not the freedom of questioning, only the freedom of saying No instead of the traditional Yes. (Mortality vs. immortality, chance vs. providence, atheism vs. theism, passions vs. reason)."[39]

Here, however, it is Strauss's reference to Heidegger that should most capture our attention, since, as we will see, the discussion of Heidegger with reference to the second cave plays a key role in the continuation of his correspondence with Krüger.

In his response to Strauss on December 4, 1932, Krüger finally voices all his doubts about Strauss's metaphor of the second cave and the meaningfulness of his attempt to recover a more natural, naive approach to philosophy. He starts by only conditionally accepting Strauss's analogy, which seems to him to be "a very fitting description" of present-day intellectual condition if one sets out from Strauss's "equation of ancient, natural, and right [*richtig*]."[40] However, he also promptly makes it clear that he cannot accept that equation because, as he puts it by taking up Strauss's Platonic terms, "the metal of the 'second' chain is so strong that the entire analogy becomes untenable."[41] According to Krüger, instead of trying to understand and criticize historicism from a Platonic standpoint, Strauss would rather have to follow the opposite path and see that it is the Platonic position that is "in need of revision." After all, as he emphatically adds adopting the words Strauss had previously used, "*the problem of 'prejudice' is even more radical than that of the* δόξα."[42]

It should be remembered that Strauss had directly connected prejudice with biblical revelation. Krüger proves to be quite aware of this connection. It is likely for this reason that he chooses to stress the whole sentence just quoted, as well as to insist on the role played by Christianity in this framework in the continuation of his letter. The role of Christianity had actually already been hinted at by Strauss himself in an allusive parenthetical quotation attached, not by accident, to his definition of modern philosophy, from its inception to Heidegger, as "progressive." But in his response Krüger further elaborates on that question, making the encounter of philosophy with Christianity an irreversible and actually enriching turning point. This is why in his view, instead of combatting historicism by trying to reach a no longer accessible Platonic natural cave, one had better reduce it "to its objective [*sachlich*] and historical core: Christ's factual [*faktisch*] dominion over the spirit of post-ancient humanity."[43] It is Plato who, in the wake of Augustine, must be led to make room for revelation, not the other way round.[44] To this end, according to Krüger historicism is to be challenged because it represents a relativistic "denaturing [*Denaturierung*] of the Christian 'bondage [*Fesselung*]' of humanity"[45]—a "bondage" that, once reestablished by the reactivation of Augustine's Platonism, turns out instead to be the only possible source of a standard able to put an end to the "anarchy of the systems."

There is no solution, therefore, from the purely philosophical point of view according to Krüger. Strauss's attempt at " 'naively' claiming the openness of the 'things themselves' for our gaze," as the derivation from twentieth-century phenomenology of that formula already shows, is doomed to failure or, at best, to constitute a "*demand* [*Forderung*] that is by no means naïve."[46] The problem of the prejudice is more radical than that of opinion. In purely philosophical terms, historicism is more profound than the Platonism that Strauss, in light of the teaching of Maimonides and his Islamic predecessors, is trying to recover: "Our factual unnaturalness makes it such that" the naturalness of thought "must be a *problem*."[47]

In Krüger's view, the only viable solution to the anarchy of present-day philosophy is therefore, ultimately, a return to revelation. Strauss shows he has fully understood his friend's basic position in his reply of December 27, 1932: "The root of our difference is that I cannot *believe*, and that I am therefore searching for a possibility of *living* without faith, whereas you assume that such a possibility doesn't—any longer?—exist."[48]

Yet faith, or the lack thereof, by no means constitutes the basis of Strauss's counterargument, which aims instead to be a truly philosophical attempt, no matter how unprecedented, to find a way out from the conundrum of historicism. Strauss indeed challenges Krüger on the only available ground: the assertion that "the problem of prejudice," which here stands for a philosophy made "deeper" by the inception of historical consciousness as a result of its encounter with Christianity, is "more radical than the problem of opinion," i.e., a philosophy capable of naively beginning its journey from the Platonic, natural cave. In other words,

Strauss is intrepid enough to challenge Krüger—along with the whole of present-day mainstream philosophy (not to mention common inveterate conviction)—on the assumption that what is deeper or more profound (*tiefer*) is eo ipso more radical (*radikaler*). Having now realized that Krüger could not be counted among those who accepted the idea of the second cave, there were, at best, three people left who shared the grounds for that attempt: Strauss, Klein, and perhaps Ebbinghaus.

Strauss's counterargument proceeds as follows: he first establishes the identity of the problem of the second cave with that of historicism and, following Krüger, traces "the 'objective and historical core' of historicism" back to "'Christ's factual dominion over post-ancient humanity.'" Then he raises the question as to what follows from this factual dominion "for the person who does *not* believe" and who, therefore, "denies the right, i.e., the divine right, of this dominion."[49]

According to Strauss, two opposite answers to this question are possible. The first is the one embodied by Heidegger and, ultimately, shared by Krüger: "Christianity has brought to light facts concerning human life that were not known, or not known sufficiently, to ancient philosophy. At least, it has understood these facts more *deeply* than antiquity." This deeper understanding of historicity first made possible by Christianity, being retained by post-Christian philosophy, makes this latter "deeper and more radical than ancient philosophy."[50]

Against this view, which "perhaps" is "right," but still needs to "be proven to be so . . . through *direct* confrontation between modern and ancient philosophy," Strauss advances a second answer, which leads to a much less trodden path. He sets out by recalling his previous definition of modern, post-Christian philosophy as "a *progress* over against ancient philosophy even if Christianity is not '*true*.'" To this assumption, he objects that post-Christian philosophy "always just leads to 'secularizations,' i.e., to positions that one cannot enter into without Christianity and in which one cannot remain *with* it."[51] This inconsistency, on which Strauss also insists in major works from the late 1920s and 1930s such as *Spinoza's Critique of Religion* and *Philosophy and Law*, leads one to raise the question: "Is there not a simply a-Christian philosophy?," or even more pointedly: "Is ancient philosophy—be it Platonic or Aristotelian—not *the* philosophy?"[52]

The point is that, even conceding that post-Christian philosophy, being characterized by historicity, is deeper, one can still question the philosophical relevance of this greater depth precisely by employing the devices made available by the development of such a historical approach.

As we have seen by referring to Heideggerian deconstruction and "learning through reading [*lesendes Lernen*]" as inspired by Ebbinghaus, one can still raise the question of the historicity of historicism. It is exactly what Strauss does in the continuation of his letter by asking Krüger: "Is the viewpoint of depth not itself already a Christian viewpoint that needs to be expelled in its turn [*ein christlicher Gesichtspunkt, der seinerseits der Ausweisung bedarf*]?" This deconstructive question further leads to the following ones: "Is depth identical with radicality? Is it not perhaps the case that 'depth' is not *actually* radical?"[53]

These appear to be no rhetorical questions, since in this letter Strauss presents his reflections, as well as his whole theory of the second cave, as a "pure *aperçu*" as long as one does not find proof that confirms it.[54] Yet in his view that insight proves to be sufficient to maintain that "the *querelle des anciens et des modernes* must be repeated," as he significantly states in an earlier draft of the same letter.[55]

The continuation of the letter is surely an attempt to do so. After observing that "depth has its home in introspection [*Selbstprüfung*]," and that introspection "presupposes a standard [*Massstab*]," whose question is the truly "radical question," he goes on to claim in his own name that "the moderns have neglected this radical question to the extent that they have promoted introspection—whether actually or only apparently."[56] Even conceding that "modern reflection or introspection or depth has disclosed . . . a whole dimension not disclosed to the Greeks," is this really—asks Strauss—"a *more radical* dimension? Do we really know more about the roots [*Wurzeln*] of life, about the questionability [*Fraglichkeit*] of life, than the Greeks?" "Or"—he concludes with an implicit reference to his review of Ebbinghaus—"is it just that something has lodged itself in front of *the* radical dimension that was the sole object of Greek philosophy, and which forces a reflective propaedeutics on us?"[57]

After these thought-provoking questions, Strauss confirms that he himself—not only Krüger—thinks that "*we must* philosophize historically" and that "'naïvete' is merely a demand."[58] But he also asks whether this condition is truly an advance in philosophical knowledge or, on the contrary, "a hateful fatality that forces us into an 'unnatural' detour."[59] Strauss's answer, in the wake of his review of Ebbinghaus and his original reinterpretation of Heideggerian deconstruction, is all the more explicit: "By 'recollection [*Erinnerung*]' we must enter the dimension in which, understanding the Greeks, we can question 'naïvely' with them."[60]

III

Strauss thus asserts the impossibility of naively philosophizing in the modern world as much as Krüger does. In this respect, he sees the difference between his friend and him mainly in the fact that he does not regard this impossibility as progress. In his view, this means that modern philosophy, contrary to its self-understanding, is neither "progress" nor "progressive." In the final version of his response of December 27, 1932, Strauss does not specifically touch on this important point, which he had previously hinted at.[61] In one of the preparatory drafts, however, he elaborates extensively on this matter. The reason why modern philosophy isn't progressive—and why it ultimately leads to a "massive 'deconstruction of tradition' [*gewaltige 'Destruktion der Tradition'*]," as he puts it in Heideggerian terms precisely at the end of this draft—is that modern philosophy eventually results, through Nietzsche, in the same question that ancient philosophy, particularly with Socrates, raised as its starting point by asking what virtue is. Strauss therefore implies that the allegedly linear and progressive development of modern philosophy proves instead to be circular, leading to the reopening of that classical philosophical question.

Strauss, as we have noticed, had already underlined the key role of Nietzsche in that deconstructive process, as the "*last* Enlightener," in "Religious Situation of the Present." In this lecture, Nietzsche's decisive function is that of "shaking" the tradition "at its *roots*," of tearing down its "pillars," namely the "prophets and Socrates-Plato," by siding with their respective opponents: the kings and the sophists.[62]

In the just mentioned draft of his letter of December 27, 1932, Strauss again takes up the image of Nietzsche as the last Enlightener who breaks down "the pillars of the European world."[63] He also reiterates the description of him as the one who rejects the prophets and Socrates-Plato by opting, this time, for the "Israelite-Jewish kings (or Caesar)" on one hand, and "Homer and Pericles" on the other. But besides conveying a more nuanced portrait of Nietzsche, in light of which this latter appears to be, no matter how opposed to Christianity, still entangled in it,[64] in this draft letter Strauss provides important details that help us understand his reference to the circularity of the development of philosophical tradition.

Anticipating what he will write to Löwith a few weeks later, Strauss now explains that, by siding with the kings and Caesar or Homer and Pericles, Nietzsche "rediscovered the '*natural*' ideal of humanity—the ideal of ἀνδρεία [courage]." In doing so, he "set the position of ἀνδρεία over against the modern Enlightenment's *denial* of ἀνδρεία."[65] This means that at the peak of modernity, as represented by Nietzsche, we find a conception of virtue that is ultimately the same as the one from which Socrates starts his philosophical journey. As Strauss puts it: "In short: Modern philosophy, taken to its *conclusion*, seems to me to lead to the point at which Socrates *begins*."[66] This is its "circularity," which enables the "repetition of the ancients at the peak of modernity" Nietzsche aimed for, no matter how polemically. Socrates in fact sets out by asking the "question about the essence of virtue."[67] And since, being in the natural cave, he deals with opinion and appearance, he starts his questioning from the simple opinion that characterizes that essentially political dimension, according to which virtue is courage. This certainly is only the Platonic Socrates's starting point, since his final word is a reinterpretation of courage that, while still recognizing (unlike modern Enlightenment) its role as a virtue, leads to its subordination to the supreme ideal of knowledge and the life devoted to it.[68] Still, this trait of his philosophical approach induces Strauss to affirm the convergence between Nietzsche's conclusion of modern philosophy and the inception of Socrates's investigation, and therewith the circular and deconstructive character of that philosophy.

In this regard, all this seems to be confirmed by what Strauss claims in the draft letter under examination, namely that Nietzsche, "after having rediscovered the '*natural*' ideal of humanity—the ideal of ἀνδρεία—did not proceed to an *unbelieving* critique of this ideal," which is clearly a reference to the Platonic critique.[69] Moreover, some a posteriori evidence supporting our interpretation can be found in the already mentioned note 2 of the introduction to *Philosophy and Law*.[70] In that context, after commenting on the Platonic critique of courage (as well as on the Enlightenment's fight against *prejudices* as distinct from *opinions*), Strauss concludes by underlining the necessity of the "'historicizing' of philosophy" in order to make possible "the ascent from the second, 'unnatural' cave . . . into that first, 'natural' cave which Plato's image depicts, to emerge from which into the light is the original meaning of philosophizing."[71]

Krüger, unfortunately, never read the remarks Strauss penned in his preparatory draft. In his response, he can therefore only deal with the critique of historical consciousness Strauss formulates in the final version of his letter of December 27, 1932. He begins by agreeing that the question of the standard (*Massstab*) is more radical than that of introspection, whereby, however, the moderns have "buried" it for him as well. Unlike

Strauss, on the other hand, he believes the question of the standard can ultimately be solved only by opening a path towards revelation. After all, Augustine's Plato is "really Platonic" in Krüger's view, as we have already seen.[72]

This assumption, however, does not mean that Krüger is ready to admit that his position rests on belief. Not only under the influence of Augustine, but also of Kant, he instead interprets such an attempt to open a path towards revelation as genuinely philosophical. For this reason, he retorts to Strauss that he himself does not fully recognize the primacy of the question of the standard over that of introspection when he characterizes his position, and describes their difference, in terms of belief vs. unbelief: "Your faith or lack thereof is something purely personal here . . . By setting your problem up one step too late, at the problem of belief or unbelief, you assume the question of the standard to be solved. You take your bearings—even if just negatively—by revealed religion."[73] This being the case, from a genuinely philosophical perspective as he interprets it, "the matter seems to be such that we must repeat the ancient and genuine philosophical questions, but in the insurmountable factual situation that philosophizing is no longer as self-evident as it was then."[74] However, to these remarks—which, taken by themselves, could lead one to think that the difference between Strauss and him concerning the interpretation of philosophy is a mere matter of words—he adds the following:

> This *new* element, this newly arisen problem for philosophy, can only be posed within a philosophy of world history, and that means within an analysis of the basis of "reflection" that is *originally* discovered in the face of revelation. Now, one can take this as a "hateful fatality" or as a glimmer of hope in the night of our perplexity . . . But if one wanted to claim to find the true and *non-arbitrarily* authoritative [*das Wahre und unwillkürlich Massgebende*] somewhere else, one would have to understand ourselves far worse than we two do.[75]

To summarize: revelation cannot be "dislodged" from the world of philosophy, as Strauss would aim to do by raising the question of the second cave. Hence, we are faced by an either-or. Either revelation is the measure, or the "anarchy" of historicism must be. *Tertium non datur*.

Strauss, however, is fully committed to the search for this *tertium*, as in it he sees the only way to keep a possibility for philosophy open. For this reason, in response to Krüger's insinuation that he is "doing something 'philosophically false'" by beginning from his unbelief, he tries to vindicate his choice by connecting his unbelieving position to the "opinion of the age" and explaining his stance in terms of Socratic ignorance: "I precisely don't *know* anything, but instead merely *opine*. First, I want to get clear on what I opine (and my δόξα is atheism)."[76] This Socratic intonation proves to be in perfect harmony with Strauss's further remark on his difference from Krüger: "So we agree that the ancient questions are the *genuine* philosophical questions. We argue about the character of modern questions. And I think that these modern questions, measured by the ancient ones, are not genuinely philosophical, but instead merely *propaedeutic*"—a remark that can easily be seen as reference to the question of *lesendes Lernen* and the second cave, which is here prudently advanced by Strauss as only his "supposition (not entirely unfounded, I hope), not real knowledge."[77]

In his following letter, Krüger challenges Strauss precisely on the distinction between opinion and knowledge, significantly addressing the issue from the perspective of the ancient Greeks. He claims that the latter could refer to the concept of δόξα, as much as Strauss does in his previous letter, "since they took fundamentally achievable ἐπιστήμη to be their standard." According to Krüger, however, "if, due to the historical experience of the world of itself and of its historicity as such, the achievement of epistemic knowledge becomes questionable in principle, then the analysis of the question-situation [*Fragesituation*] changes as well."[78] This means that—with historicistic hindsight, as it were—the Greeks' "way of *treating* the themes was *not correct* back then. It could not be. Now, it could be. The 'not correct' is a *privatio boni* [privation of good], i.e., it does not mean that Plato did not understand anything about true philosophy, but that he searched in a confused and incorrect way." For Krüger, ultimately, no matter how important philosophically, Plato represents only "the greatest relative approximation of the true way of inquiry,"[79] as we have already observed.

Replying to these essentially historicist remarks, in a letter of July 17, 1933, Strauss at first limits himself to underscoring the apparent contradiction between them and Krüger's attempt to go back to Platonism and the idea of an objective standard.[80] Then—but only in an unsent draft dated July 22, 1933—he goes on to express the entirety of his disagreement and, finally, to reduce Krüger's "philosophical" position to a matter of faith.

In his letter, Krüger had attempted to destabilize the binary opposition between δόξα and ἐπιστήμη by introducing a third concept, *Glaube* (belief), while trying to understand it from a still philosophical perspective: "A philosopher can expand the indecision of opining quite a bit, but it is always just a loosening up of the structure of knowledge [*eine Lockerung des Gefüges von Wissen*] in which one factually [*faktisch*] lives and must live." Accordingly, one never merely "opines," as Strauss put it, but already "believes," moving closer to a knowledge that, however, "is always inadequately accounted for, and in principle can never be accounted for without some fundamental obscurities."[81] To this formulation, which blurs the distinction between opinion and knowledge and ultimately makes the attempt to rationally seek an objective measure or standard meaningless, Strauss replies that "*questioning* begins when that 'structure of knowledge' in which we live proves to be brittle and full of gaps."[82] By doing so, his aim clearly is to move from belief and a never fully attainable knowledge to inquiry and doubt, which start from opinion.

The same goal seems to be behind his choice to substantiate his remarks with an example taken from the dire political situation of the day (recall that the draft is dated July 22, 1933). Referring to the "structure of the liberal-democratic knowledge," he observes that "this whole modern world is cracking at all its seams."[83] In light of the inadequate character of all modern attempts, including the anti-liberal ones, to deal with this predicament, in his view the possibility remains to "try out solutions that are in principle unmodern, and concretely that means old solutions." These solutions, however, appear to be "exposed to considerable doubts" in the modern world, due to its unbelief or historicism and relativism. "In light of these immense difficulties," Strauss concludes, "no knowledge is possible at first, only surmising and questioning."[84]

Questioning and doubt, which are intrinsically related to the opposition between opinion and knowledge, emerge, therefore, as the only reasonable philosophical path, both theoretically and practically. Why, then, does Krüger raise the question of belief? In the attempt to answer this question Strauss underlines two key aspects that distinguish belief from opinion. First, unlike opinion, which has intrinsically to do with doubt, belief fosters "*action*." Second, and more generally, "to believe is to believe *someone* [jemandem *glauben*]," whereas "ideals are never a matter of belief, but instead either of knowing or of opining."[85] Admittedly, these comments are quite difficult to understand (unsurprisingly, being part of an unsent draft). But what can their meaning be? Can it perhaps be the case that Strauss is intimating that the philosophical shift to *belief*, which Krüger also approves, has provided, however unintentionally, a suitable conceptual background for the rise of Nazism, with its emphasis on action and blind trust in the leader, as the political context of the comments may suggest?[86] Or do they rather hint at Krüger's underlying Christian faith that, in Strauss's view, impairs his ability to truly philosophize from the beginning, as a subsequent reference to Augustine may lead one to think?[87] In any event, Strauss's reaffirmation of the necessity to keep an open path for a philosophy still stemming from its Greek background and not to surrender to forms of irrational belief is clear.

With the draft of July 22, 1933, the real debate between Strauss and Krüger concerning their philosophical underpinnings, as well as the second cave and historical consciousness that make up a decisive part of them, essentially comes to an end. Even though other letters follow, their edge becomes less cutting and challenging, likely due to the acquired awareness of the irreconcilable character of the two authors' ultimate positions. Strauss, sometimes, indeed finds a polite way to voice his perplexity regarding Krüger's position.[88] But the only true exception is what he writes on December 25, 1935, again in a letter that apparently remained an unsent draft. There Strauss, commenting on a review Krüger had previously sent him, takes the themes of historicism and the second cave up again. After having praised Krüger's piece, he states: "On the other hand, you will not be surprised to hear that I cannot fully agree with you. I am less convinced than ever that historicity as such is a philosophical problem." Then, expanding on these remarks, he adds: "I have meanwhile familiarized myself a little with the beginnings of the philosophy of history in the 16th century, where the problem still appears in its ancient nakedness, and that has only bolstered my suppositions that first arose regarding Mannheim's idiocy (*Ideology and Utopia*)."[89]

Since the time of "Conspectivism" (1929), Strauss's "suppositions" about the necessity of recovering a more naive style of philosophizing had, therefore, only become stronger. The second cave and *lesendes Lernen* prove to be no passing themes. And the best indication of this are not only Strauss's several subsequent essays in which he attempts to "enter the dimension in which, understanding the Greeks, we can question 'naively' with them,"[90] but also, as we have already underlined, what he says, as late as 1959, to celebrate his lifelong friend Jacob Klein in "An Unspoken Prologue to a Public Lecture at St. John's College":

> While everyone else in the young generation who had ears to hear was either completely overwhelmed by Heidegger, or else, having been almost completely overwhelmed by him, engaged in well-intentioned but ineffective rearguard actions against him, Klein alone saw why Heidegger is truly important: by uprooting and not simply rejecting the tradition of philosophy, he made it possible for the first time after many centuries—one hesitates to say how many—to see the roots of the tradition as they are and thus perhaps to know, what so many merely believe, that those roots are the only natural and healthy roots.[91]

Strauss's view of the natural and healthy character of the Greek roots and the importance of Heidegger's deconstruction in that respect remains thus the same in his maturity as well. What possibly changes, if anything, is shown by the incidental remark "one hesitates to say how many," which should not pass unnoticed. Arguably, it is a hint of the key role of biblical revelation in the process of "entanglement" of modern philosophy—a role that Strauss, later in his life, decided to emphasize much less clearly than in his writings and letters of the late 1920s and 1930s.

IV

At the beginning of this essay, we intimated that Strauss's insights about the second, unnatural cave may have directly to do with his enigmatic remarks about the surface in *Thoughts on Machiavelli*. Whether this truly is the case, will perhaps always remain obscure. Certainly, however, the representation of philosophy emerging from the correspondence of Strauss and Krüger, as well as from the essays by Strauss we have referred to, gives an uncommon, negative sense to the idea of depth insofar as it relates to the introspection (*Selbstprüfung*) that modern philosophy inherits from Christianity. Unlike this subjectivist approach, and the historicism it eventually flows into, genuine, natural philosophizing is possible for Strauss only if we start from the surface represented by the opinion and appearance characterizing Plato's natural cave. It is only by regaining that surface, and then by dialectically moving upwards from there, that one can attempt to reach that objective, unhistorical dimension where the question of the standard (*Massstab*), neglected by modernity, becomes meaningful again.

In this regard, it seems no coincidence that Strauss, in the introduction to *Thoughts on Machiavelli*, while mentioning neither the Platonic, nor the second cave, insists nonetheless on the assumption that "there are fundamental alternatives . . . which are permanent or coeval with man," to conclude that his "critical study of Machiavelli's teaching can ultimately have no other purpose than to contribute towards the recovery of the permanent problems."[92] These permanent problems, often negated by "many of our contemporaries," seem to be possible only once we have reemerged from the depth of historicism and regained the surface of opinion, including the simple one about Machiavelli as a teacher of evil. "Not the contempt for the simple opinion, nor the disregard of it, but the considerate *ascent* from it leads to the core of Machiavelli's thought."[93] It is interesting to note that this core, according to Strauss, is a "comprehensive reflection regarding the status of the fatherland on the one hand and of the soul on the other," at the heart of which lies the fundamental question of "the one thing needful,"[94] along with that of the standard the latter implies.

Chapter IV

Natural Right in Strauss and Krüger's Exchange

> Only peace, i.e., agreement in the truth, can be the last word. That this agreement of reason is possible—I firmly believe.
>
> —GS3, 399

Strauss's correspondence with Krüger, as the previous chapter shows, is an invaluable source for those who seek to understand Strauss's complex and debated thought. Dating mostly from the early 1930s—a period in which Strauss went through a decisive *reorientation*—the exchange deals with several important themes and overall has a lively and straightforward style that proves to be extremely useful for the interpreter who wishes to grasp the guiding ideas of each of the two authors.

The correspondence's main concern arguably is historicism and the challenge it poses to any attempt to achieve an atemporal philosophical view. Evidence of this can be found not only in the letters we have examined before, but also in the essays that Strauss, in particular, mentions therein. Among these are such works as "Conspectivism," "Religious Situation of the Present," and "Review of Julius Ebbinghaus, *On the Progress of Metaphysics*,"[1] where Strauss, with remarkable clarity, faces that challenge by attempting to show that the historicist, "synoptic," and relativistic stances that characterize his and Krüger's time—no less than ours—would have to be seen as historically conditioned themselves. As he will famously restate in *Natural Right and History*, once we raise the question of the historicity of historicism itself, the latter ceases to be the last word of today's philosophy (if one may still use this term in such a historicist context).[2] Rather, historicism emerges as the expression of a specific age that has lost its ability to philosophize "naturally," an age that, being by definition transient, is destined to be superseded.

Next, and linked to this concern, natural right proves to have a prominent place in that correspondence as well. Natural right surfaces as the practical manifestation of the question of the measure or standard (*Massstab*) that most of the correspondence revolves around. Strauss himself underscores this connection when, making reference to "Foreword to a Planned Book on Hobbes"[3] in a letter to Krüger from November 16, 1931, he states that in that essay he attempts "to establish the desideratum of natural right," and that his "main goal is to emphasize that historical consciousness is the sole presupposition of today's skepticism with regard to natural right."[4]

The link of historicism and natural right is also confirmed by a comparison between the end of the "Foreword" and the almost coeval "Religious Situation of the Present," a lecture Strauss delivered in 1930 that, as observed, is largely devoted to the problem of historicism. This comparison shows that the question of historicism and the question of natural right are so intertwined in Strauss's view that, as we will now see, he even adopts similar wording for both.

The concluding remarks of the "Foreword," worth quoting at length also for what they expressly state about natural right, read as follows:

> The fact of anarchy in the natural right teaching becomes an argument against the possibility of natural right as such . . . only because the reason for the necessity of failure and therewith for the anarchy is believed to be known. The opponents of natural right admit to us, as it were, that the natural right teachers failed "only" because they proceeded from a wrong starting point; but—they mean—the wrong starting point is precisely the *quest for the* natural right, the one eternal natural right. For there is not the one eternal natural right, but rather every age (or rather every people and every class) has its ideal of right. Just as there is not the one eternal truth but merely a particular truth. Hence, it is reasonable to have a quest at most only for the *particular* ideal of right, valid for men in a *given* situation; in any case, no other ideal of right is to be found. Thus it is even possible to have a historical justification

of natural right: the natural right teachers indeed sought *the* right, but they found, or rather formulated, the ideal of right of their age. They failed—measured by *their* standard; judged by the historical consciousness, they reached the goal, the only attainable goal. After the historical contingency of all human action and thought is seen clearly, however, it would be dishonest henceforth to postulate a human absolute.[5]

If we now turn to "Religious Situation of the Present," particularly to the prosopopoeia of the Present Strauss resorts to after raising the question of the "right life," we find, among other things, the following remarks (which evidently parallel some of the above):

> At one time, later generations did not let themselves be confused by the failure of the earlier ones. Full of delusion, they said to themselves, if they failed—perhaps they approached the issue the wrong way; let's just begin from the beginning; let's begin completely from the beginning. And they began from the beginning, and they also failed. The unhappy ones did not know—what I, the Present, the powerful goddess, know—that they had to fail. They had to fail since they were seeking *the* truth. For there is not *the one eternal* truth, but each age has its truth . . . [cf. lines 1–12 in the previous quote].
>
> To be sure, they [the earlier generations] did seek *the* truth, but they found the truth without time [*ohne Zeit*]; they failed—measured by their standard; measured by *my* standard they reached the goal [cf. lines 12–20, 16–20 in particular].
>
> It is befitting for thinking beings to know what they are doing and what they can reasonably want: therefore, know and be imbued with it once and for all, that you can find only your truth, the truth of the present, and therefore can reasonably seek only it [cf. the concluding five lines, notably the last three].[6]

Strauss thus approaches the question of natural right as part of the broader question of the possibility of a meaningful philosophical thought, whose goal is an eternal and absolute truth as opposed to the idea of an ever-changing, and relative, truth of the present. This is precisely the reason why he initially became involved in the study of Hobbes. In the early 1930s, Hobbes is for Strauss not only the author who, "living in an illiberal world, lays the foundations of liberalism," which the young Strauss, no less than Carl Schmitt, wanted to overcome. He also is the thinker who, unlike the historicists and legal positivists of Strauss's time, emphasizes the role of nature as he starts from a *status naturalis* seen as an original condition of disorder that must be superseded by the intervention of culture and the civil state.[7]

In the already quoted "Foreword," Strauss eloquently underscores this key role of Hobbes by saying that "only in view of *unrest* [*Unruhe*], only *in* unrest, if not indeed in revolts [*Unruhen*] can that understanding of man be gained from which the right created for the satisfaction of man can be understood: only in this way can it be radically understood that as well as how man needs right; only in this way is *philosophic* understanding of right possible."[8] Unlike legal positivism, which, as Hans Kelsen claims, can thrive "only in relatively peaceful times" and tries to achieve a detached, but for that reason distorted and unrealistic knowledge, Hobbes starts from the recognition of "the entire dangerousness and endangeredness of man," and thereby carries out "a philosophic founding of right" by defining "natural right as the behavior appropriate to this situation of man."[9]

In a letter to Krüger from October 15, 1931, however, Strauss already shows that this Hobbesian and polemic view of natural right does not any more reflect his real position, which is now epitomized by Plato to the extent that Strauss's philosophical path concerning natural right can be described as a shift between these authors. After stating that he and Krüger "will likely come to agreement on the necessity and possibility of natural right," he goes on to declare that "now that Plato has taught me the untenability of Hobbes's premises [*Ansatz*], Hobbes no longer suffices for me as a guarantor [*Gewährsmann*] of the possibility of natural right in a world without Providence. My guarantor is—Plato. Do you happen to be familiar with the myth of the *Statesman*?"[10]

Now, when Strauss here says *Ansatz*, what does he really mean? Is he referring to Hobbes's approach in general, to the way this author tackles the philosophical problems, particularly that of natural right? Or, rather, is he referring to Hobbes's starting point, the departure of his system, namely, the state of nature? The latter answer does not seem that far-fetched once we carefully consider Strauss's final reference to the myth of the *Statesman*.

As is well known, in that dialogue Plato has the visitor from Elea tell a myth about the universe according to which there are two distinct ages or phases of its working: the age of Cronus, and that commonly attributed to Zeus.[11] Over the former, the god, along with his demons, superintends the functioning of every section of the whole's life, so that everything is in perfect order. In this age, human beings do not even need any political rule, as they are not dangerous to each other nor are they endangered, living in what is also referred to as a *golden age*. During the age of Zeus, by contrast, the universe starts to move on its own towards the opposite direction, gradually deviating from the original cosmic and providential order towards a condition of chaos. However, this is the key point: according to the myth of the *Statesman*, the universe never reaches that condition of complete disorder, since the helmsman of the universe never leaves completely after releasing the tiller, but keeps observing the whole from his vantage point. Arguably, this means, leaving metaphors aside, that according to the myth of the *Statesman*, the whole, as well as nature, is never complete chaos, is never fully devoid of rational order, even when it reaches its most unordered stage.[12]

This account clearly is of the utmost importance concerning Hobbes's depiction of the state of nature and his interpretation of natural right. According to Hobbes, the state of nature is a state of disorder, where every human being has a right to everything, but no original obligation whatsoever as far as actions are concerned.[13] For this reason, that state is a state of war, if not actual, at least potential, in which human life is "solitary, poore, nasty, brutish, and short," as Hobbes famously puts it in chapter 13 of the *Leviathan*.

According to Hobbes, thus, order is artificially established, and natural right is an originally unrestrained liberty that, if left unleashed, brings unbearable disorder. Under these circumstances, only a natural right understood as a legitimate subjective claim can be affirmed. A different situation seems instead to be the one implied in the myth of the *Statesman*: if some residual form of "providence," or rather rational order never leaves the whole and the human beings who are the most excellent part thereof,[14] even when the most disorderly and chaotic stage is reached, one can never claim a right to everything, a completely free condition no matter how unbearable that stage may turn out to be. Some sense of a rational, objective restraint, as distinct from the mere command to seek peace as a means to secure one's right, still persists; freedom is never absolute, since at least a natural and *objective* "standard," as distinct from a real law, remains available for human beings to attempt to discern.[15]

This is why, according to Strauss, Plato (particularly through the myth of the *Statesman*) is his guarantor of the possibility of natural right "in a world without Providence." Even once we rule out God and his providential justice, some standard of order still stands. This however also means that the natural right whose possibility one can argue for under those circumstances is not so much everyone's subjective claim, as the idea of what is good or by nature right for us as human beings, that is a ranking of the human ends or ways of life. The real purpose of human reason is therefore not to merely figure out how one can best assure his or her self-preservation once the legitimacy of the fight for this goal, based on the inescapable and universal passion of fear of violent death, has been recognized. Above and beyond this, reason must be exercised to attempt to fathom an objective standard and thereby figure out what is truly good for us, what is the best life human beings can live qua human beings.[16]

It is in light of this Platonic approach that one can understand the otherwise rather enigmatic beginning of the part of the same October 15, 1931, letter Strauss devotes to Hobbes and natural right. There Strauss points out that, overall, Hobbes's "'political science' represents a repetition of Socratic *techne politiké*, a repetition, however, that very much flattens [*verflacht*] the Socratic problem." Then he adds: "I believe that it will in this way become possible to determine precisely what is popularly called rationalism."[17] The reason why Hobbes's repetition flattens the Socratic problem, and why his rationalism is only popularly so-called, is that instead of asking what virtue is, that is, what the good or best possible life is, Hobbes asks only about the means to achieve an end—self-preservation and, in perspective, commodious living—that in Socratic-Platonic terms (not to say Aristotelian) is too low and vulgar an end to be chosen by human beings in the full sense of the term.[18] From Hobbes's perspective, reason remains indeed key (as shown by the series of Laws of Nature he lists), but its role is to discern the right means to the end of self-preservation, namely an instrumental role, and not to be itself the peak, the center of a life devoted to knowledge.[19] It is still rationalism, in short, but of the lowest degree once it is seen through the Platonic lenses Strauss is trying to recover.[20]

This Platonic arrangement also clearly emerges in another letter Strauss writes to Krüger, on August 19, 1932, regarding his review-essay "Notes on Carl Schmitt, *The Concept of the Political*."[21] In a previous letter of his, upon reading the "Notes," Krüger had asked Strauss whether his intention in that essay could be understood as a form of Platonism according to which what justifies the political grouping into friends and enemies is "the 'political' dialectic of the totalities struggling over the character of the 'right.'"[22] If this were the case—Krüger had observed in the same letter—it would be ultimately impossible for Strauss to avoid both Schmitt's decisionism (his "neutral affirmation of all that is 'meant seriously'") and, more generally, a fideistic approach to the question of what is right. As Krüger puts it: "How can there be a decisive concretization of the search concerning the character of the right without a 'confession of faith [*Glaubensbekenntnis*]'?"[23]

In his revealing response, as we have observed in chapter I, Strauss states that in his view "there is ultimately only *one* opposition, namely between 'left' and 'right,' 'freedom' and 'authority.' " Then, shifting to "more honest ancient terms," he significantly explains that the underpinning of that opposition is the distinction between delight or pleasure and good, that is, in the Greek terms he resorts to, between "ἡδύ and ἀγαθόν."[24] Regarding Krüger's remarks about the decisionistic or fideistic stance Strauss, in Krüger's view, would have willy-nilly to embrace, Strauss replies that "the 'confession of faith' you demand seems to me to lie in the δουναι και δεξασθαι [*sic*; "to give and receive," meaning "reason" (λόγον)] as such, in modern parlance, in 'probity [*Redlichkeit*],'"[25] concluding that "the struggle between 'left' and 'right' is the struggle between utopian dizziness and sobriety."[26]

Thus, once again, as is shown by the quotation from Plato and the Greek terms he chooses, Strauss's ultimate intention is to trace his position back to a form of Platonic rationalism according to which reason, through dialectics, is seen as able to meaningfully raise the questions of what is good and what is right also in an objective, absolute sense. In this perspective, reason with its "authority"[27] opposes the essentially hedonistic attempt to unleash individual freedom in its search for pleasure, a search that, in that respect, characterizes Hobbes's thought no less than ancient hedonism. No matter how absolutist his political system may end up being, Hobbes in fact is the author who underlines the distinction between right and law, *jus* and *lex*, coherently defining the former, which becomes the center of his system, as a "liberty to do, or to forbeare," unlike the latter that "determineth, and bindeth to one of them."[28]

The only dissonant trait in this essentially classical scenario is Strauss's reference to probity as an equivalent of the Platonic "to give and receive reason." Only three years later, in the introduction to *Philosophy and Law*, however, Strauss will emend this apparent inconsistency, pointing out that the "old love of truth" differs from the "new probity" in that it is not dogmatic in ruling out from the beginning "transcendent ideals," including the ones that substantiate, at least under the guise of open problems, Platonic rationalism with its idea of the good.[29]

What Strauss argues in his review of Schmitt's *The Concept of the Political*, when he seemingly justifies the struggle among political groups over the right, is therefore "only relevant *ad hominem*," as he puts it in a statement that alone shows how removed his view of the political is from Schmitt's. As he further explains: "In opposition to agreement at any price, conflict is truer. But only peace, i.e., agreement in the truth, can be the last word. That this agreement of reason is possible—I firmly believe [*firmiter credo*]."[30]

Strauss's attempt to remain within premodern rationalism could not be voiced more clearly. What should be stressed here, however, is the remark that conflict is truer than agreement at any price. This kind of agreement in fact is the one that characterizes the positions Strauss had stigmatized in "Conspectivism," namely a constellation of views that, having set aside as meaningless the purpose of reaching an eternal and absolute truth, placidly accepts, and tries synoptically to combine, the various stances of the age. Compared to these views, the philosophical understanding that stems from the perception of the lingering conflict among the different views and their advocates is surely truer. This is, ultimately, Hobbes's role and importance, as we have already emphasized while referring to Strauss's "Preface to a Planned Book on Hobbes." From such a polemical approach, which is also shared by Schmitt, however, no stable and objective philosophical position can emerge. As observed in chapter I, Hobbes's and Schmitt's positions remain within a decisionism that is unable to substantiate an objective view of what is good or by nature right, if only as an open question.[31] With opposite intention—the one to limit the bearing of political decision, the other to extend it—they share the same skepticism towards the possibility of rationally fathoming the content of that decision.[32]

Strauss, on the other hand, "firmly believe[s]" that such an "agreement of reason," an "agreement in *the* truth,"[33] is not only desirable, but also possible. For this reason, no matter how philosophical Hobbes's position may be compared to the synoptic stances that seek agreement at any price, a horizon beyond his ultimately liberal approach must be searched for. And the only viable path towards this horizon is through the recovery of Platonic political rationalism, which, taking its orientation by speech, does not a priori give up the attempt to discern the human good, the "*summum bonum*,"[34] as distinct from mere delight or pleasure.

Delight or pleasure (ἡδύ), nonetheless, turns out to be the ultimate underpinning of Hobbes's system. This clearly comes out in a letter from November 17, 1932 (as well as in its preparatory draft), where Strauss tries to answer a question Krüger had raised in a previous letter of his (from November 13, 1932) regarding the tenability of Strauss's attempt to directly compare Hobbes's approach with the Socratic one. Significantly, Krüger had voiced his perplexity in the following manner: "Is Hobbes's 'foundation of liberalism' really identical to the Socratic intention? After all, Hobbes's question concerning the 'right' is not the same as the Socratic question concerning the good. Even if one does not insert some 'external,' 'demanding' moralism into the ancient αγαθον [*sic*], the kind of obligation and the *ground* of the question is a different one."[35]

In reply, Strauss begins by emphatically answering Krüger's question in the negative: Hobbes's foundation of liberalism is "of course not" identical to the Socratic intention. "How can a reasonable human being, a *philosopher* (!)," he continues, "be liberal or be the founder of liberalism? Or, more pointedly: how can a philosopher, a man of science, teach like a sophist?" And to these revealing questions he adds: "Once this has become possible—and it has become possible above all on account of Hobbes—then the fundamentally *clear* situation that Plato had created by allocating ἀγαθόν to τέχνη and ἐπιστήμη, ἡδύ to sophistry and barbering professions (to professors, journalists, demagogues, business leaders, poets, etc.) becomes fundamentally unclear, with the upshot being the total lack of orientation in the 'currents of contemporary thought,' in which 'everything' becomes philosophically possible."[36]

Once again, Strauss traces the conspectivist nature of today's philosophy back to the abandonment of the Platonic approach—based on the search for the good as the foundation of both art and science—and to the consequent hedonistic turn towards individualism and relativism, which only a decisionistic act of the will can temporarily hold in check. For Strauss, Hobbes inaugurates a new sophistic approach to political philosophy, according to which it is not natural reason, but the contingent human will and a merely "instrumental" reason that can artificially establish order each time. As Strauss puts it in a later letter to Krüger (March 27, 1935) to explain an analogous utterance that occurs in the introduction to *Philosophy and Law*, the term "'sophistry' . . . is meant literally (after the Protagoras myth): to submit to what the Athenians say on the basis of an Epimethean physics (the exposedness of human beings)."37

In Strauss's view, thus, philosophy and liberalism are as incompatible as philosophy and sophistry are in Plato's account. Liberalism and sophistry share the same relativistic, ultimately hedonistic background: they start from a conception of reason and nature according to which only human *decision* can set a measure or standard (*Massstab*) and therewith *create* order. As the myth of the *Protagoras* shows, the basis for this view is a conception of the human being as by nature deprived of adequate skills to live in a complete and orderly manner. Human beings under Epimethean physics as described in the *Protagoras* are "naked, unshod, unbedded, and unarmed," a condition that reminds one of Hobbes's description of human life in the state of nature as "solitary, poore, nasty, brutish, and short."38 In both cases, only the subsequent development of art (*techne*), be it mechanical or political, allows human beings to improve their naturally exposed condition.

Strauss had already underlined the importance of the myth of the *Protagoras*, with its Epimethean physics, in a previous letter to Krüger (February 7, 1933). There, he first stresses the role of the " 'Epimethean' natural philosophy as the basis of the justification of Athenian democracy." Then he states that the myth of the *Protagoras* "shows how, in principle, modern naturalism is identical to ancient naturalism."39 However, prompted by a previous observation of Krüger's about the importance of the "second sailing" in Strauss's account,40 he this time explains (in accordance with what has been noted in the introduction) that "the knowledge of human order and factual human disorder is not tied to a prior knowledge of φύσις, as is sufficiently shown by the limitation to the δευτερος πλους [sic] in the *Phaedo* and the mythical character of the *Timaeus*, whereas the combated sophistic view naively presupposes a naturalistic cosmology."41

Krüger had prompted this remark by claiming that compared to thinkers like Löwith, who in his view fails to acknowledge the challenge of revelation thereby remaining "clueless [*ahnungslos*]" in the search for a *Massstab*, Strauss "know[s] better, and that is why for [him] the search for an atheistic philosophy is the δεύτερος πλοῦς that is *incapable* of ignoring the old ἀγαθόν in its rank."42 Unlike other atheistic thinkers of his time, as we have emphasized, Strauss attempts to recover a Platonic perspective according to which the question of the good becomes central again. The path through which that perspective can be re-enabled is the "second sailing," in which the mere observation of φύσις in its materiality is replaced by a rational inquiry, by way of dialectics, into what is "good and opportune."[43] In the second sailing, reflection on what is "by nature" as distinct from what is "by convention" is not ruled out: rather, it shifts from the sensible and material plane to the intelligible and rational one, which is absolute and eternal and which only rational discourses (λόγοι) can disclose.[44] Hence, although not a believer, Strauss is not clueless because he still trusts reason and takes his orientation by speech.[45] To take up again Strauss's explicit words: "Only peace, i.e., agreement in the truth, can be the last word. That this agreement of reason [*Verständigung der Vernunft*] is possible—I firmly believe."[46]

That this Platonic and rationalistic approach constitutes Strauss's real stance is also shown by what he claims, in his exchange with Krüger, about politics. Especially in the period around the fateful date of 1933, comments on the dire concrete political situation become more common even in this detached philosophical debate. The period, one may say, is one of those moments of truth in which real friends, and more or less opportunist turncoats, suddenly take different paths and reveal themselves.[47] At one point, Strauss even expresses relief at the simple fact that Krüger, unlike, for example, Schmitt, still corresponds with him despite his being a Jew.[48]

In a letter from July 17, 1933, which touches upon the recent German events, Strauss sets out by observing that "the gulf that others have torn open in fact now also separates us as well, since we are not pure spirits but terrestrial descendants of terrestrial beings. It is almost like in a war . . ." Then, with a disappointed mood, he continues: "There could have been a decent, just, *imperial* solution. The solution that has been opted for stems from hate, and it almost necessarily generates counter-hate. It will require a long, strenuous effort on my part to be able to deal with what has been inflicted on me and my kind."[49]

Those who are familiar with Strauss will not fail to notice the similarities, as well as the differences, of this quotation with a letter Strauss had sent not much earlier (on May 19, 1933) to Löwith. As noted in chapter II, that letter has become rather famous (or infamous), as it is usually cited to prove Strauss's proximity to fascism (if not, all the more improperly, to Nazism).[50] As is well known, in that context Strauss speaks of the "principles of the right," of "fascist, authoritarian, *imperial* principles" as the only ones from which "it is possible, with decency, that is without the laughable and despicable appeal to the *droits imprescriptibles de l'homme* to protest against the shabby abomination [*das meskine Unwesen*]."[51] To these remarks, he adds the quotation from Virgil: "Tu regere imperio . . . parcere subjectis et debellare superbos," to conclude that "there is no reason to crawl to the cross, neither to the cross of liberalism, as long as somewhere in the world there is a glimmer of the spark of Roman thought."[52]

The "fascist, authoritarian, *imperial* principles" have meanwhile given way to a "decent, just, *imperial* solution." The emphasis is always on the "imperial" character of those principles or solution. The "authoritarian" can still be seen as implied in that character. But what about the fascist side of the matter? Is this just an "ad hominem" omission due to the different type of correspondent (the believing Krüger instead of the secular, "clueless" Löwith)? Or is it rather the consequence of a change of mind on Strauss's part?

The latter explication seems to be by far the more probable. As observed in chapter II, in his response to Strauss on May 28, 1933, Löwith had in fact already questioned not only Strauss's leaning towards the principles of the right, but also, more significantly for our analysis, Strauss's interpretation of fascism. In Löwith's view, fascism is not so much the heir of Roman thought and therewith, at least indirectly, of the classical approach, as the heir of modern democracy, of which fascism is "definitely an excrescence [*Gewächs*]."[53]

Moreover, Strauss himself, in an unsent draft letter to Krüger from July 22, 1933 (which is only five days after his previous letter to him where the comparative omission of fascism occurs), proves to have meanwhile framed a more sophisticated appraisal of fascism. In that draft letter, starting from the already mentioned assessment that the modern world, based on a "liberal-democratic" structure, "is cracking at all seams," Strauss points out that "the opponents of *this* modern world, I mean those who act, propose solutions that are no less 'modern' and hence in principle have to lead to the same negative result."[54]

Now, leaving aside the incidental remark that clearly implies that there are more theoretical opponents who are immune from this faulty approach, it is important to underline that as an example of these no less "modern" and "negative" solutions, Strauss singles out nothing less than Benito Mussolini's political views. He refers to "Mussolini's Encyclopedia article on the state," likely meaning the entry "Fascism" that Mussolini, along with the neo-Hegelian philosopher Giovanni Gentile, wrote for the Italian Encyclopedia (Treccani) in 1932.[55] In this entry, especially in the first part by Gentile (but published under Mussolini's name alone) the authoritarian and ordering role of the state is highly praised and emphasized. However, the emphasis is particularly on its creative will, which establishes order over a natural setting fundamentally seen as fight and disorder.[56] That entry, in other words, does not exceed the "liberal horizon" framed by Hobbes as a consequence of his rejection of the ancient Greek paradigm. In criticizing Mussolini (and Gentile), Strauss is ultimately restating his critical appraisal of Schmitt, published in 1932, which culminates in his astonishing summary of Schmitt's approach as a "liberalism with opposite polarity," since, as we have noted, it limits itself to affirming the authority of the will of the state while liberalism wanted to limit or negate that will. The will, however, remains the same, as does the empty decisionism upon which it rests.

Strauss's solution, on the other hand, aims to be "unmodern," not ultramodern. As he puts it in the same draft letter (July 22, 1933), faced with the "negative result" that the still modern solutions epitomized by Mussolini's fascism lead to, "we . . . are inclined to try solutions that are in principle unmodern, i.e., concretely: old solutions."[57] It is significant that the draft begins with Strauss's attempt to describe the difference between him and Krüger in the following terms: "Formally, this difference consists in the fact that I am determined to depart from the Socratic-Platonic approach—and not just from this *approach*—only when I have understood the inadequacy of this manner of questioning, whereas you do not claim to want to forgo this insight but instead claim to possess it."[58] Not only in political matters, but also more generally in philosophical matters, starting with the question of a rational standard that alone can make it possible meaningfully to reject historicism and relativism, Strauss's beacon is the Socratic-Platonic dialectical approach, with its ideas of eternal and absolute knowledge (*episteme*) and good (*agathon*). This is why for Strauss even such a philosopher as Nietzsche turns out to represent an ultimately unsatisfactory position. No matter how much Nietzsche is the "*last* enlightener," who destabilizes the pillars of modernity and therewith makes a consideration of the old solutions meaningful again,[59] his "vacillating" between the attempt to reaffirm the spirit of philosophy and that of going beyond (or "behind") it, "could only be overcome by proceeding to Platonic philosophy."[60]

Unsurprisingly, then, Strauss will later define Nietzsche as the "stepgrandfather of fascism."[61] Like fascism (not to mention Schmitt's individual case), Nietzsche ultimately remains entangled in modernity, with its "philosophy of power" based on the centrality of the human will.[62] Against this kind of philosophy, resulting in a "philosophy of culture" that "forgets nature altogether,"[63] Strauss attempts to re-enable a "natural" philosophizing wherein the investigation of what is by nature good and what is by nature right becomes possible again. But on what basis and with what results?

As has been observed in the previous chapter, that basis is a critique of historicism that results in its rejection on grounds of its own historicity. As Strauss himself puts it, "if historical consciousness isn't a carriage that one can stop whenever one pleases, then one arrives at a historical destruction [*Destruktion*] of historical consciousness. The latter proves to be historically conditioned and limited to a particular situation."[64] From this perspective, Strauss's insights regarding the "second cave" undoubtedly play a central role. Indeed, it is only in light of his attempt to go back to the "first, natural cave"—which is the Platonic one—that he can meaningfully "believe in a '*natural*' basis *and* view antiquity to be the standard," as well as he can "assume—until there is evidence to the contrary—that antiquity (more precisely: Socrates-Plato) is the standard *precisely because* it philosophized *naturally*, i.e., originally inquired into the order that is *natural* for human beings."[65] The same applies to Strauss's emphasis on "learning through reading [*lesendes Lernen*]," by means of which only we can attempt to "bring ourselves into the dimension in which we, understanding the Greeks, can question 'naively' with them."[66]

As for results, Strauss's attempt to re-enable a kind of Platonic natural philosophizing is not intended as a way to set up a dogmatic approach. His endeavor to dialectically frame a ranking of the human ends or ways of life, to discern what is by nature good or right for human beings, never translates into a detailed set of rules, for example an objective natural law. As he clearly states in a letter to Krüger from August 18, 1934, Plato's main concern, even in practical matters, remains theoretical, namely the pure knowledge of the "standard [*Massstab*]" or the "principle of order [*Prinzip der Ordnung*]," as distinct from its practical application to human beings, which "only *assumes* the character of bindingness." As Strauss further explains, "Platonic philosophy is concerned with the knowledge of this 'What' that does not itself have the character of a law in the proper sense," a "What" that he will later refer to as "natural right" (*physei dikaion*) and that appears to be essentially intertwined with the good or *agathon*.[67]

Hence, Strauss ends up affirming, Socratically, that precisely because such a detailed set of rules is apparently unavailable, the highest human end is its investigation, and consequently the best possible life, at least for those who are capable of it, is the philosophic life.[68] As far as the correspondence with Krüger is concerned, the best proof of this is perhaps one of the last recorded letters the mature Strauss sent his friend in 1958. There Strauss draws a distinction between "the ἀρίστη πολιτεία and the factual 'natural community'—to say nothing of the fundamental difference between the highest πρᾶξις that is only θεορία and all other πράξεις."[69] To this emphatic celebration of the theoretic life as the best possible life, he adds that "the difference concerning 'natural communities' is . . . decisive. Their 'naturalness' is ambiguous, since only ἀριστη [sic] πολιτεία is natural in the strict sense (cf. the problem of ἀγαθὸς ἀνὴρ in distinction from ἀγαθὸς πολίτης in *Politics* III). To express the matter in the extreme Platonic term, the πόλις is the cave. There is a necessary tension between the πόλις and philosophy (hence even the ἀρίστη πολιτεία is in need of the καλὸν ψεῦδος)."[70]

We cannot comment at length on this complex passage, whose language will become typical of the mature Strauss in his books on the Greek classics of the 1960s and early 1970s. What is clear and most relevant for us to note in conclusion, however, is that in this passage Strauss insists on a different meaning of natural, which becomes perspicuous only after one has raised, by way of dialectics, the question of the standard. "Natural in the strict sense" is only the "best regime" because it is only in such a regime that, as Aristotle puts it, the best citizen and the best man can coincide.[71] And the reason for this is arguably that only in the best regime is the goal (the highest human end) the theoretic or philosophic life simply—a "life of questioning" that Strauss will come to see as essentially at odds with the political life, since this latter, being like a cave, necessarily remains bound up with religion and noble lies.[72]

Chapter V

Strauss and the "Politicization of Philosophy"

> Not the Appetite of Private men, but the Law . . . is the measure.
> —OMPT, 174

The "politicization of philosophy" this chapter focuses on needs some preliminary explanation, since this expression, as it occurs in the title, can be interpreted in at least two ways. On the one hand, it may sound as a reference to Strauss's philosophical approach, as if his own philosophy could be adequately characterized in terms of politicization. On the other, the expression may be taken as pointing to his historiographical appraisal of the tradition of philosophy or, more precisely, of a specific phase in that tradition: the modern age.

The first understanding characterizes those who, explicitly or implicitly, maintain that for Strauss philosophy (including his) is based on an act of will or belief—namely, on some kind of "decisionism"—because philosophy is unable to show its meaningfulness, let alone necessity, from a rational standpoint.[1] If this were the case, the choice for philosophy would be an eminently practical matter, based on purely moral and political grounds. Among these interpreters are not only the more or less harsh critics who accuse Strauss of attempting to resort to a kind of "rationalistic" rhetoric only for the purpose of destabilizing the liberal-democratic institutions in order to pursue a reactionary agenda. Whether they are aware of it or not, to the same group belong those who believe that Strauss is placidly accepting a stalemate between reason and revelation when, for instance, speaking of "the conflicting roots of Western civilization" (Greek philosophy and biblical revelation), he states: "No one can be both a philosopher and a theologian, or, for that matter, some possibility which transcends the conflict between philosophy and theology, or pretends to be a synthesis of both. But every one of us can be and ought to be either one or the other, the philosopher open to the challenge of theology, or the theologian open to the challenge of philosophy."[2]

To disprove the assumption that statements like this entail Strauss's ultimate acceptance of a stalemate between reason and revelation, suffice it to recall what he writes, in a 1931 letter to Krüger, after the publication of *Spinoza's Critique of Religion*, whose defense of Calvin's fideism against the dogmatic approach of modern atheism is also often quoted by the advocates of the stalemate hypothesis as proof of their being right. In his letter, Strauss exhorts Krüger not to "misunderstand [him] to have been of the opinion, at the time [he] wrote the book, that one must remain satisfied with a difference of 'standpoints' in the face of the belief character of both opposing positions (theism and atheism)," to conclude that "the fact that Nietzsche's critique exists, even if only by intention, always counted as proof to me that one cannot remain satisfied with ceremonial bows to the other position."[3]

This being the case, the first understanding of the politicization of philosophy hardly fits in with Strauss's own philosophical approach. And the very concept of politicization of philosophy as he understands it, as we shall now see, provides non-negligible evidence in that respect.

Here, therefore, I mean politicization of philosophy as a reference to Strauss's historiographical appraisal of modern philosophy. With regard to this interpretation, however, some ambiguity may also arise, since one could still think that Strauss, while dealing with the different phases in the history of political philosophy, criticizes a partisan and ideological type of political philosophy while advocating a purely theoretical and detached pattern thereof.

Although the first assumption is true (Strauss surely criticized a partisan and ideological type of political philosophy),[4] the second is not. What Strauss advocates when he criticizes, for instance in *Natural Right and History*, the "politicization of philosophy"[5] is not so much a move towards "political theory" as "a purely theoretical, detached knowledge of things political," as he puts it in "What Can We Learn from Political Theory?"[6] Rather, he suggests a view of philosophy according to which philosophy itself, understood primarily as philosophic life (*bios philosophikos* or *theoretikos*), is the very end of politics, and not the other way round.

The politicization of philosophy Strauss refers to in *Natural Right and History* is thus the interpretation of philosophy—characteristic, in his view, of the early modern thinkers—whereby philosophy comes to be seen as an instrument subservient to politics: the handmaid of politics or *ancilla civitatis*, as it were. Making reference to Julien Benda's *Treason of the Intellectuals* while addressing the problem of historicism as the "ultimate outcome of the crisis of modern natural right," Strauss observes in this regard:

> Since the seventeenth century, philosophy has become a weapon, and hence an instrument. It was this politicization of philosophy that was discerned as the root of our troubles by an intellectual who denounced the treason of the intellectuals. He committed the fatal mistake, however, of ignoring the essential difference between intellectuals and philosophers. In this he remained the dupe of the delusion which he denounced. For the politicization of philosophy consists precisely in this, that the difference between intellectuals and philosophers—a difference formerly known as the difference between gentlemen and philosophers, on the one hand, and the difference between sophists or rhetoricians and philosophers, on the other—becomes blurred and finally disappears.[7]

The key to understand Strauss's interpretation of modern philosophy as politicized is thus to understand such a difference and the reason why it could finally disappear.

I

In Strauss's view, the difference between the gentleman and the philosopher amounts to the difference between political life and philosophic life. The first is a life that remains entirely within the limits of the city and its authoritative opinions (the *endoxa*, as Aristotle used to call them). The second is the life characteristic of those who, while starting from these opinions and even playing an active role in the city (that of the umpire or the teacher of legislators), transcend those limits, since they come to consider the understanding of the whole, of what is by nature, as their most important task.[8]

By contrast, the difference between the sophist or rhetorician and the philosopher may be described, in a nutshell, as follows: both recognize the uncertain character of the opinions of the city and, consequently, raise the question of what is *by nature* as distinct from what is *by convention*. Yet, while the sophists or rhetoricians disregard the truth hidden in the opinions and try to exploit that recognition instrumentally—as a way to establish themselves within the city by increasing their power, wealth, or prestige—the philosophers, taking orientation by speech, see the same recognition as confirmation that they have to seek true knowledge of what is good and that they need to transcend the too narrow political sphere.[9]

According to Strauss, hence, the politicization of (modern) philosophy is the negation of the possibility or meaningfulness of a *trans-political*, theoretical life devoted to the search for truth and the consequent understanding of philosophy not as an independent, sovereign way of life, but as an instrument subservient to the city's well-being (this latter understood according to the city's essentially practical and hedonistic interpretation). That being the case, the questions arise: How is this understanding possible? What changed, at the beginning of modernity, so that such a politicized, essentially instrumental view of philosophy could finally prevail?

To answer these questions, it is worth considering "The Origin of Modern Political Thought," a lecture Strauss delivered in the late 1930s.[10] Since Strauss never published it, "he may have had second thoughts about some of the arguments he advanced"[11] there. Hence, this lecture should be mainly used as an aid to the understanding of such other works of Strauss's as *Natural Right and History* and *What Is Political Philosophy?* where he notably deals with the same matter. Yet even a quick glance at the lecture shows how important it is for our topic.

The basic idea one can draw from "The Origin of Modern Political Thought" is that what Strauss later called the "politicization" of modern philosophy is fundamentally brought about by two factors. The first is that according to the moderns—Hobbes in particular, whom the lecture focuses on—any attempt to discern an objective standard, a "transcendent, superhuman order or superhuman will," is doomed to failure. The second is that, no matter how atheist the modern authors may be—again, Hobbes is here presented as their paradigm—they are still under the influence of the biblical tradition, notably of the idea of divine providence. Combined together, as we shall now see, these two factors explain why for Strauss the modern project is characterized not only by the emergence of natural right as distinct from natural law, but also by the attempt to conquer nature—an attempt that clearly depends on the understanding of philosophy (and science) as an essentially practical, and practice-oriented pursuit.

Strauss regards the first factor, "the denial of any superhuman order or will," as the sine qua non for explaining the modern project as characterized by both natural right as a justified subjective claim and the attempt to conquer nature. Clearly, such a factor can be found in Hobbes who, on the one hand, rejects classical teleology to embrace a mechanistic and materialistic view of nature and the universe. On the other, while emphasizing the importance of law interpreted as a command in bringing about order among human beings, he also rules out the possibility of deriving such a law from divine revelation. However, not to be forced to embrace a kind of pure naturalism and conventionalism, for Strauss Hobbes attempts an "immanent" foundation of morality by distinguishing between right and law. According to this revolutionary view, natural right is neither pure appetite nor an objective law, but a "justified" subjective claim. This claim is justified in that it can be "publicly" defended since it derives from an irresistible passion (an "inescapable necessity," as Strauss puts it in "Anmerkungen zu Carl Schmitt, *Der Begriff des Politischen*"[12]) that is universally experienced in the warlike state of nature: the fear of violent death seen as the *summum malum*. As Strauss observes in "The Origin of Modern Political Thought":

> Thus, out of the experience of the natural state of war, the minimum claim, the absolutely justified claim, arises; and this claim is absolutely justified because it can be answered for in the face of all other men under all circumstances. In this way Hobbes succeeds in taking into account the fundamental difference between human appetite as such and right human appetite, without having recourse to a transcendent, superhuman order or will; he succeeds in what we may call an "immanent" foundation of morality. But he succeeds in this merely because he was able to discover natural right (namely: the minimum claim) as a medium between transcendent law and human appetite. In order to maintain the fundamental difference between human appetite as such and right appetite, in spite of his denying a transcendent order, he must assert

the primacy of Right before Law. And for this very reason, he had, to begin with, to distinguish between Right and Law as clearly as at least no well-known and influential thinker before him had ever attempted to do.[13]

In Strauss's view, however, this necessary condition to explain Hobbes's approach—namely, the denial of any superhuman order or will—is not, in itself, sufficient. At the end of the same lecture, Strauss underscores that, if one really wants to grasp the "bold and active"[14] character of materialistic modern philosophy as distinct from its ancient, epicurean counterpart, that denial must be supplemented by the influence still exerted, however indirectly, by the idea of divine providence. Nothing, indeed, seems to be more inappropriate to define that bold and active character than the epicurean concepts of *ataraxia* (tranquility, absence of disturbance) and *aponia* (absence of pain), not to mention the motto *lathe biosas* (live secretly).

Hobbes's rejection of the teleological conception and his acceptance of the mechanistic-materialistic view bring him back, thus, neither to conventionalism and naturalism pure and simple, nor to the reserved, "unpolitical" stance that characterized pre-modern materialism or atheism. Unlike this latter, which "was based on knowledge of the limits set to human designs" and still believed in the possibility of "*beatitudo*" and "self-sufficiency," modern Hobbesian materialism regards human life as characterized by "continuous movement and restlessness" and comes to experience nature itself as a menace: as the source of conflict, war, disorder.[15]

According to Strauss's interpretation in "The Origin of Modern Political Thought," however, such a radical change of perspective is not so much the consequence of a shift in the understanding of nature itself, as of a modified interpretation of the relationship between human beings and nature due to the enduring influence of the biblical concept of divine providence:

> Nature is, however, felt as a menace not because man has now discovered natural evils either in the world or in himself which were unknown to classical philosophy, but because man had been accustomed by a tradition of almost two thousand years to believe himself to be protected by Providence. When this belief became shattered, he could not immediately cease to hope for Providence, to expect help from it. Denial of Providence

was thus from now on related not to serene and detached philosophizing, but rather to disappointed hope in Providence.[16]

And to these eloquent remarks, making now reference to those who, living in the seventeenth and eighteenth centuries, had already been shaped by the modern, Hobbesian approach, he adds:

> Being as yet under the spell of the traditional idea of Providence, they felt the menace to their happiness, this menace which was and is always felt, much stronger than classical philosophers could do; but no longer believing in the existence of Providence, they were enabled by this very unbelief to fight that menace. Their denial of Providence was not merely a theoretical assertion, but a practical revolt against Providence. Fighting the superhuman, inhuman menace to human happiness, however, meant conquering nature, i.e., both boundlessly producing external goods and revolutionizing society. It was in this way that atheism became "enterprising," that the principles leading to the French Revolution came into being.[17]

Now, as is well known, Strauss often criticized the secularization theory in his writings from the mid-1940s onwards.[18] According to his view, that theory does not acknowledge the key function performed, in early modernity, by the conscious and deliberate attempt to oppose revelation and restore philosophy as a discipline in its own right, as a free enterprise that does not bend its knee to any form of authority (except that of "unassisted" human reason). The view that emerges from the passage we have just quoted, by contrast, appears to be more nuanced in that it implies that remnants of the biblical tradition, like the idea of providence, still play an important role, no matter how indirectly (as polemical targets) or complementary. For this reason, in his comment on the same remarks of "The Origin of Modern Political Thought," Tanguay has argued that, however critical overall, Strauss is still propounding a "weak version of the secularization thesis."[19]

Tanguay's claim is even more worthy of our consideration because, in the case under scrutiny here as well, we are confronted with a scenario that reminds one of the second cave and the moderns' entrapment in it. Modern materialism and atheism are forms of revolt against revelation and a type of philosophy—Christian Scholasticism—that is so deeply influenced by biblical revelation that it can hardly be distinguished from disguised theology.[20] While performing a deliberate break with these intertwined traditions, however, modern philosophy, to a certain degree, continued them as well. As Strauss puts it in his 1952 "Preface to Isaac Husik, *Philosophical Essays*," "Modern philosophy emerged by way of transformation of, if in opposition to, Latin or Christian scholasticism."[21] There is indeed opposition and a deliberate break, triggered by the often (and aptly) emphasized "antitheological ire."[22] But there also is a transformation of views and ideas that, by being transformed, are at the same time incorporated in the new context. No matter the differences, one cannot help but think of Hegel's *Aufhebung* in this regard (not to mention the Hegelian interpretation of modernity in particular).[23]

In "The Origin of Modern Political Thought," this dialectic of rejection and acceptance by way of transformation is openly underscored by Strauss with regard to the inception of modern political philosophy. Speaking of the indictment of classical political philosophy by such authors as Bodin and Hobbes, Strauss, on the one hand, points out that "they do not even mention the medieval tradition," adding however that "this fact does not mean that they had a better opinion of the medieval tradition than they have of the classical tradition. Quite the contrary, it means that they rejected medieval tradition even more than the teaching of classical antiquity."[24] On the other hand, to such an express argument in favor of the break thesis, he adds the following caveat: "That is not to deny that the medieval thinkers were in more than one way preparing the ground for modern political philosophy in general, and the doctrines of Bodin and Hobbes in particular, and that, consequently, from this point of view, medieval political philosophy is nearer to modern political philosophy than is classical political philosophy."[25]

The reason why medieval political philosophy is nearer to modern political philosophy than its classical counterpart is given shortly afterwards: "If there was criticism of classical political philosophy in the Middle Ages, the classical tradition was attacked in the name of another *tradition*—of biblical tradition."[26] Given the anti-traditional character of modern political philosophy, this feature clearly sets it and medieval political philosophy apart, bringing modern political philosophy nearer to ancient political philosophy. As Strauss explains: "With reference to this most important fact, we may fairly say that there is at least as deep an affinity between modern political philosophy and classical political philosophy as there is between either of them and medieval political philosophy."[27] For unlike this latter, and trying to follow in the footsteps of classical political philosophy, modern political philosophy attempts to "discuss independently of any tradition the principles of politics. Argument of authority did not carry any great weight either with Plato and Aristotle, or with Hobbes and Rousseau; but they did carry a great weight with the medieval thinkers."[28]

On the other hand, the fact that medieval political philosophy, insofar as it criticized the classical one, did so in the name of the biblical tradition proves to be of decisive importance in order for us to fully understand the modern approach, particularly as embodied by Hobbes. This is due to the fact that although Hobbes, no less than Bodin, does not even "mention in his general statements the medieval tradition," as ultimately encompassed in the classical one as far as its philosophical underpinnings are concerned, "the objections which Hobbes raises against the classical tradition are, to some extent, based on the biblical tradition."[29] Precisely for this reason, as we have underscored, medieval political philosophy (being partly based on the same biblical tradition) is nearer to modern political philosophy, and to Hobbesian political philosophy in particular, than the classical one. Hence, if we really want to understand Hobbes and therewith the origin of modern political philosophy—Strauss explains—"we have to disentangle Hobbes's own and truly revolutionary principle from its traditional presentation." In doing so, however, "we ought not to underestimate that presentation which is, as a matter of fact, the historical presupposition of Hobbes's own teaching."[30] Once again, as we have observed regarding the second cave, the modified historical setting, due to the encounter of Athens with Jerusalem, proves not to be a purely extrinsic phenomenon. Consequently, for Strauss the interpreter must undertake a difficult work of disentanglement, whose result is, however, the realization that this work can hardly be brought to full completion, since the author in question—Hobbes in our case—remains entrapped, at least to some extent, in his "historical presupposition."

II

Tanguay's suggestion that Strauss implicitly advocates a "weak version of the secularization thesis" with regard to the origin of modern political philosophy, at least in "The Origin of Modern Political Thought," proves thus to be plausible. The presuppositions and scope of this claim, however, deserve to be further investigated. For such a claim can be raised not only with regard to the concept of providence, still operating on the background of modern atheism's attempt to conquer nature and revolutionize society. As we shall now see, it can also be raised regarding Hobbes's view that the only effective and reliable "measure" of good and evil is the "Law," i.e., the expression of the sovereign's will as distinct from the subjects' independent understanding, which in Hobbes's view becomes the mere transposition of their "appetites" as "private men."

Furthermore, we will have to raise another important question if we truly want to understand Strauss's intention in "The Origin of Modern Political Thought." Following in Tanguay's footsteps, our argument so far has been that Strauss may be propounding a "weak version of the secularization thesis." However, weak secularization of what? Indeed, of the biblical view. But a mere reference to the Bible may here result ambiguous in that, as Strauss knew better than most of his (Christian or post-Christian) contemporaries, under the indistinct concept of Bible lie two threads, which only at the price of substantial simplifications can be regarded as adequately represented by the so-called "Judeo-Christian" tradition.[31] Hence, the additional task for the interpreter arises of trying to discern which of the two roots, in each case, plays a prominent or exclusive role.

But let us proceed in an orderly manner and begin by dealing with the first question, namely, to what extent Hobbes's emphasis on the key role of the law—which, in his case, means the sovereign's will—is of biblical origin.

In "The Origin of Modern Political Thought," Strauss proves to be rather explicit in this respect. He sets out by underscoring that according to Hobbes the "original error" (in quotation marks already in Strauss's lecture) of classical political philosophy and its followers is the "assumption that private men can know by themselves what is good and evil."[32] "The traditional teachers of politics," Strauss explains further, "by trying to answer by their own reason the question as to what is good and bad, tried to set up a standard by which they, and anybody else, were enabled to measure the laws."[33] By doing so, "they became teachers of disobedience, promoters of anarchy, sophists who deceived men by the specious name of liberty,"[34] as Strauss puts it summarizing Hobbes's thought. Then, he adds: "To the traditional political philosophy which was based on independent reflection of private men, which with necessary consequence led to a doctrine of rebellion, anarchy, *freedom*, Hobbes opposes a new political science which intends to establish by cogent reasons that man is obliged to unconditional *obedience*; in opposition to the classical tradition of democratic ideals, Hobbes teaches the preference of absolute monarchy."[35] However, instead of providing what one would expect in such a context—namely, an explication of the features that make Hobbes's political science truly "new"—Strauss goes on to point out, still in his own name, that "Hobbes is thus in opposition to classical thought an exponent of a doctrine of absolute obedience to the laws. He was fully aware that by being this he was following another tradition. In the same texts on which we have mainly based our characterization of Hobbes's primary tendency, he gives us sufficient hints as to that other tradition."[36] And unsurprisingly at this point, Strauss explains further:

> He [Hobbes] states that when private men claim to have an independent knowledge of good and evil, they wish to be like kings (*cupiunt esse sicut reges*); and he adds that the oldest of all commandments of God was that man should not eat of the fruit of the tree of knowledge of good and evil, and that the oldest of the temptations of the devil was: You will be as gods, knowing good and evil. Thus Hobbes seems to base and, *to some extent, he actually does base* his criticism of the classical doctrine of freedom and democracy on the biblical doctrine of obedience and monarchy.[37]

Now, how should we interpret the part—quite straightforward, to be sure—we have emphasized in the quote above? Is Hobbes not, being the author who started modernity according to Strauss at that stage of his reflection, a clear expression of a new kind of atheism and, accordingly, a thinker moved by the "antitheological ire," as we have noted? Indeed. As Strauss puts it shortly afterwards, "Of course, we must not take Hobbes's quotations from the Scripture too seriously. Far from having been a sincere believer in the Scripture, he may rightly be said to have been the harshest critic of the authority of the Scripture, and even of its specific teaching, among the many violent opponents of the Bible in the 17th and 18th centuries."[38] For this reason, Strauss continues, "Hobbes rewrites the ten commandments by replacing God by kings," and "the absolute obedience which Hobbes demands has then as its object not divine law, the will of God, but human law, the will of the sovereign power."[39] However, as Strauss also points out, "in spite of his denial of the authority of the Scripture and in spite of his very atheism, it is not a mere matter of chance or prudence that Hobbes attacks the classical tradition in the name of the biblical tradition: as we shall see soon, his own teaching would not have been possible without the Greek tradition having been undermined by the biblical tradition."[40]

Hobbes's new and original perspective is, therefore, not entirely new. As Strauss suggests, Hobbes adopts elements not only (as one would expect from a committed "philosopher") of the philosophical tradition, but of the biblical tradition as well. This latter had already been brought in (although without allowing it to destabilize the underpinnings of its overall philosophical approach) by medieval political philosophy. For this reason, as we have underscored, medieval political philosophy is, for Strauss, nearer to modern political philosophy and Hobbes than is classical political philosophy, despite its inability, or unwillingness, to "lead to a systematic criticism of the classical framework" due to the fact that all the "very important modifications," based on the Bible, it introduced were inserted "into the framework of classical thought."[41]

Certainly, that inability does not characterize Hobbes. Proof thereof emerges, for example, in what Strauss observes about his view of the principle of absolute obedience to the law compared to the conception of the rule of law as framed by Aristotle. According to the latter, as well as the whole classical tradition, law is the reflection of right order, which is independently understood by human beings. As Strauss explains:

> The conception guiding Plato as well as Aristotle and Cicero may be summed up in the formula: Law is an order, a distribution and assignation of something; it owes its validity to its having emanated from wisdom and understanding; law is right order, found out by reason, and it *is* law not because it is imposed on man by the will of authority, and not in the first instance because it is consented to by the citizens, but because it is founded on perception of what is good.[42]

In light of this conception, irrespective of their depreciation of consent, the classics regarded the doctrine of the rule of law as a doctrine of freedom, since the rule of law, in their view, amounted to the rule of reason as distinct from that of particular individuals with their, potentially intrusive and tyrannical, idiosyncrasies.

Hobbes, by contrast, while raising the question of the "authorization" of the sovereign (thereby preparing the ground for modern liberalism and democracy), plainly states that the law is "essentially a command, i.e., a precept which man has to obey merely because it is commanded."[43] In his view, "the reason for which man has to obey the law, is the *will* of authority."[44] This being the case, as Strauss puts it contrasting Hobbes's principle of "absolute obedience to the law" with the classical "rule of law" we have just described, "not the law is sovereign, but the will of men, of the men in power; and the law, far from being the sovereign, is itself completely subject to the will of the governing men."[45]

It is in light of this view that Strauss significantly observes that "the more Hobbes understood his own intention, the more he put the idea of law into the background in favor of the idea of the sovereign will," to conclude that "when Hobbes opposes to the classical doctrine of freedom . . . his own doctrine of absolute obedience to the laws, the conceptions of 'law' and 'obedience' must have undergone a fundamental change."[46]

According to classical philosophy, in fact, the view that law is ultimately a "command" of the sovereign will is, "to say the least, not in the foreground,"[47] as Strauss ironically contends. This is due to the fact that, as we have emphasized, law was regarded by the classics as "right order, found out by [a type of] reason" that, in its turn, was seen as capable of perceiving "what is good."[48] This rationalistic perspective permeates the whole tradition of natural law and, as Strauss underscores, can still be detected, no matter how transformed on its surface, at the core of the reflection of Richard Hooker.

Only one generation later, by contrast, Hobbes introduces what proves to be a radical change. In his view, natural law is not so much such a demanding and objective perception, carried out by wisdom and rational understanding, of what is good or of the right order, as a theorem (in addition, an "uncertain" one) devised by "private men" in order to achieve peace. What was the outcome of a reason seen through the strengthening lenses of classical rationalism, for Hobbes is the result, indeed, of reason, but on a reduced scale. If Hooker could still observe that law is "any kind of rule or canon, whereby actions are framed," and that natural law, consequently, is "the natural measure whereby to judge our doings," "the sentence of Reason, determining and setting down what is good to be done,"[49] Hobbes claims instead that natural laws are "not properly" laws. For they are not commands of the sovereign will, enforced by civil authority, but mere "dictates" that proceed from the natural reason of each. Natural law, in other words, is only "a precept, not imposed by the will of an authority, but 'found out by reason'; the obligation to obey it is founded not on the will of a superior, but on insight into the matter, into what is good, what is good to the obeying man: the natural laws 'are but Conclusions, or Theorems, concerning what conduceth to the conservation and defence *of themselves*.'"[50]

This devaluation of natural law, and of the rationalism that was at its basis, leads Hobbes to distinguish, in an unprecedented manner, between natural right and natural law, as well as to rely on the former only as the real foundation of his political philosophy. However, what is here worth noting first is that, although Hobbes rejects the established scholastic view that natural law was still a law not "in respect of nature" itself, "but in respect of the author of nature, God Almighty,"[51] the biblical concept of "divine omnipotence" still operates in the background of his approach in a decisive manner. As Strauss explains, "When Hobbes attacks the classical view," still present in Hooker, "according to which law is essentially dependent on understanding, and the consequence of this view that natural law is a real law, he follows a medieval tradition."[52] And to explain this remark, drawing from Francisco Suarez's *Tractatus de legibus ac Deo legislatore*, he significantly adds:

> The theological correspondence to the classical view is the thesis that the ultimate reason of natural law is divine *understanding*. To that thesis, a number of medieval thinkers had opposed the opinion that the ultimate reason of natural law is divine *will*. According to this opinion, natural law is for this reason, and for this reason only, a law because it is commanded by God who can change it or repeal it just as he likes; consequently, no action whatsoever is intrinsically good or bad, but merely as far as it is commanded or forbidden by God.[53]

As one can easily see, in this theological conundrum the struggle between Athens and Jerusalem turns out to be summed up and reduced to its ultimate terms. To the classical view that natural reason is able to glimpse an eternal and necessary paradigm that, as it were, is above the same gods[54] (therefore becoming the truly divine), the biblical view objects that nothing is above the omnipotent God. For even what is perceived as "by nature" good and evil is so just because God has ruled that way. Strauss even discloses his rationalistic leanings while emphasizing this radical (and irreconcilable) opposition: "There were other thinkers who could not accept this consequence of the latter opinion because they *realized* that the actions commanded or forbidden by natural law *are intrinsically* good or bad; they tried to avoid the danger that the intrinsic validity of the principles of morality would be denied in the name of divine omnipotence."[55] As a result, "they made natural law absolutely independent of the will of God."[56] However, having accepted the view, no less biblical, that "law is essentially a command, they could not maintain the classical view that natural law is a real law," and "came to the conclusion that natural law is no law in the proper sense of the word, that it does not command, but merely indicate and show what has to be done or omitted."[57]

Now, according to Strauss Hobbes not only "takes over" the teaching above, thereby following in the footsteps of those medieval thinkers and adopting a view of a distinct biblical origin. He also goes beyond that teaching by claiming that natural laws are not only merely "indicative" (being devoid of the command character), but also, to some extent, "*uncertain.*"[58] For in his view what was still regarded, even by most of the medieval thinkers, as the outcome of natural, universal reason, is now to be conceived of as the uncertain "conclusions of particular men, and therefore not properly laws."[59]

Strauss devotes to the explanation of this "uncertainty" some of the most enlightening and subtle pages of his whole lecture, expanding, in this respect, on what he had previously stated in his seminal book *The Political Philosophy of Hobbes.*[60] He starts from the observation that Hobbes still needs natural law in order to justify the obligation to obey the laws passed by the sovereign, which, otherwise, would be "invalid."[61] Then, he shows that this fundamental role of natural law in Hobbes's political philosophy is only apparently in contradiction with his claim that "where there is no Common-wealth, there nothing is Unjust."[62] For Hobbes introduces a difference between intentions and actions whereby he can still make that relativistic (jus-positivistic) assumption as far as actions are concerned, while allowing for a compelling moral assessment of the intentions. According to Hobbes, intentions are defensible or not, in the state of nature as well, depending on whether they emanate from fear of violent death or pride (desire to triumph). While in the first case they are just and morally defensible, in the second they are not. This assumption, as we have seen, leads Strauss to stress that the real basis of Hobbes's political philosophy is not natural law, but natural right: the right to everything (*ius in omnia*) that individuals, in the state of nature, deem necessary to secure their life. In this framework, natural law becomes only a means to such a fundamental end. If the goal is to secure one's life (or, negatively expressed, to escape violent death and the fear it necessarily sparks), the command to seek peace, in which natural law ultimately consists according to Hobbes, proves to be the logical conclusion for those who start from that premise. Hence, natural law is logically certain. Still, it remains uncertain with regards to its implementation, since, as Strauss underscores, in Hobbes's account only natural right, being based on an "inescapable necessity" prompted by the passion of fear of death, is absolutely certain and, therewith, the real foundation of Hobbes's political philosophy. In the state of nature, natural law, particularly if compared to the "inescapable necessity" on which natural right rests, proves to be weak. Yet it is strong enough, as it were, to justify the obligation of each individual to obey the civil authority once this has been created, since their goal is precisely the same: peace as the condition of avoiding violent death and, in perspective, of commodious living.

III

There are several aspects of this revolutionary view that would deserve to be underscored and commented on. Here, however, I wish to focus on the downgrading of reason this arrangement entails. Only passion, fear of violent death, is inescapable, sure and, therewith, fully reliable from the practical standpoint. Reason, although still playing an important role, becomes just the handmaiden of that passion: it is calculation, a mere means to an end, regarding how one can better achieve the goal passion has set. As a result, in this Hobbesian scenario reason is no longer considered as capable of discerning a supreme end: the *summum bonum* or *beatitudo*. The search for the *summum bonum*, the supreme good, is replaced by the attempt to avoid the *summum malum*: violent death.[63] This is the gist of the lowering of the standards Strauss often underscores when it comes to modernity. The presupposition of this lowering is the downgrading of reason we have just described in his footsteps. From Hobbes onwards, reason is regarded as no longer capable of discerning an objective standard and promoting the "understanding" of right order (as we have underscored while referring to the classical approach to law, particularly to natural law). In Hobbes's account, reason is too weak to do so: it is a mere tool, which can play a role only by being subservient to passion. By contrast, fear of violent death, along with the natural right it enables, becomes paramount. Passion now sets the goal, and reason has, henceforth, merely to comply: "He [Hobbes] opposes to the seeing, understanding obedience to right reason, the blind obedience to the will of the sovereign; and that blind obedience is derived from the fear of death which—in spite of the fact that it *makes* man prudent—is itself not prudent, not seeing, but blind. Obedience, as Hobbes understands it, and fear of death are related to each other by the fact that they both are blind."[64] To this important statement, where the word *blind* tellingly occurs even four times in few lines, Strauss adds:

> We may take it that the fear of death which is the beginning of all prudence is only the "secularized" form of the fear of God which is the beginning of all wisdom. Indeed, Hobbes coordinates the fear of "Spirits Invisible" or, rather, "the feare of that Invisible Power, which they every one Worship as God" to the natural state, just as he coordinates the fear of the sovereign power to the civil state. This, however, means, as the natural state is essentially irrational, while the civil state is essentially rational, and as men's subjection to a sovereign power arises out of natural fear, of fear of violent death, that, according to Hobbes, fear of God is the irrational, prerational equivalent to fear of death, which, in spite of its being prerational, has nevertheless the merit that it is the only means to make man rational.[65]

Once again, the dynamic of transformation of and opposition to a view of biblical origin, which for Strauss characterizes the emergence of modern philosophy, is apparently at play.[66] Hence, Tanguay's claim that Strauss advocates a "weak version of the secularization thesis" proves indeed to be plausible. Regardless of whether secularization is the best possible term to use in Strauss's case (which we will delve into later), the main question about that claim is whether, at least in "The Origin of Modern Political Thought," it does not hold true even for other aspects of Strauss's approach than his explicit remarks about the idea of providence.

Doubtlessly, what we have noted about Hobbes's view of law already proves this is the case. Nonetheless, to further address this question, as well as that of the downgrading of reason we have raised above, it is worth considering anew what Strauss observes regarding Hobbes's remark that the "original error" of classical political philosophy is to believe that "private men can know by themselves what is good and evil."[67] As we have pointed out, Strauss emphasizes the extent to which, by doing so, Hobbes is following the biblical tradition, a tradition of absolute obedience as distinct from the independent thinking that informs the classical philosophical approach. In that instance, after underscoring the similarities between Hobbes and Calvin in that respect,[68] Strauss quotes Hobbes as saying, against the rationalistic approach characteristic of classical political philosophy, that "the rules of good and evil are the *laws*"—meaning civil, positive laws—"whereas the classical philosophers"—and here come Hobbes's own words—"'make the Rules of Good, and Bad, by their own Liking, and Disliking,' by their *passions*."[69] Under the influence of the Bible, what was once regarded as the exercise of human reason, for Hobbes becomes now the mere expression of one's liking or disliking, i.e., of one's passions. And to explain further Hobbes's position on that matter, Strauss goes on to observe that "against the doctrine of 'Aristotle, and other *Heathen* Philosophers' who 'define Good, and Evil, by the Appetite of men,' he makes the objection: 'Not the Appetite of Private men, but the Law . . . is the measure.'"[70]

Liking, disliking, passions, appetite, law: everything but reason seems to be capable of being "the measure." What is the origin of this anti-rationalistic view, according to which reason can, at best, play an ancillary and downgraded role? As we have already noted, Strauss explicitly traces this Hobbesian approach, no matter how secular and revolutionary, to the biblical tradition. Arguably, however, this is only one side (perhaps, even the less noteworthy) of his interpretation of the inception of modernity and the crisis of philosophy it brings about. For while insisting on Hobbes's critique of the "*Heathen* Philosophers," Strauss keeps quoting him as saying: "And yet is this Doctrine . . . still practised; . . . and no man calleth Good or Evil, but that which is so in his own eyes."[71] Then, to stress the biblical origin of this view, he observes: "The expression 'whatsoever seemeth good in his own eyes' is obviously of scriptural origin. We need only refer to Hobbes's own quotation: 'After the death of Joshua, till the time of Saul, the time between is noted frequently in the Book of Judges, that there was in those dayes no King in Israel; and sometimes with this addition, that every man did that which was right in his own eyes.'"[72] Hence, the expression is indeed "of scriptural origin." But Strauss is here more specific than that: no matter how reminiscent of Calvin's position, the genuine root of Hobbes's view according to which what was considered by the "*Heathen* Philosophers" as the outcome of the independent inquiry of human reason is now to be regarded as mere appetite or passion is the Hebrew Bible: the Book of Judges, more precisely, and what it narrates about the period between the death of Joshua and the time of Saul in Israel.

This hint by Strauss proves not to be accidental, let alone negligible. After contrasting the rationalistic approach of classical political philosophy with Hobbes's approach based on the biblical idea of absolute obedience to the law, Strauss had already commented: "Hobbes opposes to the Greek schools of philosophy the *Jewish* schools of law. And whereas he considers the former to have been completely useless, he strongly recommends the latter."[73] To these straightforward remarks, he adds shortly afterwards: "Speaking of his doctrine of the rights of the sovereign power, he [Hobbes] says: 'But supposing that these (principles) of mine are not such Principles of Reason; yet I am sure they are Principles from Authority of Scripture; as I shall make it appear when I shall come to speak of the Kingdome of God, (administered by Moses,) over the Jewes, his peculiar people by Covenant.' "[74]

Now, as we have already underscored, Strauss swiftly warns the reader not to take Hobbes's quotations from the Scripture "too seriously," since Hobbes remains "the harshest critic" of the Bible and its teaching among its opponents of the seventeenth and eighteenth centuries. What he states in a note attached to the revealing quotation from Hobbes's *Leviathan* above, however, should not pass unnoticed. There Strauss observes that "it may be added that the interpretation, given by Hobbes as well as by other absolutist writers, of the biblical right of kings . . . is based on the teaching of the Talmud," to conclude with the following, telling remark: "The influence of Jewish law on the political discussions of the 16th and 17th centuries deserves a special study."[75]

If Strauss ever conducted such a study in a systematic manner (as he likely did), he never published its results, at least in any explicit form. Had he done so, he would presumably have had to observe, in his own name, that a key aspect of early modern political philosophy (which, be it not forgotten, marks for him the beginning of the crisis of political philosophy) is enabled by views that are of biblical origin, some of them distinctly Jewish. This might have been an uncomfortable comment to make for a person like Strauss who, throughout his life, felt that he belonged "to the Jews, no matter what."[76] For even in the late 1930s such a comment could easily be misinterpreted, by superficial or biased readers, as a broad indictment of the biblical or Jewish background, and not, as Strauss meant it, as a quintessentially philosophical observation. Strauss's discretion on this sensitive matter can thus be understood. It did not prevent him, nonetheless, from giving his audience hints like those in the quotations above, as well as the others in "The Origin of Modern Political Thought" we are now going to focus on.

Before suggesting that the Jewish legal tradition, in particular, influenced the political discussions of early modern political thinkers, Strauss had arguably already singled out a Jewish locus in at least another instance. Notably, this occurs when he points out that for Hobbes, by attempting to know through independent, rational inquiry what is good or evil, as classical political philosophy did, "private men . . . wish to be like kings."[77] In that context, as we have underscored, while highlighting the fact that, in doing so, Hobbes was "fully aware" that he was following "another tradition," Strauss traces this tradition back to "the oldest of all commandments of God,"[78] namely, not to eat of the fruit of the tree of knowledge of good and evil. And it is, significantly, right after this remark that Strauss observes that the tendency to play the "biblical doctrine" of absolute obedience to the law against the "classical doctrine" of free and independent inquiry can be detected in other texts by Hobbes, to emphatically conclude that "Hobbes opposes to the Greek schools of philosophy the Jewish schools of law."[79]

When hearing such remarks, all those who are familiar with Strauss cannot but think of the opposition between "Athens and Jerusalem." Indeed, they have good reasons to do so, their only possible mistake being that they may not be reading what Strauss thereby states literally enough, to wit, as a specific reference to the Jewish heritage within the biblical tradition (Jerusalem) as distinct from a broad mention of the so-called Judeo-Christian tradition.

This possible mistake seems to be confirmed by what Strauss observes regarding the "disappointed hope in Providence" as the reason behind the modern attempt to conquer nature and revolutionize society, which in turn leads philosophy towards its "politicization."

We have already insisted on this point, which occurs right at the end of Strauss's lecture. This time, I will therefore limit myself to highlighting the fact that, also in that instance, Strauss seems to underscore the specifically Jewish side of the matter. As the reader will recall, Strauss explains the difference between ancient, restrained atheism and modern, enterprising atheism—which comes to see the denial of providence as no longer a "merely theoretical assertion," but as a "practical revolt against Providence"—in terms of their different attitude towards nature. Unlike ancient atheism, which could still see in the theoretical knowledge of nature a means to achieve beatitude, modern atheism begins to feel threatened and frightened by nature. Nature, however, is "felt as a menace not because man has now discovered natural evils either in the world or in himself, which were unknown to classical philosophy."[80] Rather, as we have observed before, for Strauss this shift of attitude is due to the fact that "man had been accustomed by a tradition of almost *two thousand years* to believe himself to be protected by Providence."[81] Now, since Strauss is here referring to the seventeenth and eighteenth centuries,[82] this nowadays routine expression to mean the beginning of Christianity cannot be understood in that manner without further ado. As a true beginning of that timespan, in fact, Strauss may well be aiming at a period that antedates the inception of the Christian era by around three centuries.[83]

This hypothesis is made stronger by what Strauss observes, right afterwards, about "man" still influenced by that bimillenary tradition, notably by the belief in providence. As we have noted, at first he stresses the disappointed and reactive mood of such man: "When this belief became shattered, he could not immediately cease to hope for Providence, to expect help from it. Denial of Providence was thus from now on related not to serene and detached philosophizing, but rather to disappointed hope in Providence."[84] Then, he adds the following remark: "What was in earlier times nothing more than the complaint of suffering, not yet enlightened, Job, became now, as it were, the keystone of philosophy."[85]

Strauss's emphasis is, hence, on a central figure of the Jewish biblical heritage: Job. No matter how subsequently flown into the Christian tradition (in that respect, Judeo-Christian tradition), this figure, along with the distinctly Jewish elements recalled above, seems to be considered by Strauss in its Jewish specificity (and not, apparently, just because Strauss himself happened to be a Jew). If so, modern political philosophy (and modernity more in general), with its emphasis on activism and decisionism, could be interpreted, with regard to these characteristics, in terms of the encounter of the philosophical tradition, with its enlightening thrust, with the "Jewish schools of law" and Job's unredeemed suffering—a suffering now regarded as utterly absurd and therefore no longer bearable.[86]

IV

In this scenario, only two elements of religious background among those "sublated" by modernity would not be of specific Jewish origin, according to Strauss's account. The first is the opposition between state of nature and civil or political state. As we have already underscored,[87] in *Natural Right and History* (that is to say, however, more than a decade later than "The Origin of Modern Political Thought") Strauss points out that Hobbes draws this opposition from Christian theology, according to which the state of nature is that which precedes, and is superseded by, the state of grace. In Strauss's account, this view is transformed by Hobbes in that he "replaced the state of grace by the state of civil society."[88] In doing so, however, Hobbes kept the polemical stance towards nature that was characteristic of the Christian approach, which saw the state of nature as intrinsically defective (notably, as a result of the Fall), thereby preventing himself from attaining "a pure and whole knowledge" of nature itself.[89]

The second element is Hobbes's "immanent foundation of morality," based on the distinction between intentions and actions and the consequent affirmation of natural right as the "absolutely justified claim." As early as 1935, in *The Political Philosophy of Hobbes* Strauss had already underscored the Christian origin of such a distinction, while also showing the similarities between Hobbes and Kant concerning the "immanent" character of that foundation.[90]

Having said that, it is worth noting that for Strauss the separation between the objective sphere of actions and the subjective sphere of intentions (or, at least, of private beliefs more in general) seems not to be as exclusively related to the Christian background as one may think at first sight, especially relying on statements like those from *The Political Philosophy of Hobbes* we have just referred to. At least in an early work of his, Strauss proves to have somewhat agreed, in this respect, with a different interpretation, namely, that by Paul de Lagarde.[91] Lagarde was a German nationalist and antisemite biblical scholar and orientalist of the nineteenth century whom Strauss, in his youth, credited for having "set the highest standard in honesty and seriousness in the political arena," a standard Strauss commended "for emulation by the Zionists" (whom, at that time, he belonged to).[92] No matter how divergent in their ultimate goals,[93] Lagarde's German nationalism and the political Zionism the young Strauss endorsed agreed that the solution of the "Jewish question" advanced by modern liberalism was ultimately unfeasible. Unlike this solution, based on the separation between state and society, as well as on the reduction of the Jewish national character to a matter of merely private concern, according to Lagarde (as Strauss summarizes him) "the [German] state must . . . either assimilate the Jews (or, rather, prepare the ground for assimilation, which, itself, actually lies beyond the possibilities of the state), or expel them."[94]

However radical, this position—which arguably leaves no other solution than the emigration of the Jews in light of the doubts voiced in the parenthetical remark—could not totally displease a political Zionist like Strauss at the time. The same position also appears not to be entirely at odds with the "imperial solution" that Strauss, about a decade later, would praise as a possible "decent solution" of the Jewish question in Germany.[95] Needless to say, this position contemplates as the only possible either-or that of complete assimilation, meaning Germanization and Christianization, or expulsion, thereby ruling out, in principle, any hypothesis of discrimination on racial basis within the state, let alone of extermination.[96]

This is not, however, the aspect of the matter that should now be emphasized, no matter how interesting it may be. What, rather, needs here to be underscored is that in "Paul de Lagarde" Strauss appears to agree with Lagarde's interpretation of modern liberalism, and by implication of modernity as a whole, as a form of "secularized *Judaism*."[97]

According to Strauss, Lagarde sees as "characteristic features of Judaism . . . its being devoid of reality and its 'materialism.'"[98] While the first feature is due to the loss of independence as a kingdom and the inception of the exile, which make the Jews dependent on other political communities for their most basic and urgent needs, the second is understood by Lagarde as "the putting of the law before the spirit, of the finished matter before the process, and of culturedness [*Gebildetheit*] before the acquisition of culture [*Bildung*]."[99] The Judaism that is shaped by the experience of the exile, in other words, becomes for Lagarde "essentially pharisaic," namely, purely concerned with respect for forms and external rules, irrespective of the individuals' innermost beliefs. Regarding this aspect of the matter, Lagarde is at one with such "anti-anti-Semitic" authors as Nietzsche, Mommsen, and Wellhausen.[100] And Strauss, at least at the time, is ready to give them some credit in that respect.[101]

As a result, Lagarde's next step also becomes less far-fetched from Strauss's standpoint. After having reduced postexilic Judaism to Pharisaism, Lagarde, in Strauss's summary, contrasts it with Christianity. Unlike Paul's interpretation of the latter, through which "Judaism gained mastery over the gospel" by objectivizing it,[102] for Lagarde Christianity ultimately is "evangelical piety" and an ever-regenerating spiritual process. "In the community that is materialistic and devoid of reality [*entwirklicht-*

materialistische Gemeinschaft], and as its antithesis," as Lagarde puts it in Strauss's account, "there arises in the line of the prophets Jesus: he contrasts the election of Israel with the divine sonship of all human beings, the synagogue-state with the kingdom of God, descent from Abraham with spiritual rebirth."[103] The conclusion of Lagarde's argument could not be more radical: "There is no reconciliation between Judaism and Christianity; Judaism is the anti-Christian principle pure and simple," and the so-called Judeo-Christian tradition ultimately a misrepresentation, at best favored by the overwhelming influence of "Paulinism."[104]

It is only after bringing up such a striking theological background that Strauss, always reconstructing Lagarde's thought, comes to the political implications of his summary and to the question of liberalism in particular. Against that background, he asks: "How was it possible for the Jews to become emancipated in Germany?"[105] This emancipation turns out to be nothing other than the result of the Jewish influence on the Christian and German world: "The Jews owe their admission [*Aufnahme*] to the circumstance that the Jewish spirit has gained mastery over Germany; for liberalism is nothing but secularized Judaism."[106] For liberalism "too," as Strauss adds to explain these categorical remarks, "is characterized by a superstitious belief in the rigid, objective, unique, and isolated fact [*Aberglaube an die starre, objektive, einmalige, einzelne Tatsache*]. Only thus have the Jews been able to gain influence over the Germans, without rebirth in the German spirit. Germanism on the basis of the Jewish religion: this is a contradiction in terms."[107]

So far, Strauss has apparently limited himself to reconstructing Lagarde's views.[108] But regarding (at least) the final statement, he now emphatically comments: "Indeed [*In der Tat*]!" Then, clearly still arguing in his own name, he observes: "Thus, and only thus, may one put the question: how could the so-called assimilation take place in spite of the inner alienness of Germanism and Judaism? And the answer to this question cannot but take the general form given to it by Lagarde [*wird nicht umhin können, die allgemeine Form derjenigen Lagardes zu tragen*]: only through a kind of 'Jewification [*Verjudung*]' of the German spirit was this assimilation possible."[109]

Now, by introducing a term like *Verjudung*, the young Strauss in the mid-1920s was dangerously handling a weapon that would become tragically powerful in the weaponry of the anti-Jewish propaganda, especially once joined by its correlative concept of *Entjudung*: "de-Judaization." As we have observed before regarding the either-or of assimilation or expulsion, he could not even imagine, at that time, that these ideas would be interpreted in racial-biological terms and used as a justification for the attempt to annihilate his people.[110]

The fact remains, nonetheless, that the young Strauss ultimately agrees with Lagarde's view that liberalism is "secularized Judaism," since "it too is characterized by a superstitious belief in the rigid, objective, unique, and isolated fact."[111] As a "pharisaic" political regime, liberalism focuses on an external and purely formal law-abidingness, in which the innermost convictions and beliefs, provided they do not interfere with the objective sphere of actions, are not publicly probed. As a convinced and proud political Zionist, who wanted his people to wholly regain the "sense of reality" it had lost since the exile,[112] Strauss is even ready to acknowledge the opportunistic nature of the too easily assimilated and liberal Jews whom Lagarde dispraised for their allegedly merely formal and artificial culturedness. Although underscoring Lagarde's superficiality in that regard ("We do not deem it necessary to specify to what extent Lagarde ignored essentials when he contented himself with pointing to the spirit of culturedness"),[113] Strauss seems to agree with him on the substance of that matter: "But most certainly this spirit was an important moment in nineteenth-century German Judaism: *Gumpelino!*"[114]

All this is of particular importance to us because Strauss, when writing "The Origin of Modern Political Thought" towards the end of the 1930s, could hardly have entirely forgotten what he had maintained, in 1924, about liberalism as "secularized Judaism" and Jewish emancipation as the result of "Verjudung."[115] This is even more plausible when we consider that, in the lecture, he hints at the Jewish background of Hobbes's essentially modern perspective. Admittedly, in "The Origin of Modern Political Thought" Strauss focuses on Hobbes as the initiator of modern political philosophy, and liberalism ultimately plays no role in that work. One should not forget, however, that for Strauss Hobbes is (and remains also after he began to consider Machiavelli as the first of the moderns)[116] a proto-liberal thinker, nay, the true "founder of liberalism." As he famously states in *Natural Right and History*: "If we may call liberalism that political doctrine which regards as the fundamental political fact the rights, as distinguished from the duties, of man and which identifies the function of the state with the protection or the safeguarding of those rights, we must say the founder of liberalism was Hobbes."[117]

In light of this background, what should we conclude regarding the alleged Jewish origin (as distinct from a more broadly Judeo-Christian origin or a specifically Christian one) of modern political philosophy and liberalism as shaped by Hobbes? Bearing in mind that, in Strauss's view, Hobbes's approach remains philosophical in principle, since he tried to enfranchise human reason from its subordination to revelation, and that the influence still exerted by the biblical tradition must be regarded as Hobbes's residual entanglement (whether conscious or unconscious)[118] in some of the conceptual categories of that tradition, one can attempt to answer the question as follows.

"Hobbes's decisionism,"[119] which is his belief (shared by Schmitt's merely "inverted" liberalism) that human reason cannot independently discern what is good or evil (at least when it comes to actions), but has to depend on the will of a sovereign power (in the absence of God, the human sovereign), is of distinctly Jewish origin. The same can ultimately be argued, as we have pointed out, regarding the other main root of the politicization of philosophy in modernity, namely, the "disappointed hope in providence" that transforms the restrained, even "coward"[120] epicurean in a Baconian and Hobbesian activist who aims to master nature and, looking ahead, revolutionize society.

As regards the primacy of right over duty, as well as the "immanent" foundation of morality that Hobbes, well before Kant, lays down, the scenario seems, however, more nuanced. On the one hand, the distinction between intentions and actions, on which that "immanent" foundation ultimately rests, appears to be of Christian origin. As already noted, Strauss openly states this view in *The Political Philosophy of Hobbes*.[121] Likewise, his early essay "Paul de Lagarde" seems to suggest the same line of reading insofar as it follows Lagarde's description of the genuine Christian approach, unlike the "objectified" and essentially "pharisaic" postexilic Judaism (not to mention Paulinism), as characterized by inwardness. Moreover, we should not forget, in this regard, what we have observed while focusing on Strauss's correspondence with Krüger, where the whole topic of depth or profoundness is traced back to Christianity in particular, by Krüger no less than Strauss.[122]

If we shift from the moral and theoretical aspects of this matter to its distinctly political features, however, the above-sketched differences cease to be so sharp. It is "Paul de Lagarde" that points more clearly towards this direction, notably where it states that liberalism is secularized Judaism because it shares the latter's emphasis on what is objective and exterior, namely, human actions as distinct from intentions.[123] From a legal-political standpoint, as Hobbes shows, an almost exclusive emphasis on external actions, on a purely formal law-abidingness, implies the intangibility of inwardness. This attitude may indeed be regarded as the legacy of a typically Christian stance, in light of the originally unpolitical character of this religion.[124] But the same attitude, if we give enough credit to "Paul de Lagarde," turns out to characterize (actually, to be originated by) the postexilic Jews, whose Judaism becomes depoliticized and can survive only at the price of its privatization.

Ultimately, this seems to be the meaning of the remark restated by the young Strauss that "liberalism is secularized Judaism" because "it too is characterized by a superstitious belief in the rigid, objective, unique, and isolated fact."[125] Is this "objective fact," translated from the religious into the political and legal sphere, not the action that is required to formally comply with the law, regardless of its innermost intention?[126] If this is the case, the correlated character of Christian inwardness and postexilic Jewish objectivization, once it is addressed from a political perspective, emerges with greater clarity. As a result, elements that appear as essentially Christian prima facie, especially if approached from the moral standpoint as Christianity understands it (from the point of view of intentions rather than actions), become able to be integrated in a (postexilic) Jewish framework from the political perspective—a perspective that also according to the "liberal" Hobbes cannot but focus on actions.

However important, the only purely Christian element still retained, although duly transformed, by early modern political philosophy would thus be the opposition between the state of nature and the state of grace, the latter being replaced by the civil state in Hobbes's account.[127] As we have underscored, Strauss openly traces this view back to Christian theology in *Natural Right and History*, implicitly emphasizing the role of this view with regard to Hobbes's still polemical stance towards nature. Be this as it may, for Strauss the Jewish heritage, whether alone or together with Christianity, proves to play a prominent role in the process of "weak secularization," as it were, that brings about modern political philosophy. If need be, additional, though indirect proof of this can be found by contrasting the ways in which Strauss refers to the question of secularization in such different and distant works of his as "Paul de Lagarde" and "Perspective on the Good Society."[128] While in the former, as we have observed, he summarizes (and ultimately agrees with) Lagarde as claiming that "liberalism is secularized Judaism," in the latter, likewise reporting others' views (this time in a more detached fashion, to be sure) he limits himself to asking: "But is modernity secularized Christianity?" "Mr. Cohen," Strauss concludes laconically his summary of the views of one of the speakers at the Jewish-Protestant Colloquium he reports about, "seemed to doubt this."[129] And Strauss must presumably have agreed with him, due to both the "grave differences" that are blurred and concealed, in his view, by the concept of "the Judeo-Christian tradition"[130] and the doubts he may have had concerning the concept of secularization later in his life.

V

In order to conclude this chapter on the politicization of philosophy, as well as the comment on "The Origin of Modern Political Thought" this topic has brought about, we still need to complete our analysis of the difference between "bold and active,"[131] intrinsically politicized modern philosophy on the one hand, and reserved, essentially theoretical ancient philosophy (both idealistic and materialistic) on the other.

As we have underscored, in "The Origin of Modern Political Thought" Strauss claims that it is the "disappointed hope in Providence" that ultimately prevents modern philosophy from going back to ancient "unenterprising" materialism, prompting it to become, instead, "enterprising and designing" and to attempt to conquer nature as well as revolutionize society.[132] The influence of the biblical tradition in this regard, and the "entanglement" of the philosophical one in it, would thus be limited to the concept of providence. Now, leaving aside, for the moment, the question of the nature of such an entanglement, can one really be content with this interpretation only?

My doubts concern what Strauss observes about ancient, epicurean atheism and materialism. As we have seen, this approach appears to be coherently conventionalist, much more so than Hobbes's. Unlike Hobbes, who affirms that prior to civil society no action can be seen as unjust but grants that intentions are already justifiable or not depending on their being based, respectively, on fear of violent death or pride (i.e., on their being the expression of man's natural right or mere "will to triumph"), ancient, epicurean materialism states that "'nothing is just or unjust' before there are covenants made."[133] This assumption leads ancient materialism to affirm a form of straightforward naturalism, unlike Hobbes who attempts and realizes, as the first thinker ever, an immanent foundation of morality by stressing the role of the unavoidable and therewith universally justifiable fear of violent death.

At closer inspection, however, the conventionalism or naturalism of ancient materialism is arguably not as straightforward as it may seem. As we have underscored, for Strauss "pre-modern atheism was based on *knowledge of the limits* set to human designs."[134] According to this view, happiness was regarded as "self-sufficiency" and independence from external goods. This, however, means that human happiness was still conceived of as a kind of *beatitudo*, as the fulfilment, by way of knowledge and reason, of what befits human beings qua human beings.[135] There are still "limits" given by nature to what the latter may do or desire according to pre-modern atheism as Strauss describes it. It would be an unwise and Sisyphean attempt, from that perspective, to unleash human desires to the point of perpetually and restlessly (recklessly) seeking "power after power."[136] Human beings and their reason, as it were, still have a given place in the whole that cannot be ignored, no matter how blind and mindless the whole's components may be.[137] The perspective from which human beings approach nature is, therefore, still rationalistic and theoretical. This being the case, pre-modern naturalism seems to presuppose a notion of nature (more precisely, of what is by nature) as order, however weak or residual. It implies the notion of a measure that must be acknowledged and in light of which there still is a supreme good, *beatitudo* or "interior happiness," whose fulfilment is achieved by the exercise of human reason and the objective knowledge it enables.[138]

This possibility is rejected by Hobbes. As we have noted, although he distinguishes (but only "immanently") between natural right and mere appetite, in his view "the idea of *beatitudo*," based on the perception of objective "limits set to human designs," is "incompatible with human life, with its continuous movement and restlessness."[139] What was regarded as a "limited" condition within the whole becomes now a limitless, ever progressing attempt to secure oneself against a disorder brought about by a hostile nature.[140] As Strauss puts it, Hobbes replaces "the traditional idea of *beatitudo* by the modern idea of progress."[141] "Hobbes's very starting-point," he goes on in the same context, "is that death is the greatest and supreme evil, not counter-balanced by a supreme good."[142]

Now, why cannot Hobbes simply go back, in the wake of ancient materialism, to the idea of interior happiness or beatitude that rests, in its turn, on the idea of a limited human condition and on a kind of objective order, however residual this may be? Why must he instead see beatitude as replaced by never-ending progress and conceive of human life as "continuous movement and restlessness," thereby enabling—if not in his own doctrine, at least as a further possible development—a view of human nature as indefinitely "malleable"?[143] Is the residual "disappointed hope in Providence" enough to explain all of this?

Arguably, the disappointed hope in providence would suffice to explain Hobbes's position if he had only denied "superhuman will." But according to Strauss Hobbes also denied any "superhuman order." Pre-modern atheism can indeed be said to have rejected the same will; but not, at least completely, the idea of a superhuman, natural order whose knowledge leads to happiness, as we have underlined when referring to the idea of "limits set to human designs."[144] Hobbes's possible entanglement in the belief in providence can explain only his position, as well as his disappointed and polemical reaction, concerning God's will. In itself, however, it seems insufficient to fully account for his inability to recover the notion of a natural order—an order that, although in a weaker form than that characteristic of Greek "idealistic" tradition, for Strauss still tends to characterize ancient materialism.[145]

If this is the case, an additional cause of Hobbes's inability to recover the notion of any superhuman, natural order has to be sought. In light of what we can also read in "The Origin of Modern Political Thought," the biblical notion of divine "omnipotence" seems to be the best candidate.

In "The Origin of Modern Political Thought," Strauss addresses this question only with regard to the theme of natural law. In his account, as we have underscored, Hobbes does not consider natural law to be fully biding because it is not a command, namely, the expression of a sovereign will. In denying the character of law to natural law—Strauss underscores—Hobbes follows "a medieval tradition" for which natural law, if regarded as fully biding, would amount to a limitation of God's omnipotent will.[146] This interpretation directly opposes the classical view according to which natural law depends on independent, rational understanding of right order.

Now, this idea of omnipotence can hardly be seen as operating only in that specific context. Once it is accepted, its importance becomes so overwhelming that no sphere can be regarded as immune from its influence. Strauss himself hints at this feature of divine omnipotence when, in another context, he underscores the relevance of the medieval debate around the eternity or the created character of the world.[147] Is the idea that nature is created out of nothing not precisely the opposite of the motto *ex nihilo nihil fit* attributed to ancient materialism?[148] In "The Origin of Modern Political Thought," Strauss claims that the change of attitude towards nature in modernity is not the consequence of the discovery by man of "natural evils, either in the world or in himself, which were unknown to classical philosophy," but only of a "disappointed hope in Providence."[149] However, what should one say about the fact that, following the encounter of Athens with Jerusalem, nature itself, as well as what is by nature, comes to be seen as the mere product of the omnipotent will of an inscrutable God who, in light of his unlimited "power," may have made it differently? Is this view not, after all, at the core of modernity's "idealistic" or "phenomenalist" approach to natural science?[150]

The theoretical perspective that was still somewhat inherent in ancient materialism becomes utterly meaningless to modern materialism. The radically practical and anthropocentric view that characterizes the latter may indeed be the consequence, as Strauss expressly puts it in "The Origin of Modern Political Thought," of the disappointed hope in providence that, in its turn, is the indirect result of the biblical approach. But the bold and active, conquering attitude towards nature seems to be fully intelligible only by adding to that disappointed hope the idea, ultimately enrooted in the same biblical perspective, that nature and the world are created, particularly for human beings' sake, who are the peak of creation. Nature can be mastered, and no longer merely contemplated, because it has lost its eternal, necessary, and intrinsically knowable character.[151] The theoretical perspective that still appeared as meaningful to ancient materialism, with its resulting acceptance of the idea of *beatitudo* and of natural limits that human beings have to acknowledge, becomes untenable to modern materialism, which comes now to see nature as a practical resource to exploit in order to foster unlimited human progress, making human life "continuous movement and restlessness." The same line of reasoning applies to society. This is now regarded as artificially created (and as such, capable of being "revolutionized") by means of a pact that is meant as the only possible way to establish order over the original disorder characteristic of the state of nature.

Be this as it may, the more such concepts as *power* and *will* come to the foreground, the more nature—*physis* in Greek, a term with no equivalent in the Hebrew Bible[152]—fades away. This is perhaps the reason why, at the beginning of his 1954 essay "On the Basis of Hobbes's Political Philosophy," where he claimed to have condensed his deepest understanding of Hobbes and "modern natural right," Strauss blames Nietzsche for having ignored Hobbes, like Nietzsche himself a "philosopher of power."[153] The same holds for Strauss's attempt, in the same place, to trace back the origin of technology not so much, like Heidegger, to the

Greek philosophical thought, as to the "origins of that philosophic tradition which Nietzsche continued or completed: the British tradition."[154] For it is this latter, which is the modern tradition insofar as it was originated by Hobbes, that explains why and how philosophy became a weapon, making the purely philosophic life meaningless and obliterating the distinction, on which that life rested, between philosophers, on one hand, and gentlemen or sophists, on the other.

VI

In this chapter, we have maintained that, despite Strauss's skepticism concerning the concept of secularization, it is possible to show that he himself resorted to arguments that remind one, to some extent, of that concept—a claim that Tanguay, relying on "The Origin of Modern Political Thought" in particular, summarizes by saying that Strauss maintained a "weak version of the secularization thesis."[155]

Now, as Tanguay himself reminds us, Strauss clearly voiced his skepticism regarding the theory of secularization, notably in a 1946 letter to Löwith where he speaks of "fable convenue" regarding the interpretation of modern Enlightenment as "Christianly *motivated* [*christlich motiviert*]."[156] In the same letter, he argues that "modern science, that is, modern philosophy, is *fundamentally* to be understood inner-philosophically and inner-theoretically," to conclude that this "holds likewise for practical-political philosophy," as he claims to have shown in a seminar paper from the previous year.[157]

It is worth noting, nonetheless, that in the same letter Strauss concedes to Löwith that "biblical-scholastic motives only"—but definitely—"co*ll*aborated [*haben nur* mit*gewirkt*]"[158] in the genesis of modern philosophy—a concession that appears to be consistent with what he will publicly observe in his 1952 "Preface to Isaac Husik, *Philosophical Essays*": "Modern philosophy emerged by way of transformation of, if in opposition to, Latin or Christian scholasticism."[159] Evidently, this shows that Strauss harbored, even after the 1930s, a view of modern philosophy according to which, despite its head-on and polemical opposition to the biblical tradition (and to some extent, precisely because of such a polemical opposition), key elements of that tradition concurred to shape it.

On the other hand, this assumption seems contradicted by what Strauss observes in the seminar paper "Natural Right (1946)," which he cites in the above-mentioned letter to Löwith to support his inner-philosophical and inner-theoretical understanding of modern political philosophy as well. In that paper, Strauss indeed reiterates the gist of the arguments he had advanced in "The Origin of Modern Political Thought" to explain the bold and active character of modern atheism, including the pivotal role of the disappointed hope in providence.[160] But right after such a reiteration, he adds the following remark: "This, however, cannot be the last word on the subject. For there are reasons to suppose that the theological garb owing to which the doctrine of the rights of man achieved its victory was really not more than the protecting coloring of an essentially untheological effort."[161]

Whatever these reasons—which, unfortunately, Strauss does not explain in the continuation of his paper—this remark alone, along with the fact that he never published either "The Origin of Modern Political Thought" or "Natural Right (1946)" in his life,[162] should make us rather cautious about the opportunity to resort to the concept of secularization and its likes as far as Strauss is concerned, at least from the mid-1940s onwards.

Nonetheless, Strauss's admission, in his 1946 letter to Löwith, that "biblical-scholastic motives," at any rate, "*co*llaborated"[163] in the genesis of modern philosophy, as well as his remarks, along the same lines, in his 1952 "Preface to Isaac Husik, *Philosophical Essays*," makes such an opportunity worthy of being contemplated. It might be no coincidence that in "Natural Right (1946)" Strauss limits himself to stating the above-mentioned remark on the merely "protecting" character of modernity's entanglement in the biblical tradition, notably in the idea of providence, without then giving any further detail about that supposition. After all, the view that a "Christianly motivated" Enlightenment was only a "fable convenue"—the meaning of which expression does not differ that much from the idea of "protecting coloring"—did not prevent him from acknowledging that "biblical-scholastic motives" at least "*co*llaborated" in its genesis.

The main question, with regard to this key feature of Strauss's thought, seems thus to boil down to a better understanding of the way in which such a "*co*llaboration" may have taken place in his account. It is fair to say that, notably in his maturity, one of Strauss's main concerns when it comes to explaining the genesis of modern philosophy is to underscore, as clearly and strongly as possible, both the radically anti-theological drive and the awareness that, in his view, the early moderns displayed even when following doctrines of biblical origin. There seems to be a limit, however, as to the extent to which such an effort can reasonably be pursued, if one does not want to subscribe to a full rejection, on the assumption of its being purely exoteric, of the difference between ancients and moderns Strauss himself so painstakingly affirmed. In this regard, Strauss's 1938–1939 "rediscovery" of esotericism,[164] no matter how paramount, cannot be used as a picklock to dissolve any difference of perspective characterizing the history of philosophy. Furthermore, remarks such as those the mature Strauss makes in the "Preface to Isaac Husik, *Philosophical Essays*," cannot be easily dismissed.

Arguably, an important part of the reservations the mature Strauss raised concerning the concept of secularization is due to the ambiguity of that term, which, in his view, did not distinguish clearly enough among such different meanings as "sublimation," "rejection," and "modification" of the biblical doctrine.[165] Another key aspect, in Strauss's view, was surely that, unlike "more of less thoughtless people," those whom he regarded as the "heroes of modern philosophy," i.e., such thinkers as Machiavelli and Hobbes, could hardly have inadvertently switched "from a religious understanding of certain phenomena" to a "fundamentally nonreligious understanding." Out of this premise, Strauss saw himself "forced" to reject any explanation resorting to the concept of secularization and "to try to understand" the revolutionary approach of those thinkers, in its stead, in more "secular" terms.[166]

It seems thus possible to maintain that some of Strauss's reluctance, in his maturity, to recur to the secularization theory is to be explained by means of his programmatic effort to understand the founders of modern philosophy in purely rational, inner-philosophical terms. Whether this attempt was entirely viable (Strauss himself, for instance in his letter to Löwith of August 20, 1946, seems a little uncertain on that), and whether it is consistent with his apparent distinction between philosophical antiquity and modernity, may here be left open questions. The same applies to the question, which we have not failed to hint at in this chapter, whether Strauss may have had other or additional reasons to increasingly tone down, notably from the mid-1940s, his use of concepts and tools belonging to the secularization theory.

Be this as it may, it is interesting to note, in conclusion, that in a course on natural right Strauss delivered at the University of Chicago as late as 1962—where "Hobbes's revolutionary political philosophy,"[167] understandably, features prominently—Strauss, on the one hand, insists on his "inner-philosophical" approach to the genesis of modern philosophy, thereby reaffirming his overall skepticism concerning attempts to interpret that author in terms of sheer secularization. More than once, on the other hand, he cannot help but concede that there are clear similarities, not to say kinship, between Hobbes's doctrine and the theological tradition, whether biblical or specifically Christian. He does so, for instance, when he traces the origin of Hobbes's view of the state of nature, despite its originality, back to its Christian theological background.[168] Another clear example of this tendency can be seen in Strauss's remark that "Hobbes finds the badness of man not in sensuality or bestiality but in pride, and it is easy to say that there is something connecting him here with the biblical tradition,"—a remark that significantly follows his observation that "the very title of the *Leviathan* is taken of course from the Book of Job, but with most special regard to the verse where the Leviathan . . . is described as the king of the children of pride."[169]

The list could be extended further, notably with a mention of the fact that, in this late course of his, Strauss explains the "universal doubt" that is at the basis of modern science and characterizes Descartes as well as Hobbes by ascribing to the former thinker the need to counter the hypothesis of a deceiving "*omnipotent* god."[170] It is for such reasons, one may surmise, that Strauss begins his treatment of Hobbes's revolutionary view, as well as of modern philosophy as a whole, by plainly acknowledging that its understanding in terms of "secularization of biblical beliefs . . . is a defensible assertion," although he qualifies this statement by noting that such an assertion "is not good enough because we must make clear what it implies." Once again, his main aim seems to be to understand modern philosophy "inner-philosophically and inner-theoretically," despite all the "biblical-scholastic motives" that have, at least, "*co*llaborated."

Chapter VI

The "Pit beneath the Cave" and the Problem of Natural Right

Wir *müssen* fragen, ohne fragen zu *können*.

—GS2, 447

One of the fittest remarks on Strauss, to my knowledge, is by the Italian legal philosopher Bruno Leoni. Along with the historian and classicist Arnaldo Momigliano, Leoni was among the few Italian scholars who showed genuine interest in Strauss during the 1950s and 1960s.[1] For the rest, Strauss's reception in Italy, mainly brought about by the translation of *Natural Right and History* in 1957, was rather cold at the beginning, sometimes even harshly critical.[2] Guido Fassò, for example, who was an influential professor in legal philosophy at that time, wrote two very negative reviews of Strauss's book.[3] And Norberto Bobbio, perhaps the most important legal and political philosopher in Italy over that period, although less biased than his colleague Fassò, showed little interest in Strauss's reflection on natural right.[4] This critical reception, after all, was even to be expected, due to the overwhelming influence in Italy at that time of positivism and historicism, the two major positions Strauss argues against in his book.

Now, according to Leoni, Strauss was a *"rara avis"*[5] (rare bird) among twentieth century political philosophers. By saying so, Leoni was referring to Strauss's criticism of Weber and his rejection of the latter's distinction between factual judgments and value judgments.[6] But the expression *rare bird*, which one may venture to render in a more Nietzschean fashion as "untimely thinker," also applies to Strauss concerning other aspects of his original and challenging thought, especially once it is addressed from the typical twentieth-, now twenty-first-century philosophical perspective. In particular, Strauss must have appeared a *rara avis* also concerning his interpretation of natural right, as is shown, for example, by the reception of *Natural Right and History* mentioned above or, to add some anecdotal evidence, by what Berlin once recalled about him:

> He did try to convert me in many conversations when I was a visitor in Chicago, but he could not get me to believe in eternal, immutable, absolute values, true for all men everywhere at all times, God-given Natural Law and the like. . . . He . . . appear[s] to me to believe in absolute good and evil, right and wrong, directly perceived by means of a kind of a priori vision, a metaphysical eye—by the use of a Platonic rational faculty which has not been granted to me.[7]

No matter how inaccurate (Strauss never believed in "God-given Natural Law") and ironic in its conclusion, this remark shows the extent to which Strauss was regarded as peculiar by the mainstream twentieth-century thought, whether pluralist as in Berlin's case (Strauss would have said "relativist"[8]), positivist, or historicist. Seen through these lenses, he was indeed a *rara avis*, to quote Leoni again, since he was as worthy of interest and curiosity as he was eccentric and isolated.

As is well known, against this relativist, positivist, and historicist background, Strauss attempted, if not to fully recover, at least to "revitalize"[9] the philosophical inquiry concerning such themes as the best way of life and natural right. As Berlin himself put it ironically, but again conflating currents of thought that Strauss regarded as radically at odds, "Plato, Aristotle, the Bible, the Talmud, Maimonides, perhaps Aquinas, and other scholastics of the Middle Ages knew what was the best life for men. So did [Strauss], and his disciples claim this today. I am not so privileged."[10]

Such a "revitalization of earlier ways of thinking,"[11] particularly of the quest for the best way of life and the inquiry into natural right, is thus a distinctive trait of Strauss's "untimely" approach that deserves to be carefully investigated. This chapter aims to foster that investigation by trying, in particular, to answer two major questions. The first concerns the specific meaning of natural right in Strauss's account and its relation to the topic of the best way of life. As part of this question, Strauss's critique of legal positivism and historicism will be addressed, as well as his attempt to recover an interpretation of natural right that, deconstructing the conceptual categories of modern natural law, leads to the rediscovery of the essence of the classical approach.

The second question concerns the conditions of possibility, as it were, and the implications of Strauss's attempt to revitalize such an approach. Unlike the first question, which evidently corresponds to the second part of the title of this chapter ("the problem of natural right"), the relationship between this second question and the first part of the title ("the pit beneath the cave") may be less clear. This possible obscurity begins to fade away as soon as one replaces this expression by another Strauss uses, still in his published works, to address the same question: the second, unnatural cave.[12] For it seems reasonable to hold, at least as a preliminary assumption, that it is only by "ascending" from this "second, 'unnatural' cave" into that "first, 'natural' cave which Plato's image depicts"[13] that one can again raise, in a meaningful way (as Strauss aimed to), the question of the best way of life and of natural right. Both that cave and this question, after all, revolve around what is "by nature," a concept without which the "original meaning of philosophizing" remains inaccessible, "philosophy" becomes a sort of empty word capable of designating the most disparate intellectual pursuits, and the idea of natural right is nothing more than a "salutary myth."[14]

What Is Natural Right According to Strauss?

The Role of Natural Right in Strauss's Political Thought

As noted in chapter II, one of the most debated and controversial issues in Strauss's thought in recent years has been his stance towards liberal democracy. Thanks to the publication (or re-publication) of his early writings, as well as, in particular, of his letters, what was previously regarded as Strauss's clearest and most significant statement in that respect ("We are not permitted to be flatterers of democracy precisely because we are friends and allies of democracy"[15]) no longer appears as his final and unambiguous word. Strauss interpreters have thus begun to dig deeper into this important aspect of his political thought. In particular, the already mentioned letter to Löwith of May 19, 1933 (that is, written shortly after the Nazi seizure of power in Germany) has come to be regarded as a key document, since it appears to convey a much more conservative, not to say revolutionary (from the right) perspective.[16] In addition, Strauss's 1923 essay, "Antwort auf das 'Prinzipielle Wort' der Frankfurter,"[17] has been increasingly regarded as relevant. For in it, after endorsing, although not without reservations, the political stance represented by "Breslau" and its leader Walter Moses—which goes so far as to negate the private sphere— Strauss specifies that this stance should be understood as "pagan-fascist."[18] Finally, Strauss's 1941 lecture, "German Nihilism," has been adduced as proof that Strauss was not, at best, a "true" friend and ally of liberal democracy. For at the end of the lecture, despite praising the Anglo-Saxons, and Churchill in particular, over the Germans and Hitler, he does so not so much because the former are the heirs of modern, liberal Western civilization, as because, as we have noted, he sees in them the incarnation of the ancient Roman "imperial" spirit, which Strauss epitomizes by quoting the Virgilian maxim: *parcere subjectis et debellare superbos*.[19]

Given the often ideological character of the debate on Strauss (especially in the US, where the political relevance of his legacy is more sensitively felt), the availability of these new sources has had the side effect of exacerbating the controversy about Strauss's real political thought.[20] Some critics, relying on these sources, have even argued that Strauss was, and remained, not so much a friend and ally of democracy, as one of its most resolute and dangerous enemies: a kind of fascist under cover who wanted to establish an authoritarian regime in his new home country by way of subtle propaganda.[21]

Against charges of this sort, Catherine Zuckert argues that the key to understanding Strauss's political perspective is to take into account his interpretation of natural right. Referring to an important but enigmatic letter to Scholem of June 22, 1952, she points out that "as Strauss suggested" in that context, "he understood 'the principles of the right' to consist in a true knowledge of politics or—as he often put it—of natural right."[22] Although one may disagree with Zuckert's interpretation of Strauss overall as sometimes too "edifying,"[23] in this case I believe she is correct: Strauss's interpretation of natural right is key to understanding his stance towards politics, as well as his specific political views. Strauss himself, after all, emphasizes the connection, at least as far as the classics are concerned, between what he defines as "natural right" and the best regime. In addition, he insists that the inquiry into natural right is not so much an exclusive concern of a "philosophy of law" narrowly understood, as it is, more broadly, the central topic of political philosophy itself, as is shown, for example, by Plato and Aristotle.[24]

On the other hand, what Strauss understands by natural right from that perspective by no means coincides with the typical modern understanding of that concept. Of this modern understanding—the one which, for example, lies at the heart of the US Declaration of Independence—Strauss was not only emphatically critical in *Natural Right and History* ("the modern interpretation is a seminary of intolerance and leads to nihilism"), but he even once defined as "laughable and despicable [*lächerlich und jämmerlich*]" the appeal to what in 1933 came closest to it, the "droits imprescriptibles de l'homme."[25]

Hence, while Zuckert's suggestion regarding the relevance of Strauss's reference to natural right proves insightful, it is important to take it as only a starting point for further analysis. For two questions immediately arise. First, what does natural right mean in Strauss's account, particularly in its "classic" interpretation? Second, what are the grounds for Strauss's criticism not only of legal positivism and historicism, which reject the concept of natural right altogether, but also of the modern interpretation of natural right?

NATURAL LAW, NATURAL RIGHT, NATURAL RIGHTS

To begin with, it is important to notice that in Strauss's view "natural right" has to be clearly distinguished from "natural law." Generally speaking, Strauss understands natural law as a comprehensive moral law that has power or is valid by nature. In his view (insofar as we can reconstruct it from his comments on other authors), this concept cannot be approved from a philosophic standpoint (no matter how important or useful the same concept may be from the practical perspective[26]).

In the introduction to *Persecution and the Art of Writing*, for example, Strauss states that the notion of "natural law," particularly in its Christian version, amounts to the notion of "rational commandments," that is to say, to the notion of a fully binding "moral law."[27] Understood in this demanding manner, for Strauss this notion was rejected by the *falasifa* (the medieval Islamic philosophers) due to their "philosophic intransigence."[28] (According to them, consequently, the principles of morality are not rational, but only "probable" or "generally accepted"). The same notion, however, was characteristic of the *kalam*, i.e., of "what one may call Islamic theology," as Strauss explains in the same context.[29]

Alongside the case of the Islamic medieval philosophers, the notion of natural law was also significant in the Christian medieval philosophic tradition and, before that, in Stoicism. Strauss, however, proves to regard these traditions as philosophically weak and ultimately untenable. Regarding the Christian medieval philosophic tradition, particularly Thomism, Strauss casts doubts on its philosophic relevance in the very few pages he devotes to Thomas Aquinas in *Natural Right and History*: "At any rate, the ultimate consequence of the Thomistic view of natural law is that natural law is practically inseparable not only from natural theology—i.e., from a natural theology which is, in fact, based on belief in biblical revelation—but even from revealed theology."[30] Moreover, he expressly parallels the Thomistic approach with *kalam* (a form of theology as distinct from philosophy, as we have seen) at the beginning of "The Law of Reason in the *Kuzari*,"[31] where he also defines "Natural Law" as "a term which is as indispensable," presumably from a political perspective, "as it is open to grave objections."[32]

Furthermore, this time with reference to the Greek understanding, in "On Natural Law" (1968) Strauss observes that the notion of natural law—in Greek, *nomos tes physeos*—would appear to be a contradiction in terms rather than a philosophically meaningful concept. For in Greek that expression would sound like "convention by nature," as *nomos* and *physis*—"convention" (not only law) and "nature"—are two antithetical concepts:

> By natural law is meant a law which determines what is right and wrong and which has power or is valid by nature, inherently, hence everywhere and always. . . . The notion of natural law presupposes the notion of nature, and the notion of nature is not coeval with human thought; hence there is no natural law teaching, for instance, in the Old Testament. Nature was discovered by the Greeks as in contradistinction to art (the knowledge guiding the making of artifacts) and, above all, to *nomos* (law, custom, convention, agreement, authoritative opinion). In the light of the original meaning of "nature," the notion of "natural law" (*nomos tēs physeōs*) is a contradiction in terms rather than a matter of course. The primary question concerns less natural law than natural right, i.e., what is by nature right or just: is all right conventional (of human origin) or is there some right which is natural (*physei dikaion*)?[33]

To this observation, one might add that already in *Natural Right and History* Strauss interprets the "Stoic natural law teaching" (with natural law understood as a fully binding moral law) in purely "exoteric" terms, since it is "based on the doctrine of divine providence and on an anthropocentric teleology."[34] In his view, after all, Cicero "was an Academic skeptic and not a Stoic."[35] This being the case, Cicero could not accept these doctrines clearly at odds with such a skeptical approach, except for purely practical considerations.

Now, as emerges clearly at the end of the passage of "On Natural Law" above, not to mention what Strauss states in the preface to the seventh impression of *Natural Right and History*,[36] his real topic, his "primary question," is natural right. He openly stresses this point, for example, in a letter (undated, but from the period 1956–1958) to Helmut Kuhn, who had reviewed the German translation of *Natural Right and History*.[37] There Strauss observes: "I begin my discussion with the remark that I spoke in the very title of my book [*Natural Right and History*] of natural right and not of natural law."[38] As Strauss points out in the same letter (and as he suggests in the above-mentioned preface), however, in dealing with natural right one faces a "fundamental ambiguity," as one has to deal with two "essentially different" interpretations of natural right: the modern interpretation and the pre-modern, classical interpretation.[39]

Indeed, natural right is one of the major themes of early modern philosophy, particularly of Hobbes who, as we have observed, is the first to clearly distinguish between right and law.[40] According to Hobbes, right is a liberty, or better stated a subjective and justified "claim" (in German, *subjectives Recht*)[41] since it is based on a universal passion, the fear of violent death. As such, it is justified because that fear, from which it originates, can be defended in the face of every other human being, i.e., "immanently" but universally. For this reason, Strauss underscores that early modern philosophy, as represented by Hobbes, avoids relapse into pure naturalism.[42] For natural right, no matter how absolute—in Hobbes, it is even a *jus in omnia*—never loses the trait of something legitimate, i.e., of something justifiable in a moral sense.

The concept of natural law, understood as an objective, rational norm, also plays an important role in Hobbes's approach, as we have seen in the previous chapter. But the fundamental concept, in his revolutionary view, is natural right as a subjective claim, with natural law only derivative. As Strauss puts it, Hobbes's cornerstone is the idea of a *summum malum* (violent death), and not of a *summum bonum* (virtue, happiness, etc.). For Hobbes assumes, as we have underscored, that any possible source of superhuman order, either in the form of God's revelation or as a natural objective standard, is unavailable, leaving as the only remaining solution to the moral problem (in order not to embrace a form of naturalism or pure conventionalism and irrespective of its political ineffectiveness) the immanent justification of what is subjectively right as prompted by that *summum malum*. This perspective on "right" as a subjective and justified claim is reflected in the technical language Strauss resorts to, for example, in *Natural Right and History*, where, when referring to modern natural right, he coherently uses the term *right* as a countable noun, since there can be a plurality of claims or rights so understood.

This is not the case, however, with pre-modern, classic natural right. As we have seen in the quotation from "On Natural Law" above, *natural right* in this sense is the literal translation of *physei dikaion*. This is also confirmed in the "Letter to Helmut Kuhn," where Strauss, contesting Kuhn's claim that pre-modern natural right begins with Stoicism, points out that "natural right (*jus* or *justum naturale, physikon dikaion* or *to physei dikaion*) is, I contend, an important and even central theme of both Plato and Aristotle."[43] Understood in this sense, natural right means "what is by nature right or just." It is thus approached from an objective perspective, as a standard or paradigm, and coherently Strauss uses the term *right* in the expression "natural right" as an uncountable noun when referring to the classic view in *Natural Right and History* and elsewhere.

As previously noted, however, natural right as an objective standard is not "natural law," i.e., a comprehensive moral law based on divine providence or an anthropocentric teleology.[44] What is, then, by nature right according to the classics, Plato and Aristotle in particular? Apparently, Strauss's answer points to an objective order or hierarchy of human ends, as well as of the human types corresponding to those ends, as distinct from a comprehensive moral law:

> The variability of the demands of that justice which men can practice was recognized not only by Aristotle but by Plato as well. Both avoided the Scylla of "absolutism" and the Charybdis of "relativism" by holding a view which one may venture to express as follows: There is a universally valid hierarchy of ends, but there are no universally valid rules of action . . . when deciding what ought to be done, i.e., what ought to be done by this individual (or this individual group) here and now, one has to consider not only which of the various competing objectives is higher in rank but also which is the most urgent

in the circumstances. What is most urgent is in many cases lower in rank than the less urgent. But one cannot make a universal rule that urgency is a higher consideration than rank. For it is our duty to make the highest activity, as much as we can, the most urgent or the most needful thing. And the maximum of effort which can be expected necessarily varies from individual to individual. The only universally valid standard is the hierarchy of ends. This standard is sufficient for passing judgment on the level of nobility of individuals and groups and of actions and institutions. But it is insufficient for guiding our actions.[45]

According to the classics, this "highest activity" is philosophy itself. To make it the "most urgent" or "most needful thing," one needs the proper social and political context, that is to say, one needs what the classics referred to as the "best regime." It is for this reason that, according to Strauss, "the classic natural right doctrine in its original form . . . is identical with the doctrine of the best regime,"[46] and that the best regime can be defined as "the object of the wish or prayer of gentlemen as that object is interpreted by the philosopher."[47] It is, in fact, a regime in which virtue (*areté* or human excellence) is the highest end, but in such a way that the highest virtue is not so much political or moral virtue, but intellectual virtue: wisdom itself.[48] Against this background, we can now better understand why the classics rejected the view of right that would become characteristic of modernity:

> Since the classics viewed moral and political matters in the light of man's perfection, they were not egalitarians. Not all men are equally equipped by nature for progress toward perfection, or not all "natures" are "good natures." While all men, i.e., all normal men, have the capacity for virtue, some need guidance by others, whereas others do not at all or to a much lesser degree. Besides, regardless of differences of natural capacity, not all men strive for virtue with equal earnestness. . . . Since men are then unequal in regard to human perfection, i.e., in the decisive respect, equal rights for all appeared to the classics as most unjust. They contended that some men are by nature superior to others and therefore, according to natural right, the rulers of others.[49]

Now, to revitalize the classical perspective on natural right as an objective standard, Strauss needs to challenge the presuppositions of modern natural right according to which no superhuman source of order is available (not only in the form of divine revelation and providence, rejected even by the classics, but also as nature, *physis*, regarded as a standard or paradigm, in light of which it becomes meaningful to speak of "human perfection"). Even before that, however, Strauss has to take issue with modern science and historicism, which regard any attempt to raise the question of what is by nature right as meaningless.

We can find evidence of this predicament in *Natural Right and History*. At the end of the introduction, while referring to the different parties involved in the debate regarding natural right, Strauss states:

> But both armies and, in addition, those who prefer to sit on the fences or hide their heads in the sand are . . . in the same boat. They are all modern men. We are all in the grip of the same difficulty. Natural right in its classic form is connected with a teleological view of the universe. All natural beings have a natural end, a natural destiny, which determines what kind of operation is good for them. In the case of man, reason is required for discerning these operations: reason determines what is by nature right with ultimate regard to man's natural end. The teleological view of the universe, of which the teleological view of man forms a part, *would seem* to have been destroyed by modern natural science.[50]

At the end of chapter I of the same book, moreover, we find clearly expressed the idea that historicism represents the denial not only of the possibility of natural right, both in its classic and modern interpretations, but also of philosophy itself. For philosophy, in its original sense, means awareness of the fundamental and permanent problems as distinct from knowledge of their definitive solutions. But even philosophy so understood is impossible if historicism is right in asserting that it has discovered "a dimension of reality that had escaped classical thought, namely the historical dimension." Revealingly, Strauss ends the paragraph from which the latter quotation is taken with the following words: "We have to raise the question whether what is called the 'discovery' of history is not, in fact, an artificial and makeshift solution to a problem that could arise only on the basis of very questionable premises."[51]

The "Pit beneath the Cave" / 151

Those who seek to grasp the "problem of natural right" must therefore dig deeper into these "premises." This means for them to try to fully understand the meaning and importance of the so-called pit beneath the cave in Strauss's account. We will attempt to do so in the second part of this chapter. First, however, for the sake of completeness, it is worth briefly focusing on Strauss's criticism of legal positivism and modern natural right.

Strauss's Criticism of Legal Positivism

When analyzing Strauss's criticism of legal positivism as it can be reconstructed through the remarks he made, at different times, about this approach, one is left with the impression that Strauss had a twofold strategy. On the one hand, especially after the tragic experience of Nazism—which, as we have noted, he regarded as the "most dishonourable form" of German nihilism[52]—he tried to show that legal positivism, not to say positivism tout court, bore some responsibility for that event, in that it cultivated an intellectual soil suitable for the rise of that extreme kind of tyranny. This is mainly a political, not to say rhetorical, argument. It can be found especially in *Natural Right and History*, when, for example, Strauss accuses Kelsen of having omitted in *General Theory of Law and State*, published after World War II, a most instructive passage of his 1925 book *Allgemeine Staatslehre* where Kelsen criticized as "natural law naivety [*naturrechtliche Naivität*]" the statement that despotism is not a legal system (*Rechtsordnung*) and where he found good aspects in dictatorship.[53] Another instance of this kind of argument is when, addressing Weber, Strauss warns that by considering his doctrine of the polytheism of values one will "reach a point beyond which the scene is darkened by the shadow of Hitler."[54] As is well known, however, Strauss explicitly rejects as fallacious any *reductio ad Hitlerum*.[55] We have thus to leave aside these political and rhetorical refutations (however sound they may have appeared to Strauss from a practical standpoint) to focus on his purely philosophical critique. First, however, it is important to underscore the vital character of this critique for philosophy itself. In Strauss's view, the main problem with positivism is that, along with historicism, it deprives philosophy of its genuine meaning.[56] If trying to establish that a given order is by nature right or wrong is only "natural law naivety," as Kelsen put it, or even worse, an "ideology," philosophy itself, at least in its original sense (according to which it is much more than "methodology"), becomes meaningless. Strauss, therefore, had to counter positivism by attempting its philosophical refutation. With respect to legal positivism in particular, he made this attempt, for example, in the already mentioned "Foreword to a Planned Book on Hobbes," a remarkable document from the early 1930s, originally not meant by Strauss for publication and, consequently, never published in his lifetime.[57]

In this essay, Strauss argues in two ways. First, he states that the point of departure for legal positivism, which he there understands as the attempt to obliterate the question of the political foundation of the legal sphere, is a relatively quiet situation. For Strauss, whose interpretation verges on Schmitt's in this regard, this situation is the only one in which the political qua political can almost be forgotten. But precisely for this reason, it is also the least adequate to obtain a true knowledge of the "legal," understood as the "right order of living together [*die rechte Ordnung des Zusammenlebens*]."[58] As we have already emphasized, retorting to Kelsen who, in his 1928 work *Die philosophischen Grundlagen der Naturrechtslehre und des Rechtspositivismus*, had acknowledged that an objective and scientific view like legal positivism can only prosper during relatively quiet times, Strauss observes in the same essay: "Only in view of *unrest* [Unruhe], only *in* unrest, if not indeed in *revolts* [Unruhen], can that understanding of man be gained from which the right created for the satisfaction of man can be understood: only in this way can it be radically understood that as well as how man needs right; only in this way is *philosophic* understanding of right possible."[59]

The second way in which Strauss, in "Foreword to a Planned Book on Hobbes," tries to counter legal positivism is by pointing out that its alleged scientific understanding is not so much objective and absolute, as the historically conditioned outcome of a specific worldview. As previously explained, Strauss here deploys an argument of Nietzschean and Heideggerian inspiration that could be fatal to philosophy as well, since it could lead to the recognition of its own perspective and historically conditioned character. Yet, Strauss aims to suggest that at least an undogmatic, "natural" form of philosophy can survive this criticism. Indeed, for Strauss the historicist argument (that every interpretation is historically conditioned) allows one to consider positivism, not to mention historicism itself, as a contingent interpretation. If so, one can begin again the exercise of philosophy in its original sense, as a life devoted to questioning what is by nature right: "After the belief of the last century started to waver, doubt was stirred in 'culture' as well as in right and the science of right; now neither the authority of positive right nor the competence of positive science of right stands indisputably firm in matters of natural right. The question of natural right urges itself forward in its natural sharpness."[60]

Strauss's Criticism of Modern Natural Rights

Although in Strauss's early critique of legal positivism a modern theorist of natural right like Hobbes is singled out for praise because he recognized the "unquiet" original situation of human beings in the "state of nature,"[61] Strauss, as we have seen, is far from considering Hobbes's interpretation of natural right as satisfactory. Contrary to the pre-modern approach, Hobbes recognizes as the original phenomenon not an objective norm, the *lex naturalis* (not to mention here the natural right equivalent to Plato's and Aristotle's *physei dikaion*), but a subjective claim, the *jus naturale*. This view, which was developed by Locke and flourished within modern liberalism, is called by Strauss "political hedonism,"[62] i.e., a form of hedonism that, unlike the classical one, no longer leads to "the most uncompromising depreciation of the whole political sphere."[63] On the contrary, the individual, with his or her original rights, is now regarded as the real "sovereign" of that sphere. The same occurs with nature, of which human beings make themselves masters in order to obtain the *commoda hujus vitae*, the goods of this life, the only ones truly available to them.[64]

Strauss was clearly against this view. As we have seen in chapter II, in this regard the ancient liberalism he sought to revitalize represents the opposite of modern liberalism, based on the primacy of individual rights and on an unrestrained mastery over nature. Implicitly agreeing with the authors of the Conservative revolution in Germany and their inspirer Nietzsche, he sees behind this view not so much an ever more prosperous future for mankind, but the shadow of the "last man." Moreover, Strauss tends to consider political hedonism and modern liberalism, if not duly restrained by more aristocratic means, as ultimately untenable, as shown, for example, by the fall of the Weimar Republic.[65]

From this perspective, Strauss's approach is similar, once again, to that of Schmitt. They both were implacable adversaries of modern liberalism, at least, as far as Strauss is concerned, until the early 1930s. But in order to understand Strauss's complex stance on natural right and politics in general, it is also important to pinpoint their differences. As observed in chapter I, these differences notably emerge in "Notes on Carl Schmitt, *The Concept of the Political*." In this essay, while agreeing with Schmitt in his opposition to modern liberalism and its "mercenary morality," Strauss clearly distances himself from him. In particular, he accuses Schmitt of merely trying to affirm "the political" denied by liberalism, but in such a way as to remain entrapped in liberalism's conceptual framework. According to Strauss, in other words, Schmitt could not free himself from the premises of modern constructivism, or from what he also tellingly defines, in a letter to Klein, "Hobbes's decisionism."[66] Schmitt, in his view, could indeed say "no" to the political hedonism characteristic of modern liberalism, but only by way of a "decisionistic" affirmation of "the political." For this reason, as we have underscored, Strauss regards Schmitt's view as "liberalism with the opposite polarity [*Liberalismus mit umgekehrtem Vorzeichen*]."[67] Against this liberalism turned upside down, and not only against its original model, Strauss suggests the reopening of the question of nature, which, from a political perspective, boils down to "the question concerning the right order of living together, concerning its 'natural' order, concerning *natural right*."[68]

Is Natural Right an Essentially "Political" Right?

In light of the difference between natural law and natural right within pre-modern thought—namely, between a comprehensive law and a mere standard indicating a ranking of human ends and of the ways of life corresponding to those ends—it is impossible to interpret Strauss's view of natural right in a comprehensive moral sense. It is not accidental, in this regard, that in *Natural Right and History* Strauss claims that the classical reflection on natural right culminates in the doctrine of the best regime. What matters the most, for the classics as Strauss interprets them, is not so much what ought to be done in, and by, any given political community in any given situation, as who should govern such a community or, at least, set its tone.[69] What ought to be done in any given situation, especially for a skeptical philosopher, always remains a problem largely depending on contingent circumstances. Yet, for Strauss those who are able to raise and rationally address this problem, along with the other questions the philosophic life revolves around, are arguably better suited to rule than others. At least, since they, qua philosophers, cannot but consider the political life as only a means, however important, to their supreme end, which is the philosophic life itself, they should be regarded as entitled, by natural right, to set the tone of the city by determining its supreme ends. As Strauss puts it in *Thoughts on Machiavelli*, "Philosophy transcends the city, and the worth of the city depends ultimately on its openness, or deference, to philosophy."[70] Only in a city where the best regime has been realized does "the object of the wish or prayer of gentlemen"—virtue—become the supreme goal, but only "as that object is interpreted by the philosopher"[71]—namely, as knowledge itself or the search for it. If so, natural right as Strauss understands it may be defined, at least preliminarily and in the absence of a better term, as "political." For it has to do with the ultimately "political" question (at least according to the modern interpretation of that concept) of who should rule the city, if not directly, at least indirectly by setting its supreme ends.[72]

In order not to become a matter of force or fraud, however, this interpretation must be defended in a context where the question of the primacy of the philosophic life over the political life is raised in a philosophical manner as Strauss understands it. This means that this question must lead to the attempt to determine a ranking of human ends that is valid by nature and defensible on rational grounds.[73] It is not sufficient to claim that the best possible life is the philosophic life because one needs to know what one does not know. For one has first to show that such a knowledge is possible, as well as good for those who seek it.[74] In order not to be a delusion, or a trivial intellectual pursuit among many others, the philosophic life must thus be shown to be "the *right* life,"[75] that life in which the problem of what is by nature is meaningfully raised and which represents the fulfillment of the highest human possibilities. This life, in other words, seems to be fully possible only under pre-modern premises, according to which the city is regarded as the Platonic cave that philosophy can and must leave, by way of dialectics, in order to carry out its heliotropic contemplation. As Strauss explains in the passage from *Thoughts on Machiavelli* quoted above, indeed "the worth of the city depends ultimately on its openness, or deference, to philosophy." But "the city cannot fulfill its function if it is not closed to philosophy as well as open to it; the city is necessarily the cave."[76]

These remarks point to the problem of the tense practical relationship between philosophy and politics—a problem that, as Strauss intimates in the same context, can ultimately be solved only by resorting to a "noble rhetoric."[77] This theme, no matter how important in Strauss, goes beyond the scope of the present work.[78] What is here important to focus on is, rather, the cave regarded as the natural starting point of philosophy. Only the Platonic, natural cave (characterized as it is by "appearance and opinion" as distinct from "prejudices") provides a suitable context for philosophy as Strauss understands it.[79] In a different cave, like the one

Strauss, in his published writings, calls the "pit beneath the cave" or the "second, 'unnatural' cave,"[80] such an attempt to "philosophize naturally"[81] proves vain. For the only kind of philosophy, if any, that remains available in that unnatural cave is a "decisionism" where any attempt to establish a ranking of human ends, as well as the primacy of philosophy itself, cannot but rest on an act of will or belief based on mere preferences.

The Pit beneath the Cave and the Natural Cave

The expression *natural cave* (in German, *natürliche Höhle*) cannot be found in "Religious Situation of the Present" (1930) or in the slightly later "The Intellectual Situation of the Present" (1932), but only in *Philosophy and Law* (1935)[82] and "How to Study Spinoza's *Theologico-Political Treatise*" (1948).[83] It is, however, in the first two lectures, along with such other essays from the same period as "Conspectivism"[84] (1929) and "Review of Julius Ebbinghaus, *On the Progress of Metaphysics*"[85] (1931), that Strauss is more outspoken regarding this theme. Hence, not only for chronological reasons, it is useful to begin with these works in order to explain what Strauss meant by that expression and what it implies.

"Religious Situation of the Present"

In "Religious Situation of the Present," as the title suggests, Strauss starts from the question concerning the religious situation of the beginning of the 1930s, particularly of young German Jews like himself to whom the lecture is addressed. Yet, he immediately explains that this question, once it is interpreted in philosophically meaningful terms, amounts to the question of "the right way of life," namely, something that can hardly be distinguished from what we have observed regarding classic natural right and its hierarchy of ends: "There can, however, be no doubt about what *the* question is that is and must be the most important one for us: it is the question what is the *right* life [*das* richtige *Leben*]? how *should* I live? what matters? what is needful? Thus, our modern topic of the 'religious situation of the present' boils down to the old, eternal question, *the* primordial question [die *Urfrage*]."[86]

Now, by resorting to the rhetorical device of the prosopopoeia, Strauss shows, as we have seen in chapter III, that "the present"—namely, the "historical consciousness" characteristic of historicism—represents the main obstacle to the revitalization of this kind of "primordial," "naive" questioning. Hence, it is with that historical consciousness, which holds that "there is not the one eternal truth, but each age has its truth," that one must first deal with, precisely as he will maintain in *Natural Right and History*.[87]

In this regard, Strauss observes that it would be a relapse into dogmatism to take for granted, without any further examination, that there is a principle according to which all human knowledge is "present," i.e., historically conditioned. "Our *fate* is *not* our *task*,"[88] he emphatically observes. For the fact that every attempt to ask and answer the *Urfrage* has failed so far does not philosophically, that is essentially, prove that that questioning is impossible or meaningless. This being the case, for Strauss one has to try to better understand why the present epoch has become historicist in such a dogmatic way. To this end, one needs to free oneself from the present and its historicist perspective and try, instead, to see the present itself "just as it *is*, free from the dominant views, which we must first examine."[89] One needs, in other words, what Strauss, notably in some of the letters from the early 1930s we have analyzed in the introduction to this book,[90] associates with the approach characteristic of twentieth-century phenomenology: a fresh, even naive perspective, which is able not to succumb, right from the beginning, to the historicist view. As Strauss puts it in "Religious Situation of the Present":

> We turn to the matter, that is, the question concerning the right life, with the will to answering it. But in order not to suffer shipwreck as thousands have suffered shipwreck *before* us, we do want to hear the *warning* of the present, the call: watch out. We will not listen to the present if it turns this failure into a theory; if it asserts the *inevitability* of failure. In order to be able to get beyond the present, we must take the warning of the present seriously, we must be in a position to interpret more closely the experience on which the present insists.[91]

This is precisely what Strauss tries to do in the continuation of his lecture. While investigating the presuppositions of the present and its historicist stance, he underscores that the situation of the present and our inability to ask the question regarding how one should live are not due to subjective reasons, to the "individual inadequacy" of those who ask. Rather, they are due to objective "serious reasons," to certain "artificial difficulties" of philosophizing that have been added to its "*natural* difficulties," the latter being those Plato described in the allegory of the cave. Although these natural difficulties, as "difficulties natural to man as man," fully account for the "anarchy of the opinions" from which philosophy begins, only the artificial difficulties, which "are not 'natural' but become effective only under certain presuppositions," explain why philosophy, in its original, "naive" meaning, has come to be considered as impossible.[92]

Now, referring to Maimonides, Strauss points out that these artificial difficulties are the consequence of the appearance of the Bible in the world of Greek philosophy, namely, in a world where, as Strauss observes in "Conspectivism," the notion of science (including philosophy) first arose and established its foundations.[93] As Strauss puts it in "Religious Situation of the Present": "Let us sum up: by the fact that a tradition resting on revelation has entered the world of philosophy, the difficulty of philosophizing is fundamentally augmented, the *freedom* of philosophizing fundamentally limited."[94]

As Strauss explains in the same lecture quoting the *Guide of the Perplexed* (I.31), what actually affects such a philosophizing and increases its natural difficulties is that, after the Bible has entered the world of philosophy, human beings have become accustomed, through "habituation" and "schooling," to opinions that are regarded as based on revelation, that is, on an "unconditionally" authoritative and binding source.[95] Due to this fact, these opinions have become more than naturally questionable opinions. They have become "prejudices": "In order to render possible philosophy in its natural difficulty, the artificial difficulty of philosophizing has to be eliminated [*aus der Welt geschafft werden*]; there has to be a struggle against prejudices. In this, modern philosophy is fundamentally different from Greek philosophy: the latter struggles only against appearance and opinion; modern philosophy's struggle begins prior to that against prejudices."[96]

This being the case, for Strauss the whole fight of the Enlightenment can be summarized in Maimonides's observation regarding this additional, "artificial" difficulty encountered by philosophy after the appearance of the Bible in its world. Seeking to recover Greek philosophy, the Enlightenment must first embark on a struggle against "prejudices" understood in this specific sense. In Strauss's view, however, in doing so the Enlightenment remains "entangled [*verstrickt*]" in the conceptual framework of the tradition it faces, largely based on the Bible. As a result, the Enlightenment gains the freedom of polemically answering "no" to the questions characteristic of the tradition, but not the freedom of questioning.[97] For this reason, it remains even more deeply entrapped in the "presuppositions" of the tradition originated by the encounter between Greek philosophy (Athens) and the Bible (Jerusalem).

One may think that the relevant aspect of those prejudices (what makes them prejudices) is only their being based on revelation, i.e., an unconditionally authoritative source.[98] But this appears to be only one side of Strauss's argument. For already in "Religious Situation of the Present," he hints at the necessity of taking into consideration also the specific "content," as it were, of the "presuppositions" of the tradition in which the Enlightenment, as well as modernity as a whole, remains entangled. It is worth noting that Strauss, as examples of that entanglement, among others, gives the "internalizing" of some traits of the original belief in the biblical God and the problem of creation.

Regarding the first example, Strauss sketchily points out that the belief in the biblical God is replaced by an anthropocentric reinterpretation whose fundamental traits are the "self-redemption of mankind, self-assurance of immortality . . . assuming the role of providence."[99] A common characteristic of all these traits is that they rest on a special role played by the human being within the whole—a special role that, for Strauss, can largely be traced back to the conception of man as "created in the image of God" and protected by his "providence."[100]

Regarding the problem of creation, although, again, in a sketchy manner, Strauss observes that, according to the Bible, creation is the consequence of a free decision of God: "God has created the world in complete freedom, out of love; he rules over it in complete freedom . . . In his freedom he can perform miracles. Miracles are not in themselves 'more divine' than the usual course of the world; but there is no reason for saying that God could not and would not perform miracles."[101]

This aspect of the question is, for us, of the utmost importance, since it is in light of it that we can fully understand the incompatibility of the Greek conception of nature, on which science and philosophy originally rested, with the biblical view. It is not accidental, in this respect, that at the very beginning of "The Origin of the Idea of Natural Right," chapter III of *Natural Right and History*, Strauss underscores that in the Old Testament, "whose basic premise may be said to be the implicit rejection of philosophy," there is no equivalent for the Greek term, and concept of, nature.[102] As he will explain in "Progress or Return?," the Greek concept of *physis* is the philosophical, "rational" equivalent of the pre-philosophical, "mythical" concepts of *Ananke* (Necessity) or *Moira* (Fate).[103] It is characteristic of the Greek view, at least since Homer, that even the gods are subject to this kind of "impersonal necessity"[104] or "impersonal powers."[105] Hence, they are not omnipotent. This means that according to the Greek understanding—philosophical and rational after the discovery of the concept of nature, pre-philosophical and mythical before that fundamental event—there is something stable, necessary, and eternal (a-temporal, to use the language of modern historicism) that, being unchangeable for both humans and gods, can become the object of a meaningful theoretical investigation. As Strauss explains in "Progress or Return?" by referring to Maimonides's view:

> The issue as he [Maimonides] stated it was as follows: philosophy teaches the eternity of the world, and the Bible teaches the creation out of nothing. This conflict must be rightly understood, because Maimonides is primarily thinking of Aristotle, who taught the eternity of the visible universe. But if you enlarge and apply it not only to this cosmos, to the visible universe in which we live now, but to any cosmos or chaos which might ever exist, certainly Greek philosophy teaches the eternity of the cosmos or chaos; whereas the Bible teaches creation, implying creation out of nothing. The root of the matter, however, is that only the Bible teaches divine omnipotence, and the thought of divine omnipotence is absolutely incompatible with Greek philosophy in any form.[106]

If so, the dependence of the world, as well as of the whole, on God's will and omnipotence—even their usual, regular course—makes them unavailable for a meaningful theoretical investigation. For that dependence deprives knowledge of its "natural" object and of the source of any possible stable, rational order or standard.[107]

It is precisely for this reason that modern physics, trying to restore "true" science while being still under the influence of the biblical conception, must now "understand nature completely on its own term [*völlig aus sich selbst*]," as Strauss puts it in "Religious Situation of the Present."[108] Remaining entangled in that conception, however, it must search for a stable order for its knowledge not so much in an objective, eternal, and necessary nature, as the Greeks understood it, but in a new type of nature. According to modern physics, therefore, nature becomes "a construct of human intellect [*Verstand*]."[109] For it is now the human being who, deprived of any source of a rational superhuman order (like nature in the Greek sense) while attempting to protect his knowledge from the possible disruption of God's omnipotence, must "create" order, therewith remaining entrapped in a radical idealism or phenomenalism. Analogously, "the whole of culture, and with it religion, is understood as a construct of the human mind [*Geist*]."[110] This however implies that the world and the whole "in themselves" remain inaccessible, since they are now perceived as beyond human reach and still, as it were, clothed in the darkness of God's omnipotence and inscrutability.[111]

When it comes to political philosophy, this new understanding of nature and science, as previously observed regarding *Natural Right and History*, creates the conditions, first, for the modern interpretation of natural right, according to which right is a subjective, justified claim, instead of an objective standard (at least conceived of as the best way of life, as a hierarchy of human ends). Eventually, however, the same understanding leads, for Strauss, to historicism. If nature, in this case human nature, is a residual, derivative concept, and the human being has to build his world and his own "artificial" order, human nature itself turns out to be indefinitely "malleable," and human beings are more the result of their "history" than of their "natural," merely primitive, beginning.[112] History, regarded as the manifestation of man's essential freedom rather than of his eternal nature, comes thus to the foreground, and eventually this view turns itself into a "philosophy of history": "The entanglement in the tradition is further intensified by a *theory* that *legitimizes* this entanglement. While the Enlightenment itself was wholly convinced that history was accidental, that the victorious party was not in the right just because it happened to be victorious, in the nineteenth century the belief that world history is the world's court of judgment becomes dominant."[113] From there to radical historicism it is a short step, as Strauss underscores in *Natural Right and History*.[114] Once this stage has been reached, the entanglement in the tradition is complete, and philosophy, in its original Greek sense, becomes impossible:

> Thus: the question πως βιωτέον [sic; how should one live?] is hard to answer today not merely on account of the natural difficulties, not merely on account of the dominance of a tradition of which we are aware as being a tradition, but on account of our total entanglement in the tradition, which goes so far that we cannot express ourselves purely and freely, that

every attempt to express and determine what we have seen and experienced is impossible at first. But what then can we do now?[115]

In "Religion Situation of the Present," the answer to this question is provided, to begin with, by Nietzsche. By rejecting the two pillars on which the tradition rested, the "prophets and Socrates-Plato," Nietzsche performs the role of the "last Enlightener" who destabilizes the tradition at its roots and, thereby, makes the *Urfrage* "How should one live?," "What is the right life?," possible again: "The tradition has been shaken at its roots by Nietzsche. It has altogether forfeited its self-evidence. We stand now in the world completely without authority, completely without orientation. Only now has the question πως [sic] βιωτέον regained its full sharpness. We *can* again pose it. We have the possibility of posing it in full seriousness."[116]

Thanks to Nietzsche's completion of the Enlightenment, thus, it is possible to "begin *entirely* from the beginning," free from "any polemical passion against the tradition," which has now become "completely questionable."[117] It is one thing, however, to ask the *Urfrage*; it is another thing to try to answer it. Not only the historicist "Present" Strauss enacts by means of its prosopopoeia, but also Nietzsche, as the last "Enlightener," would prevent us from raising that question in a philosophically relevant manner. The reason is that in destabilizing the pillars of tradition, Nietzsche, as Strauss underscores, also rejects "θεωρεῖν" and the "good-evil" distinction,[118] which appear to be indispensable presuppositions in order for that question to be meaningfully raised. If, thus, we really want to attain that goal, for Strauss (who, in this regard, appears to begin to distance himself from Nietzsche[119]) we need, first, to regain the condition of "natural ignorance" enjoyed by Plato's cave dwellers. For it is only in this cave, freed from the artificial difficulties originally brought in by revelation, that we can restart to devote ourselves to the theoretical, philosophic life, and investigate whether this life truly is the answer to the primordial question, πῶς βιωτέον.

"The Intellectual Situation of the Present"

The conclusion of "Religious Situation of the Present" is, ultimately, the final point Strauss also reaches in the slightly later "The Intellectual Situation of the Present": "If then the Enlightenment's fight against prejudices is only the fight against *the* historical difficulty of philosophizing, then the true goal of this fight is only: the recovery of philosophizing in its natural difficulty, of natural philosophizing, that is, of Greek philosophy."[120] The same holds for both the key role played by the quotation from Maimonides (*Guide of the Perplexed*, I.31) about the biblical origin of the "prejudices" fought by the Enlightenment[121] and the reference to the opposition between a first, natural cave and a second, unnatural cave. "In other words," as Strauss now puts it, "the natural difficulties of philosophizing have their classical depiction in Plato's allegory of the cave. The historical difficulty may be illustrated by saying: there *now* exists another cave *beneath* the Platonic cave."[122]

Despite this overlap, however, in "The Intellectual Situation of the Present" there are some elements that, if not entirely new, at least shed new light on our primary question: the meaning and scope of the moderns' entanglement in the second cave. To begin with, it is important to observe that in this lecture—more precisely, in the "Plan of the Lecture in Draft" attached to it—Strauss explicitly defines the second cave, or "the cave *beneath* the Platonic cave," as "the cave of modernity."[123] This is relevant because it shows that for Strauss the second cave is not just that in which the human beings of the present find themselves as a result of historicism, as it may seem, at first glance, from "Religious Situation of the Present."[124] The first, decisive entanglement in the tradition, the first step into the second cave, on the contrary, takes place at the inception of modernity, with the attempt, carried out by the Enlightenment of the seventeenth and eighteenth centuries, to free science and philosophy from the restrictions brought in by Christian Scholasticism.[125] As Strauss will reaffirm, about two decades later, in "Preface to Isaac Husik, *Philosophical Essays*," "Modern philosophy emerged by way of transformation of, if in opposition to, Latin or Christian scholasticism."[126]

This revealing remark becomes clearer if one considers what Strauss explains about this matter in "The Intellectual Situation of the Present." In this lecture, Strauss attempts to disprove the historicist "belief" that the present age, despite its "radical ignorance" and consequent "inability" to raise the question about the right life, has progressed further ahead than any previous stage of the philosophical tradition. As he puts it criticizing the historicist view, "Being fundamentally *ignorant we cannot come to knowledge since we know too much*." "Since we *believe* we know too much," Strauss however hastens to retort, to conclude that "we will not be able to remove our radical ignorance until this belief that we know [*Glaube zu wissen*] is abolished [*aufgehoben*]."[127]

Now, in order to perform such an *Aufhebung*—which, in a fashion that reminds one of Hegel, rejects while retaining some of the insights of the rejected, in this case of historical consciousness—Strauss resorts to an act of what, in "Review of Julius Ebbinghaus, *On the Progress of Metaphysics*," he defines as "learning through reading."[128] In the present context, this means to learn by way of a historical reading of the documents of the past that, however, remains free from the presumptuous "Glaube zu wissen" of historicism. Hence, it is indeed an approach—this is the retaining part—based on "historical consciousness," that is, on the insight that we now need historical studies to gain access to previous stages of human thought with which we have severed any direct connection. But it is also a rejection, in that it avoids the dogmatic belief that the historicist "present" is intrinsically superior to any previous age, with the implication that nothing beyond a merely antiquarian knowledge of the past can be achieved.

Applying this anti-historicist pattern of historical consciousness,[129] this time to early modernity, Strauss shows that, in contrast to the prevailing impression that modernity as a whole has always been progressive—which would make the claim to superiority of the present plausible—one can detect a "reversionary character [*Rückgangscharakter*]" at its very inception. Indeed, it is true that "the modern centuries are dominated by the pathos of progress in knowledge and through knowledge," that at the beginning of the modern development stands the fight against the "stagnating" scholastic science, which, instead of investigating nature itself, to the astonishment of the early modern physicists, transmitted and explained Aristotle.[130] As Strauss observes, unlike Christian Scholasticism, which regarded science as "essentially completed" and was "pursued by monks," modern philosophy, being once again the concern of "free citizens," like the Athenians of whom "Thucydides writes that they are always ready to *hope*," displayed a totally different approach: "plus ultra."[131] However, despite this intention and the overall impression that "the moderns got further than the ancients," for Strauss, in the early modern centuries, "the conviction of the *authoritative significance of the Greeks* keeps breaking through."[132] As he further explains, ". . . the fight against the Middle Ages appears as an attempt to recover Greek freedom, Greek science. At the beginning of modern philosophy stands the Renaissance, the renaissance of *antiquity*. In fact, the fight against the Scholastics is in considerable part conducted in *the* manner of opposing *genuine* Greek science—whether it be Aristotle himself, or Plato, or Democritus and Epicurus—to the *corrupt* Greek science of Scholasticism."[133]

Now, it is worth noticing that for Strauss the key element of this effort to recover Greek science, and thereby to oppose Christian Scholasticism, is the attempt of the moderns to go back to nature. As we have seen, modern scientists, for instance, were puzzled by the fact that scholastic physics was transmitting and explaining Aristotle rather than investigating nature. While emphasizing the "reversionary character" of modern philosophy, Strauss generalizes this remark and observes that "even the fiercest opponents of the Greeks believed themselves able to put into effect the progress they had in mind only after they had laid the foundation for it by a *return*, namely, by a return to *nature*."[134]

This is why the fight against prejudices becomes so important in the seventeenth and eighteenth centuries. As we have observed with reference to Maimonides, "prejudices" strictly understood are the consequence of "artificial" or "historical" difficulties that, due to the appearance of the Bible in the world of Greek philosophy, have been added to the "natural" difficulties originally characterizing that world. The return to nature attempted by early modernity, thus, is possible only by way of a preliminary fight against prejudices. As Strauss puts it in "The Intellectual Situation of the Present," "the word 'prejudice' is indeed the Enlightenment's polemical keyword . . . One must *free* oneself from prejudices, and this freeing is accomplished by *retreating* to a plane, or even a point, from which one can finally progress free of prejudice once and for all."[135] That here Strauss also thinks of nature as the point to which the Enlightenment wanted to return or retreat, in order to be finally able to progress free of prejudice, is confirmed by the already mentioned "Plan of the Lecture in Draft." There, under the bullet point corresponding to the part we are dealing with, Strauss observes that "While the progressive tendency is primary, modern philosophy is always characterized by a countermovement—and not only as a condition independent of it, but as its condition proper." To this remark, he schematically, but clearly adds: "State of *nature. Liberation from prejudices*," to conclude that "the meaning of modern philosophy must be understood in light of this *fundamental* intention of this philosophy."[136]

The "state of nature," at least as regards "political philosophy," appears thus to be the plane to which the Enlightenment wanted to retreat in order to free itself, once and for all, from each and every prejudice. For this reason, when, in the body of the lecture, Strauss refers again to the modern attempt to return to nature, he mentions Rousseau's "call" to that return as only "*one* example of that and not even the best one."[137] Hobbes, who, not accidentally, is the focus of his coeval essay "Notes on Carl Schmitt, *The Concept of the Political*," would arguably have been a better example in that respect. At any rate, the reference to the "state of nature" turns out to be key in order for us to understand what Strauss adds shortly afterwards. Having explained the "reversionary character" of early modernity by way of its attempt to retreat to the "state of nature"— or to start again to investigate nature itself as far as modern physics is concerned—Strauss observes: "Today's reader of a writing from the Age of Enlightenment in which prejudices are fought so fiercely will often have to smile when he realizes just how strong were the prejudices of the supposedly prejudice-free gentlemen of the Enlightenment. One could even say: the century of the Enlightenment was the century of prejudices."[138]

As we shall explain further, Strauss is here likely referring to "prejudices" that characterize the early modern interpretation, of nature in particular.[139] By this I mean that also these prejudices are arguably to be understood in light of the quote from Maimonides about the biblical origin of "prejudices" strictly understood, which, not by chance, follows shortly afterwards in the text.[140] If so, the "present-day reader [*der heutige Leser*]" he mentions at the beginning of the quote above does not seem to be the reader of the historicist "present." At least, he or she does not seem to be such a reader according to the historicist interpretation of historical consciousness, which regards as ultimately impossible the attempt to free oneself from the prejudices of one's age and go back, thereby, to a condition of "natural ignorance." "Prejudice" is in fact a historical concept, not a natural one. As Strauss underscores, it is older than modern philosophy, but, being ultimately based on revelation, it is not coeval with human thought.[141] As such, it cannot have a "universal significance," but only a historical, artificial role first enabled by the encounter of Greek philosophy with the Bible and then consolidated, within modernity, by both the Enlightenment and (but only as a further development) historicism.

This is why for Strauss the "overcoming [*Aufhebung*]" of historical consciousness, as previously observed, may represent a way out of that apparently insurmountable impasse. As he puts it towards the end of the lecture, "If then only historical consciousness has taught us [*belehrt*] about the universal significance of the category of 'prejudice,' the *overcoming* [Aufhebung] *of historical consciousness* would bring with it the *overcoming* [Aufhebung] *of the universal significance of 'prejudice.'*"[142] By shifting from historicism to historical "learning through reading," thus, for Strauss one can finally see that prejudice itself is only a historical category ultimately brought in by revelation. If so, once one has dismissed historical consciousness in its dogmatic, historicist interpretation, prejudice will be overcome in its universal, insurmountable meaning, thereby enabling again a purely natural approach to philosophy based on appearance and opinion.

In "The Intellectual Situation of the Present" Strauss drafts a whole paragraph, meant as an alternative introduction to his lecture, which, under the title of "Fate as Principle," attempts the justification of this shift. Evidently, this paragraph expands on the remark "our fate is not our task" he puts forth in "Religious Situation of the Present." Addressing the problem of the alleged impossibility, within the historicist present, of meaningfully raising the "question concerning what is right [*die Frage nach dem Richtigen*]," it culminates in the following observation: "It is not the knowledge of historicity as such that leads to the explicit question concerning the present ideal of life, and therefore concerning the situation of the present, but *incorporating* the knowledge of historicity, historical consciousness, into the question, making it the element, the presupposition, the *principle* of the question—when this knowledge in fact pertains only to the conditions and fates of questioning."[143] To this remark, Strauss significantly objects: "But if the primary question [*die ursprüngliche Frage*] of the human being who does not live in a binding given order [*verbindliche gegebene Ordnung*] is the question concerning a binding reasonable [or rational: *vernünftig*] order, it is this *question* alone that must [*darf*] primarily occupy him and not the fate and condition of this question."[144]

The *Urfrage*, now *ursprüngliche Frage*, about "how one should live" remains, thus, the question to ask, at least preliminarily, in order not to remain entrapped in the dogmatic historicist approach and to begin to "philosophize naturally" again. However, not to relapse into the dogmatism of the historicist of the present (but only, as it were, "with the opposite polarity"), one cannot completely disregard the "condition of this question." This is why, in Strauss's approach, the problem of the second, unnatural cave, as well as that of the *Aufhebung* of historical consciousness by way of "learning through reading," plays such an important role, as we shall see in greater details soon. At present, however, it is worth underscoring the extent to which Strauss himself, in his lecture, while advising his audience not to be preliminarily hindered in their "naive" questioning by a dogmatic historicist approach, resorts to such a simple stile of reasoning (and not, as it seems, for purely rhetorical purposes).

This occurs, for instance, when Strauss, after explaining the meaning and scope of the question concerning the intellectual situation of the present from the perspective of twentieth-century European Jewry, points out that this question, no matter how much it may appear "straightforward," is "however *not natural*." For "at any time there existed an 'intellectual situation of the present'; but no one concerned himself with it." "Thoughtful people [*die Nachdenkenden*] concerned themselves with the eternal," Strauss observes afterwards, to conclude that the "interest in the intellectual situation of the present is not *natural* to man but tied to certain *historical* conditions."[145]

Later on, having underscored (unlike in "Religious Situation of the Present") the role of Weber, along with historicism, in bringing about a condition of "polytheism of values" and "*anarchy*," where the question concerning *the* right life is regarded as no longer meaningful, Strauss again points out that "the fact cannot be completely forgotten that in earlier times eternal, unconditional principles knowable to reason *itself*, and hence an order [*Ordnung*], were held to be possible and necessary."[146] "This belief," he concedes, "is now considered *naïve*."[147] For this reason, "historical consciousness leads to the awareness of superiority over the European past and the awareness of the complete equality of non-European ideals; and in many cases: contempt for the European past and prostration before everything exotic."[148] To this relativistic stance, however, in a manner reminiscent of twentieth-century phenomenology, Strauss emphatically retorts: "Now, it is natural [*natürlich*] to man to treasure and *cultivate* what is his own, what is handed down to him by his forebears, whereas he *confronts* what is foreign proudly, suspiciously, cautiously, at most with respect and admiration. Measured by this natural stance [*natürliche Stellung*], the stance dominant in Europe today appears as antinatural [*widernatürlich*], *perverse* [*pervers*]."[149] In light of this, the conclusion Strauss draws about the "unnatural" character of that situation could not be more straightforward: "Our inability to live, which manifests itself in our inability to question, is our unnaturalness, the unnaturalness of our world [*unsere Unnatürlichkeit, die Unnatürlichkeit unserer Welt*]."[150]

What immediately follows in the lecture also provides us with remarkable examples of Strauss's attempt to recover such a "natural stance." Despite the "unnaturalness of our world" he has just underscored, for Strauss "we, too, are still in a certain way natural beings [*natürliche Wesen*]." "And even if, in this respect," as he significantly puts it, "we had to despair in the face of ourselves, the fact that even today children are generated naturally and born naturally could reassure us."[151] To the further objection that "these children become corrupted soon enough by the dominant unnaturalness," he finally rejoins that "there remains the hope, so long as there are human beings on earth, that some day human beings will be able to be natural again."[152]

It is, however, what follows that should draw, in particular, our attention. For, after reiterating that "we, too, are still natural beings," Strauss emphatically observes:

> That we are still natural shows itself in the fact that we, confronted with the ignorance of what is right, escape into the *question* concerning what is right [Frage *nach dem Richtigen*]— escape from the unnaturalness of our situation. The *need* to know, and therefore the questioning, is the best guarantee that we are still natural beings, humans—but that we *are not capable of* questioning is the clear symptom of our being threatened in our humanity in a way that humans have never been threatened.[153]

If so, the only way for humans to regain a condition of "naturalness," where raising the question concerning what is right becomes possible again, is by "*calling historical consciousness into question.*"[154] As we have observed, the "overcoming" of historical consciousness, and the metaphor of the first, natural cave, precisely serve this purpose. For it is only by way of that overcoming that one can attempt to reach the natural cave, where, having dismissed as artificial and transient the "historical difficulty of philosophizing" that characterizes the "cave *beneath* the Platonic cave," one can finally attempt the "recovery of philosophizing in its natural difficulty, of *natural* philosophizing, that is of *Greek* philosophy."[155]

Introduction to *Philosophy and Law*

The introduction to *Philosophy and Law* is usually regarded as important because there Strauss explains that the Enlightenment critique of orthodoxy, from a logical standpoint, was successful only as a defensive critique, due to the fact that the premise of revelation (an omnipotent and inscrutable God) is irrefutable. It is also commonly mentioned because Strauss, in it, affirms that the culmination of that critique is "atheism out of probity," which turns out to be a descendant of biblical morality. This being the case, the introduction is often regarded as embracing a solution according to which the opposition between orthodoxy and atheism is a stalemate, where neither can go beyond the assertion of its own belief, with the result of an implicit victory of orthodoxy, for which, unlike philosophy, being based on belief is a kind of truism.

This reading is undoubtedly plausible. Towards the end of the introduction, after all, Strauss himself puts forward a statement like the following, where the above seems to be confirmed:

> Thus at last the "truth" of the alternative "orthodoxy or Enlightenment" is revealed as the alternative "orthodoxy or atheism" . . . The situation thus formed, the present situation, appears [*scheint*] to be insoluble for the Jew who cannot be orthodox and who must consider purely political Zionism, the only "solution of the Jewish problem" possible on the basis of atheism, as a resolution that is indeed highly honorable but not, in earnest and in the long run, adequate. This situation not only appears insoluble but actually is so, as long as one clings to the modern premises.[156]

The statement, however, starts to appear less definitive as soon as one notices—as we, by now, should be able to do promptly—that here, once again, Strauss is addressing the issue from the perspective of the "present situation [*gegenwärtige Lage*]"[157] of German Jewry, precisely like in the two lectures discussed above. In particular, the final reference to "the modern premises" should not pass unnoticed in that regard. For, as we shall now see, this appears to be an implicit reference to the entanglement of modernity—from its inception, and not only in its final stage characterized by atheism out of probity—in the biblical tradition, along the lines of what we have observed about the opposition between the first and the second cave.

In the introduction to *Philosophy and Law* Strauss addresses the question of that opposition in a remarkably explicit manner. He sets out by explaining that the aim of his book is to "awaken a prejudice" in favor of the view that "Maimonides' rationalism is the true natural model, the standard to be carefully protected from any distortion, and thus the stumbling-block on which modern rationalism falls."[158] He then points out that "the critique of the present, the critique of modern rationalism as the critique of modern sophistry, is the necessary beginning, the constant companion, and the unerring sign of that search for truth which is possible in our time."[159]

After these introductory remarks, which, however innovative,[160] ultimately sound as consistent with what we have so far observed regarding the second cave, Strauss begins to refer, once again, to the Enlightenment. Here the movement Descartes and Hobbes initiated in the seventeenth century is regarded as that which has shaped "the present situation of Judaism," as well as "all phenomena peculiar to the present."[161] In particular, tackling orthodoxy in its "external," original meaning, for Strauss the Enlightenment managed to "undermine" the foundation of Jewish tradition. This eventually led to the latter's attempt, deemed as the only possible counterattack under those conditions, to reestablish that foundation on a "higher" level based on the "internalization" of the fundamental tenets of orthodoxy.

As one would expect, Strauss takes issue with this attempt.[162] In his view, "all 'internalizations' of the basic tenets of the tradition rest at bottom on this: from the 'reflexive' premise, from the 'higher' level of the post-Enlightenment synthesis, the relation of God to nature is no longer intelligible and thus is no longer even interesting."[163] To this revealing remark, which already points to the core of the question of the second cave, he adds that in order to realize that the "internalizations" are actually disavowals, one has to resort to "historical reflection." For only in this manner—namely, by way of what we have previously called, in Strauss's footsteps, "learning through reading"—one can attempt to free oneself from the "mode of thought" created by that process of internalization, which in turn is triggered by the success of the Enlightenment critique of orthodoxy.[164]

The ground is thus prepared for the introduction of the topic of the second cave. To this end, Strauss observes that the justification of "internalizations" against the "orthodox, 'external' view" ultimately rests on two mistakes. The first consists in appealing to "witnesses" that "belong to an undeveloped stage of the formulation of belief."[165] The second is due to the reliance on "extreme statements that have been ventured within the Jewish tradition."[166] In both cases, according to Strauss the original meaning of those "witnesses" or "statements," which are torn from their context, is irremediably changed. In addition, in doing so one proves to be already following the method of the Enlightenment. For, as Strauss observes regarding the second mistake (the appeal against the orthodox view to "extreme statements" that can be found within the Jewish tradition), ". . . precisely this is characteristic of the Enlightenment: that, in its supposedly or only ostensibly 'immanent' criticism and development of the tradition, it makes extremes of the tradition into the foundation of a position that is actually completely incompatible with the tradition."[167]

Strauss reiterates, and expands on, this important remark in a long note that starts with the observation that this characteristic "extends also to the philosophic tradition."[168] From this perspective, where the Enlightenment does not simply restore "older positions"—arguably, those characteristic of the Greek approach[169]—it makes "extremes of the tradition (or polemics against extremes of the tradition) into the foundation of a position that is completely incompatible with the tradition."[170] As a result, Strauss further explains, although "the Enlightenment's aim was the rehabilitation of the natural through the denial (or limitation) of the supernatural," "what it accomplished [*ihre Leistung*] was the discovery of a new 'natural' foundation which, so far from being natural, is rather the residue, as it were, of the 'supernatural.'"[171]

Now, despite its obscurity, the latter remark appears to be a rather explicit manner of stating that the Enlightenment, while attempting to free itself from the prejudices enrooted in the Bible, remains entrapped in them, leading to a position that, instead of being the recovery of the Greek approach, is still under the decisive influence of the biblical tradition. This impression is confirmed by the fact that, like in the previously examined essays, in the continuation of this note Strauss emphasizes the role of Nietzsche as the "last Enlightener." The same occurs with the necessity to resort to "learning through reading" (here called " 'historicizing' of philosophy") and, most importantly, to the problem of the second cave as a possible way out of the philosophical predicament of modernity. As he now puts it, "Only the history of philosophy makes possible the ascent from the second, 'unnatural' cave, into which we have fallen less because of the tradition itself, than because of the tradition of the polemics against the tradition, into that first, 'natural' cave which Plato's image depicts, to emerge from which into the light is the original meaning of philosophizing."[172]

Regardless of the similarities with the previous descriptions, however, what should catch our attention the most is that Strauss, in the present context, adds some points that turn out to be particularly important for our analysis. First, he explains that modern philosophy, rather than understanding the "extreme" by starting from the "natural" regarded as the "typical," understands the typical from the extreme, thereby introducing a new view of the "natural" that appears to be inconsistent with any attempt to find order in nature itself. Second, to substantiate these remarks, Strauss puts forth some examples, among which it is here worth mentioning "natural right" and the "idealistic turn of philosophy." Regarding the first, he succinctly observes that "the extreme case of necessity [*der extreme Fall des Notrechts*] is made into the foundation of natural right"—a remark that clearly refers to Hobbes's view, notably of the *ius in omnia* in the state of nature. Regarding the second, Strauss points out that "the polemic against the extreme possibility of miracles becomes the foundation of the 'idealistic' turn of philosophy"[173]—a comment that is in perfect keeping with what we have previously observed about the idealism or phenomenalism of modern natural science as a way to shield itself from God's omnipotence and inscrutability.[174]

All these remarks by Strauss are further developed in the continuation of the introduction. For instance, after pointing out that the Enlightenment's defensive critique succeeded, at least "provisionally," because it showed the "unknowability" of miracles, Strauss explains that this position is the result of the "idealistic" turn of modern science. At that stage of the argument, he does not clarify the role of omnipotence in that turn, limiting himself to the observation that unlike "pre-Enlightenment science," "the new science, which proved itself in the battle against orthodoxy, if it did not indeed have its very raison d'être in that battle, stood in often concealed but, at bottom, always active and thus always re-emerging opposition to belief."[175] This "polemical" stance, which, as we have seen, is one of the traits Strauss singles out to explain the modern entanglement in the second cave, "brought it about that fundamental teachings of the tradition, deemed knowable by the premises of the older science, were now considered more and more to be merely believed."[176] Significantly, as an example of that development Strauss refers to "the undermining of natural theology and of natural right," which, in his view, was not only prepared, but ultimately accomplished in the Age of Enlightenment through the rejection of the teleological view of the whole.[177] The final result of this process, Strauss explains, is that "unbelieving science and belief no longer have, as in the Middle Ages, the common ground of natural knowledge."[178] Consequently, this "unnatural" situation makes any attempt to carry out "a meaningful quarrel between belief and unbelief" ultimately impossible,[179] thereby depriving science and philosophy of the chance to refute orthodoxy.

As is well known, in light of the impossibility of achieving such a direct refutation due to the "idealistic" character of modern science, for Strauss the Enlightenment attempts the "civilization" of the world, according to which "man" has to become the master, theoretically and practically, of nature and his life. In Strauss's own words, "the world created by him had to erase the world merely 'given' to him; then orthodoxy would be more than refuted—it would be 'outlived.'"[180] According to Strauss, however, the problem with this attempt is twofold. First, it ultimately proves to be vain: "Finally the belief is perishing that man can, by pushing back the 'limits of Nature' further and further, advance to ever greater 'freedom,' that he can 'subjugate' nature, 'prescribe his own laws' for her, 'generate' her by dint of pure thought."[181] Second, and even more important for us, that attempt, at closer inspection, proves to be baseless. The reason is that modern natural science, unlike pre-modern science, is unable, due to its understanding of nature, to justify any ideal of life. As Strauss observes, "it was believed that the new concept of nature was the adequate foundation of the new ideal precisely because the old concept of nature had been the adequate foundation of the old ideal."[182] But this assumption, being based on the "old concept of truth" implicitly rejected by the "idealist" and constructivist modern science, turned out to be "a delusion": "It had yet to be ascertained that the 'end-free' and 'value-free' nature of modern natural science can say nothing to man about 'ends and values,' that the 'Is,' understood in the sense of modern natural science, involves no reference to the 'Ought,' and that therefore the traditional view that the right life [*das richtige Leben*] is a life according to nature becomes meaningless under the modern premise."[183] Interestingly, Strauss attaches to this eloquent remark—which clearly shows to what extent he regarded the problem of natural right as related to the reinterpretation of nature in the second cave—a note about Nietzsche. To prove that Nietzsche, despite his being "the last Enlightener" who makes the attempt to recover the first cave conceivable, remains entrapped in such a view of nature as unable to show the right life, Strauss refers the reader, precisely in that respect, to Aphorism 9 of *Beyond Good and Evil*. There, while criticizing the Stoic attempt to live "according to nature," Nietzsche describes nature as "without purposes and consideration." He consequently emphasizes the role of human "preferences" from the moral perspective and concludes by underscoring the "tyrannical drive" of philosophy in its attempt to carry out a spiritual "creation of the world."[184]

This being the case, the new science can by no means be the foundation of the modern ideal of civilization. In fact, for Strauss it is the other way round. It is the ideal of civilization that brings about modern science not only as a tool to achieve the mastery over nature, but also as a shield to protect science itself against the possibility of miracles and of an omnipotent and inscrutable God.[185] As we have seen in "Religious Situation of the Present," modern physics understands nature "completely in its own terms," as "a construct of human intellect," precisely in light of the fact that, according to the biblical account, "miracles are not in themselves 'more divine' than the usual course of the world."[186]

In the introduction to *Philosophy and Law*, Strauss elaborates on that insight. He points out that the mere "unknowability" of miracles was already implicit in the "idealistic" character of modern natural science.[187] Then he asks the following, thought-provoking questions: "Is it not, ultimately, the very intention of defending oneself radically against miracles which is the basis of the concept of science that guides modern natural science? Was not the 'unique' 'world-construction' of modern natural science, according to which miracles are of course unknowable, devised expressly for the very purpose that miracles *be* unknowable, and that thus man be defended against the grip of the omnipotent God?"[188] If so, as Strauss seems to imply, modern natural science, with its idealism and constructivism, ultimately is another example, perhaps the most consequential, of that polemical stance towards the biblical tradition that, in his view, is the main cause of the descent into the second cave, in which philosophy, understood as "by nature" the best way of life, is no longer possible.[189]

Be that as it may, for Strauss only the "ideal of civilization" remains the true modern ideal. Unlike "freedom as the autonomy of man and his culture," which, belonging to a later stage of modernity, can forget nature altogether and ends up seeing culture as "the sovereign creation of the spirit,"[190] the ideal of civilization is essentially based on the attempt to subjugate nature. This, however, now is "modern" nature, the one that, as we have underscored, is interpreted by modern science as "end-free" and "value-free." Significantly, while commenting on the ideal of civilization as that which does not forget "the state of nature" as its real presupposition, Strauss defines this nature as "overpowering [*übermächtig*]" and describes "the primary ideal of civilization as the self-assertion of man against" it.[191]

Now, why does Strauss resort to such an expression to define nature? What is its real meaning? A few years earlier, in "Notes on Carl Schmitt,

The Concept of the Political," Strauss had already explained that unlike the pre-modern view, according to which nature is "exemplary order [*vorbildliche Ordnung*]," modernity regards nature as "disorder to be eliminated [*zu besaitigende Unordnung*]"[192]—an interpretation not difficult to understand if one considers the "state of nature" we have described above, particularly in Hobbes's view. This nature as "disorder to be eliminated" now becomes "overpowering nature [*übermächtige Natur*]." Is this an allusion to the fact that the "world-construction" of modern science, as we have underscored, rests on an interpretation of nature whereby human beings can be "defended against the grip of the omnipotent [*allmächtig*] God?"[193]

Although arguably pointing to the same biblical background, Strauss's view seems to be slightly different. We can reconstruct this view by referring to what he points out, towards the end of the introduction, regarding the difference between the original Epicurean approach to "religious delusion" and that of modern Enlightenment. Although "the Epicurean critique is the foundation, or more exactly the foreground, of the Enlightenment critique," for Strauss the Enlightenment understands "man's happiness" and "tranquillity" in a "fundamentally different way from original Epicureanism [*Epikureismus*]."[194] As we have observed in the previous chapter, rather than as *ataraxia* and *aponia*, modern Enlightenment "understands 'tranquillity' in such a way that the civilization, the subjection, the improvement of nature [*die Zivilisation, die Unterwerfung, die Verbesserung der Natur*], and particularly of human nature, becomes indispensable for its sake."[195] To this end, the Enlightenment must teach humans to reject the religious delusions not so much for their terrifying character, as because, qua delusions, they "steer [them] away from the real 'this world' to an imaginary 'other world.' "[196] "Liberated from the religious delusion," Strauss famously concludes this point, "awakened to sober awareness of his real situation, taught by bad experiences that he is threatened by a stingy, hostile nature [*karge, feindliche Natur*], man recognizes as his sole salvation and duty [*Rettung und Pflicht*] not so much 'to cultivate his garden' as in the first place to plant himself a 'garden' by making himself the master and owner of nature."[197]

Now, in this final quote, which concludes Strauss's description of the modern "ideal of civilization," the "overpowering nature" mentioned above interestingly becomes a "stingy, hostile nature" that leads man to search for his "salvation" by planting himself a "garden" instead of by "cultivating his garden." This being the case, what garden is here Strauss referring to? Moreover, how should we understand the "awakening to sober awareness of his real situation," as well as the "bad experiences" that lead man to realize that he is "threatened" by that "stingy, hostile nature"? A possible answer to the first question, at least as far as the first garden ("to cultivate his garden") is concerned, is that Strauss is referring to Epicurus's garden, whose mere "cultivation" would no longer be regarded as sufficient by modern Enlightenment.[198] But the emphasis on "salvation" and "duty," as well as on the necessity for man to "plant himself" a garden, apparently gives the whole passage, at least as far as this second garden is concerned, a biblical flavor.[199] As a result, the garden now man feels the need to plant seems to be a purely secular reinterpretation of "the Garden of Eden."[200] As Strauss puts it in a previous part of the same introduction, "man had to establish himself theoretically and practically as master of the world and master of his life," to conclude that "the world *created* by him had to erase the world merely 'given' to him."[201] The same might hold for the "awakening" and the "bad experiences," which remind one of the biblical account of the fall, as a result of which the ground is "cursed" and covered with "thorns and thistles."[202] In this case, however, the conditional mode is required, since Strauss, although in a much later work of his, proves to hold a similar view of epicureanism and its interpretation of nature.[203]

Be this as it may, if, according to Strauss, the garden that the moderns seek to plant is a secular reinterpretation of the Garden of Eden, the whole Cartesian and Baconian project of the mastery of nature would have to be regarded as an attempt to "transform," while polemically "opposing," that biblical background (*Hintergrund*), which would rest at the core of the Enlightenment behind an Epicurean "foreground [*Vordergrund*]."[204] This conclusion would fully vindicate what Strauss observes in "The Intellectual Situation of the Present" regarding the "strong prejudices" of the "supposedly prejudice-free gentlemen of the Enlightenment,"[205] as we have previously underscored. In addition, it would confirm the extent to which the entanglement in the biblical "prejudices" affects the modern understanding of nature and impairs the possibility of recovering the conditions represented by the first, natural cave. It does not seem accidental, in this respect, that the introduction to *Philosophy and Law* ends with a reference to Maimonides's premodern rationalism as a tentative solution to the insoluble problem, under modern premises, of the opposition between "atheism and orthodoxy."[206] Likewise, it seems no coincidence that Strauss, also in *Philosophy and Law*, not only quotes Maimonides, *Guide of the Perplexed*, I.31, but also reiterates that precisely that kind of rationalism encounters a "*historical* difficulty," based on revelation, that is added "to the *natural* difficulties of philosophizing, which are given with the 'cave'-existence of man."[207]

"How to Study Spinoza's *Theologico-Political Treatise*"

In "How to Study Spinoza's *Theologico-Political Treatise*," originally published in 1948, Strauss deals with the question of the second cave—or the "pit beneath the cave," as he puts it there[208]—while discussing Spinoza's view of philosophy and hermeneutics. "Spinoza's rules of reading," Strauss observes, "derive from his belief in the final character of his philosophy as *the* clear and distinct and, therefore, *the* true account of the whole."[209] For this reason, Spinoza appears not to be concerned with the problem that his books might "not be directly intelligible at all times," due to the possibility, nowadays regarded as obvious, that "the whole orientation of a period may give way to a radically different orientation."[210]

Spinoza's hermeneutics is thus based on the rejection of the principle that the "gulf" between orientations of different periods can be bridged only "by means of historical interpretation."[211] Although criticizing the dominant historicist approach, Strauss proves to defend that principle, thereby acknowledging that Spinoza's "rules of reading" are in need of emendation. In his view, however, this correction is necessary precisely to grasp, in a period dominated by historicism, the extent to which Spinoza's philosophy rests on the assumption that it conveys "*the* true account of the whole." As Strauss puts it, by implicitly referring once again to the concept of "learning through reading,"

> Reading of old books becomes extremely important to us for the very reason for which it was utterly unimportant to Spinoza. We shall most urgently need an elaborate hermeneutics for the same reason for which Spinoza did not need any hermeneutics. We remain in perfect accord with Spinoza's way of thinking as long as we look at the devising of a more refined historical method as a desperate remedy for a desperate situation, rather than as a symptom of a healthy and thriving "culture."[212]

The stage in thus ready for the introduction of the topic of the second cave, the "desperate situation" for which Strauss's "learning through reading" represents the "desperate remedy." "Spinoza knew that the power of the natural obstacles to philosophy, which are the same at all times, can be increased by specific mistakes,"[213] Strauss now observes in a way clearly reminiscent of Maimonides's distinction between natural and artificial, or historical, difficulties of philosophizing. As a confirmation of this reading, in a note attached to this remark, Strauss not only refers the reader to Spinoza's *Theologico-Political Treatise* to substantiate his claim, but also suggests a comparison precisely with *Guide of the Perplexed*, I.31, where that distinction, as we have underscored, is introduced by Maimonides.

Unlike in the cases previously analyzed, to explain Spinoza's views Strauss now points out that "superstition, the natural enemy of philosophy, may arm itself with the weapons of philosophy and thus transform itself into pseudo-philosophy."[214] Moreover, since there is an "indefinitely large variety" of pseudo-philosophies, unlike the true philosophical account that always remains one and the same, the ways through which that account can be grasped will change. "It is conceivable," he goes on clearly referring to historicism, "that a particular pseudo-philosophy may emerge whose power cannot be broken but by the most intensive reading of old books. As long as that pseudo-philosophy rules, elaborate historical studies may be needed which would have been superfluous and therefore harmful in more fortunate times."[215]

Now, these "more fortunate times" are clearly those represented by the first, natural cave. As Strauss now explains expressing his view "in terms of the classic description of the natural obstacles to philosophy,"

> People may become so frightened of the ascent to the light of the sun, and so desirous of making that ascent utterly impossible to any of their descendants, that they dig a deep pit beneath the cave in which they were born, and withdraw into that pit. If one of the descendants desired to ascend to the light of the sun, he would first have to try to reach the level of the natural cave, and he would have to invent new and most artificial tools unknown and unnecessary to those who dwelt in the natural cave. He would be a fool, he would never see the light of the sun, he would lose the last vestige of the memory of the sun, if he perversely thought that by inventing his new tools he had progressed beyond the ancestral cave-dwellers.[216]

Although, unlike historicism, learning through the reading of "old books" is not such a "perversion," it thus still remains an artificial tool devised in order to reach the level of the natural cave. This clearly means that for Strauss that learning is only propaedeutic. It is meant to re-enable philosophy in its natural difficulties by way of historical studies. But, in itself, it is incapable of being the "natural philosophizing" Strauss aims at. As he restates criticizing science and history, the "twin-sisters" of the present that reject the ideal of a "true and final" account of the whole, "once this stage is reached, the original meaning of philosophy is accessible only through recollections of what philosophy meant in the past, i.e., for all practical purposes, only through the reading of old books."[217] This reading, if properly conducted, for Strauss leads to the "revitalization of earlier ways of thinking,"[218] according to which, unlike what "science and history" claim, a true and final account is possible. The "intelligent" historical study of earlier thought, in other words, leads to the "self-destruction"[219] of the historicist approach ultimately shared by those "twin-sisters," as well as to the revitalization of approaches, like Spinoza's, which still cling to the idea of an eternal truth.

Now, according to Spinoza, who, as we have underscored, did not acknowledge the need for "historical studies," the natural alternative is that between superstition and philosophy, since these both attempt to provide a final account of the whole.[220] An opposition between philosophy and pseudo-philosophy, that is between philosophy and a superstition that takes up the weapons of philosophy, would thus be artificial and unnatural in his view. In this regard, however, it is important to notice that, compared to the classical opposition between opinion and philosophy, Spinoza's account of the natural opposition seems already a transformation of what would take place in the first, natural cave. For the opinions that characterize the latter do not claim, qua opinions, to be the "final" account. Only "authoritative" opinions do so and, as we have stressed, the "authoritative" character is what, to begin with, distinguishes opinions from the "prejudices" based on revelation.

Is this a clue that Strauss regards Spinoza as a "modern man" already descended into the "pit beneath the cave," irrespective of his claim that the final account is possible? This impression seems to be confirmed by what Strauss observes regarding Spinoza's interpretation of science in the autobiographical "Preface to the English Translation" of *Spinoza's Critique of Religion*. There Strauss clearly states that, although Spinoza "attempts to restore the traditional conception of contemplation," "he restored the dignity of speculation on the basis of modern philosophy or science, of a new understanding of 'nature.'"[221] For this reason, while rejecting the early modern attempt to achieve the mastery over nature ("one cannot think of conquering nature if nature is the same as God"[222]), for Strauss Spinoza "was the first great thinker who attempted a synthesis of pre-modern (classical-medieval) and of modern philosophy."[223] It is worth noting, in this regard, what Strauss observes, in the same context, regarding the practical consequences of that attempt: "Whereas for the classics the life of passions is a life against nature, for Spinoza everything that is is natural. For Spinoza there are no natural ends and hence in particular there is no end natural to man."[224] This being the case, in his account "man's end is not natural, but rational, the result of man's figuring it out, of man's 'forming an idea of man, as of a model of human nature.' "[225] Hence, for Strauss Spinoza "prepares the modern notion of 'ideal' as a work of the human mind or as a human project, as distinguished from an end imposed on man by nature."[226] He thereby shows traits of thought that clearly align with the "cave of modernity,"[227] under the conditions of which the original interpretation of philosophy as *the* right life, or *the* best possible life, seems to be no longer possible.

Conclusion

In the previous chapters, we have tried to show the full extent to which the concept of nature, and of what is by nature, is crucial in Strauss's characteristic effort of revitalizing what he regarded as a genuine type of philosophizing. It is highly significant, in this respect, that he often refers to this type of philosophizing as a form of "natural philosophizing" tout court. We have also emphasized that the scope of Strauss's attempt to recover such a genuine philosophical approach is rather broad, spanning from theoretical knowledge of the whole to the practical questions of the best possible life and natural right understood as a standard.

Another key element of the interpretation proposed in this book is that such a natural approach to philosophizing is indissolubly associated, in Strauss's view, with ancient Greek philosophy. Strauss even states this assumption in plain words when, at the end of "The Intellectual Situation of the Present," he describes the true goal of the Enlightenment, and implicitly his, as the "recovery of philosophizing in its natural difficulty, *of natural philosophizing, that is of Greek philosophy*."[1]

This feature turns Strauss's essentially philosophical approach, at least preliminarily, into a historical effort aimed at reviving a style of philosophizing that, when that effort was carried out by Strauss no less than today, was regarded as irremediably outdated due to its naivety and lack of profoundness (to say nothing of its questionable character from a practical standpoint). This is where Strauss's attempt to recover Greek, natural philosophizing meets the question of the second, unnatural cave we have focused on especially in the last chapter. The reason for this is that in order to recover natural philosophizing, its "conditions of possibility," as it were, must first be regained. These are now no longer available, in Strauss's view, due to the "historical consciousness" that is at the basis not only of historicism but also, ultimately, of positivism (notably in its

Weberian version).² At closer inspection, however, the rise of history over nature can be seen as a consequence of the demotion of the latter that characterizes the biblical approach, whether Christian or more specifically Jewish, with its idea of God's omnipotence and inscrutability.

The task therefore arises to recover such an original concept of nature, along with the natural philosophical approach it enables, by way of a "historical deconstruction [*Destruktion*]" that, unlike Heidegger's, pursues an entirely opposite, anti-historicist objective: not so much the indictment of Western rationalism as a whole, but its rehabilitation, at least of its original, *natural* approach. At this juncture, as we have observed in the introduction, the influence of twentieth-century phenomenology on Strauss, whether Heideggerian or Husserlian or both and aside from his originality in reinterpreting its tenets, emerges as palpable and represents one of the authentic pillars of his whole philosophical undertaking. The outcome of this undertaking—and this appears to be Strauss's own work—is, however, the conceptualization of the recovery of the first, natural cave, i.e., the Platonic cave, as the point of departure for any genuine and natural approach to philosophizing. As we have observed, the reason behind this conceptualization is that, unlike the second, unnatural cave where, due to the overwhelming influence (direct or indirect by way of polemic) of biblical revelation, "prejudices" hold sway, the first, natural cave is characterized by the presence of mere "appearance and opinion." According to Strauss, as has been claimed, particularly, in the introduction, these are the starting point for any meaningful philosophical path because it is only by taking its orientation by speech, and the common opinions the latter starts from, that philosophy, by way of dialectics, can aim not only to divine a standard, but also to meaningfully raise the question thereof. Otherwise, one is left with a type of rationalism that, like Hobbes's, can be compared to a form of (irrationalistic) sophistry and can, therefore, be regarded as "cluelessness," as Krüger puts it in reference to Löwith after significantly praising Strauss's adoption of the Socratic "second sailing."³

This idea of cluelessness is arguably what one remains with if the approach we have now described as Strauss's genuine perspective is rejected as too dogmatic or "metaphysical"⁴ to be truly so. Admittedly, Strauss himself makes every effort to relax the metaphysical connotations of a philosophical approach like his that aims at the recovery of Greek, natural philosophizing. As is often, and correctly, emphasized, his philosophy can be described as a form of "zetetic skepticism," to use a famous expression of his. As Strauss himself, albeit in passing, apparently suggests at least once,[5] however, a sort of "metaphysical eye," to borrow from Berlin, seems to characterize his approach, no matter how weak and skeptical that eye has come to be.

After all, this is implied in the concept of zetetic skepticism as distinct from the more radical (and clueless) skepticism Strauss found at the basis of both history and science—i.e., historicism and positivism—which he once described as the "twin-sisters" of the present age characterized by the denial of a "true and final" account of the whole.[6] In this regard, the fundamental thesis of this book is that a mere elenctic justification of philosophy by means of the refutation of revelation—supposing this is truly possible—would not suffice, in and of itself, to give Strauss's philosophical approach the strength and objective orientation it requires even only to be able to speak, in a meaningful manner, of "fundamental and *permanent* problems." The only way to regard as sufficient such an elenctic justification apparently is to claim that, by refuting biblical revelation, the Greek approach, based on nature and the resulting recognition of the paradigmatic character of what is *by nature* as distinct from what is *by convention* or *will* (even divine will), would be restored to its original rank. Such a refutation of the tradition based on biblical revelation (including, in this perspective, modern philosophy) by way of its "historical deconstruction," however, would ultimately amount to subscribing to what we have noticed regarding the recovery of the first, natural cave, as distinct from the second, unnatural cave, as the only genuine path toward natural philosophizing. It would, therefore, count as an implicit recognition of the soundness of the fundamental thesis put forward in this book.

That Strauss, at any rate, was fully aware of the ontological, not to say metaphysical implications of his philosophical approach is shown by what he observes, in a remarkably clear manner, in response to Kojève's intrinsically historicist objections in the debate that followed the publication of *On Tyranny*:

> The utmost I can hope to have shown in taking issue with Kojève's thesis regarding the relation of tyranny and wisdom is that Xenophon's thesis regarding that grave subject is not only compatible with the idea of philosophy but required by it. This is very little. For the question arises immediately whether the idea of philosophy is not itself in need of legitimation. Philosophy in the strict and classical sense is quest for the eternal order or for the eternal cause or causes of all things.

It presupposes then that there is an eternal and unchangeable order within which History takes place and which is not in any way affected by History. It presupposes, in the words of Kojève, that "Being is essentially immutable in itself and eternally identical with itself."[7]

Although without using the key term *nature* and frankly acknowledging, immediately afterwards, the lack of "self-evidence" of such an ontological presupposition, this quote proves that, even without openly mentioning it, Strauss was well aware of the metaphysical scope of his own approach. We have seen that his attempt to recover Socratic dialectics, with its characteristic refusal to embrace a fully developed cosmological view,[8] can largely be regarded as a way to make those ontologico-metaphysical implications less demanding, and their lack of self-evidence in a time of historicism less destabilizing. Even as a form of Socratic dialectics or zetetic skepticism, however, philosophy as Strauss understands it seems unable to do completely without the presupposition described in the quote above, however weak and residual this may have been made. This is why Strauss regarded as so urgent the refutation, by way of historical deconstruction, of historicism itself so as to regain more favorable conditions for the exercise of philosophy, even and precisely in a dialectical form. These conditions, as we have emphasized, are those one can find in the first, natural cave, which only, being characterized by "appearance and opinion" as distinct from "prejudice," can reenable philosophy in its genuine and "natural" sense.[9] Strauss was of course fully aware of the difficulty and "untimeliness" of such an attempt. As we have seen, he once even described the "more refined historical method" that his attempt required in the age of historicism as "a desperate remedy for a desperate situation."[10] But he also kept believing well beyond his youth, as his "golden sentence" shows, that "the problem inherent in the surface of things, and only in the surface of things, is the heart of things"[11]—a quote where the surface appears to be the phenomenological equivalent of the "appearance and opinion" characteristic of the first, Platonic cave, and thus the starting point for any genuine and "natural" philosophizing.

One may, of course, object that such a "metaphysical" interpretation, however weak and residual, of Strauss's philosophical intention is based on a fundamental misunderstanding of his true perspective, since it supposedly mistakes remarks Strauss meant as exoteric for his real, esoteric views. Does he not claim, after all, that "it would be *unwise*"—meaning, according to this possible interpretation, practically unsound as distinct from theoretically wrong—"to say farewell to reason"?[12] Did Strauss not just want to "awaken a *prejudice*" in favor of the view that "Maimonides' rationalism is the true natural model, the standard to be carefully protected from any distortion, and thus the stumbling-block on which modern rationalism falls"?[13] Even taking into account that at least the latter remark was made by Strauss before his rediscovery of esotericism in the late 1930s, I am ready to acknowledge that this reading remains an open possibility. However, those who claim that this is the right interpretation of Strauss's thought will have to be ready to also admit that he was arguing exoterically not only in most, if not all, of his published writings (which is quite possible given his own description of exotericism), but also in those private communications of his in which he was apparently more frankly and freely discussing the presuppositions of his philosophical approach and his true intention. Perhaps even more relevant than this, the same interpreters will have to be ready to admit that Strauss too—and not only Löwith according to Krüger's definition—was "clueless," due to the fact that a mere "elenctic" justification of philosophy by way of the refutation of revelation, if one disregards its "ontologico-metaphysical" implications, would not in itself restore the conditions for a genuine and "natural" exercise of philosophy as Strauss understands it. Would the problems investigated by such a merely "elenctically" justified philosophy truly be "fundamental and *permanent* problems"?

If the answer to this question is "no," as it seems reasonable to conclude, those who believe that the interpretation proposed in this book mistakes some of Strauss's exoteric remarks for his real, genuine views (however "tentative" and even "desperate" these may have been)[14] will have to side with Stanley Rosen when he claims that philosophy itself, in the end, was Strauss's "noble lie."[15] No matter how consistent and fascinating Rosen's reading may be, I am still inclined to believe that Strauss was genuine when he declared that, deprived of the "way of thought of natural understanding," he was attempting "to *learn* from the ancients" how to recover it and that taking orientation by speech is the only possible path towards the standard, even towards the mere question thereof.[16]

Notes

Preface and Acknowledgments

1. See, for example, PPH, 75, 77–78; SCR, 12, including note 26, and its whole chapter V on Spinoza's "Critique of Orthodoxy"; Leo Strauss, "Farabi's Plato," in *Louis Ginzberg Jubilee Volume* (New York: The American Academy for Jewish Research, 1945), 357.
2. Cf. PAW, 22–37.

Introduction

1. English translation from *The Independent Journal of Philosophy* 5/6 (1988): 184.
2. Cf. Heinrich Meier, *Leo Strauss and the Theologico-Political Problem* (Cambridge: Cambridge University Press, 2006), 65.
3. NRH, 81.
4. SCR, 31. See chapter I below.
5. The whole extant correspondence between Strauss and Löwith can be found in GS3, 607–97. English translations of parts of it, by Susanne Klein and/or George E. Tucker, have been published as Karl Löwith and Leo Strauss, "Correspondence Concerning Modernity," *Independent Journal of Philosophy* 4 (1983): 105–19, and as "Correspondence" in Vol. 5/6 (1988): 177–92, of the same journal.
6. See, in particular, GS3, 666, where Strauss emphasizes that, in his view, Löwith's interpretation of philosophy still remains within the limits set by historicism, without thus being able to overcome it. See also GS3, 614.
7. For some of these matters, see, for example, chapter II, pp. 62–67, below.
8. GS3, 612–14.
9. Karl Löwith, "Kierkegaard und Nietzsche," *Deutsche Vierteljahresschrift für Literaturwissenschaft und Geistesgeschichte* XI (1933): 43–66.

10. GS3, 613. If not otherwise indicated, the English translations of Strauss's letters to Löwith are mine.

11. GS3, 613.

12. GS3, 613.

13. GS3, 613. For other occurrences of the term *integer*, either in German or in Latin, in Strauss's works, see GS3, 238, and FPP, 12. In the latter case, the term is openly associated with Husserl's phenomenological approach: "Husserl is the only one who really sought a new beginning, *integre et ab integro*."

14. GS3, 613.

15. GS3, 613–14. In the expression "positive, konkrete *Anschauung* von Natur," I have translated *Anschauung* with "view," rather than with "intuition," because Strauss himself, writing in English some years later, employs the expression "*natural* view of the world" in a similar context where phenomenology is explicitly mentioned (LIGPP, 136). By underscoring the term *Anschauung* in his letter, Strauss may well have wanted to evoke the same phenomenological approach under which both he and Löwith received a significant part of their philosophical education in the 1920s. In their correspondence, cf., in this regard, GS3, 656, 692. Even the first part of the quote—notably "being 'somehow' aware" of unbiasedness, with the procedure this entails—arguably displays phenomenological connotations (Cf. GS3, 692). Although facilitated by both Husserl (FPP, 17, 35; LIGPP, 137) and Heidegger (GS3, 650; JPCM, 450; LIGPP, 134–35), not to mention Nietzsche (GS3, 648, 688; LIGPP, 137–38), the conclusion of the quote pointing to the recovery of pre-Christian, Greek philosophy seems to be, however, specifically Strauss's, as I argue at the end of the present introduction.

16. GS3, 616.

17. GS3, 616.

18. GS3, 615.

19. GS3, 616.

20. GS3, 616, 646, 650.

21. Cf. GS2, 14, note 2 (PL, 136, note 2).

22. GS3, 620.

23. GS3, 620.

24. GS3, 620–21.

25. GS3, 621.

26. GS3, 650. Cf. GS3, 655, where Strauss repeats his *post scriptum* with some alterations and an interpolation that seems to be motivated by the increasingly tense political situation. For a better understanding of such an interpolation, cf. GN, 360.

27. Löwith and Strauss, "Correspondence," 180 (trans. slightly modified) (GS3, 645–46).

28. Löwith and Strauss, "Correspondence," 184 (trans. slightly modified) (GS3, 650).

29. Löwith and Strauss, "Correspondence," 184 (GS3, 650).
30. Löwith and Strauss, "Correspondence," 181 (GS3, 646).
31. Löwith and Strauss, "Correspondence," 184-85 (GS3, 650).
32. Löwith and Strauss, "Correspondence," 185 (GS3, 650). Cf. GS3, 675.
33. Strauss underscores the difference of his "deconstructive" approach from Heidegger's, with the utmost clarity, in a letter to Löwith of August 15, 1946: "The conception I sketch has nothing *at all* to do with Heidegger, as Heidegger gives merely a refined interpretation of modern historicism, 'anchors' it 'ontologically.' For with Heidegger, 'historicity' has made nature disappear *completely*" (Löwith and Strauss, "Correspondence Concerning Modernity," 107; GS3, 662; cf. GS3, 674, 676-77). For an overall more positive assessment of Heidegger's approach, however, see GS3, 674-77, 684-86, 688, 690. Cf. RCPR, 29; LIGPP, 134-37.
34. GS3, 648. Cf. Neil G. Robertson, *Leo Strauss. An Introduction* (Cambridge: Polity Press, 2021), 43.
35. GS3, 649-50.
36. GS3, 653-54, 659, 664-65.
37. For the use of these terms by Strauss, see, for example, GS3, 229, 232-33. Cf. chapter I below.
38. GS3, 688 (the original letter is in English). Cf. GS3, 661 (*in fine*), 693.
39. CM, 11 (my emphases).
40. GS3, 614.
41. See, for example, note 33 above.
42. Löwith and Strauss, "Correspondence Concerning Modernity," 106 (GS3, 661).
43. NIPPP, 326-67, where Strauss extensively criticizes John Wild, *Plato's Theory of Man. An Introduction to the Realistic Philosophy of Culture* (Cambridge: Harvard University Press, 1946), whose very subtitle must have already perplexed him.
44. GS3, 659. Cf. NIPPP, 330-32.
45. Löwith and Strauss, "Correspondence Concerning Modernity," 107 (GS3, 662). See Carlo Altini, *Una filosofia in esilio. Vita e pensiero di Leo Strauss* (Roma: Carocci, 2021), 243. Cf. GS3, 190 (PPH, 168), where Strauss had already come close to the concept of "natürlicher Verstand" by speaking of "gesunder Menschenverstand" (*common sense* in PPH), which, in agreement with tradition, had understood "human nature" as "given and immutable."
46. Löwith and Strauss, "Correspondence Concerning Modernity," 109-10 (GS3, 664-65).
47. Löwith and Strauss, "Correspondence Concerning Modernity," 111 (GS3, 666).
48. See, in particular, chapters III and VI below.
49. The juxtaposition of the terms *einfach* and *Anschauung* in this sentence may remind one of the "principle of principles" Husserl puts forward in *Ideen*

I, paragraph 24 (Edmund Husserl, *Ideas Pertaining to a Pure Phenomenology and to a Phenomenological Philosophy. First Book: General Introduction to a Pure Phenomenology* [The Hague: Martinus Nijhoff, 1982] 44), where both terms are used in a sense that does not seem to be entirely different. If Strauss's emphasis on being "einfach" in understanding truly has Husserlian connotations (as it seems arguable), it would, however, be important to acknowledge that Strauss relaxes the limits of what is to be regarded as a legitimate source of knowledge compared with Husserl's "egological" perspective.

50. Löwith and Strauss, "Correspondence Concerning Modernity," 112 (GS3, 668).

51. Löwith and Strauss, "Correspondence Concerning Modernity," 109–10 (GS3, 664–65).

52. Löwith and Strauss, "Correspondence Concerning Modernity," 112 (GS3, 668).

53. Löwith and Strauss, "Correspondence Concerning Modernity," 112 (GS3, 668).

54. Plato, *Phaedo*, 99d–100a. Cf. GS3, 426.

55. Cf. FPP, 219.

56. GS3, 7.

57. Aristotle, *Nicomachean Ethics*, 1094b 20; GS3, 159 (PPH, 139).

58. GS3, 110–11, 157–58; cf. 182 (PPH, 92–93, 137–38; cf. 161).

59. GS3, 667, 348–64 (HCR, 94–109).

60. GS2, 9–10, and note 1 (PL, 21–22, and 135, note 1). On this, see also chapter IV, note 37, below.

61. GS3, 159–60 (PPH, 139–40).

62. GS3, 161 (PPH, 141).

63. GS3, 161 (PPH, 141). There should be no need, at this point, to remind the reader of the importance of the concept of *Unbefangenheit* in the previously analyzed correspondence between Strauss and Löwith, where it not by accident surfaces with reference to the search for an unpolemical grasp of nature as a standard.

64. PPH, 142–43 (GS3, 162–63).

65. PPH, 143 (GS3, 163). Cf. NRH, 124. Strauss's view that the "truth is hidden in what men say [*die Wahrheit ist verborgen in dem, was die Menschen sagen*]," besides Socrates's dialectics, may also remind one of Heidegger's concept of *Wahrheit* as *aletheia*. Also in this instance, however, Strauss's approach seems to depart from Heidegger's in that it attempts to remain within the limits set by Platonic rationalism.

66. PPH, 144–45 (GS3, 165, which has a more complex wording: "Die Tugend, die sich nicht in den *Werken* der Menschen findet, findet sich nur in der *Rede*, in der Sprache, in dem in der Sprache verkörperten, 'ahnenden,' 'grundlegenden' Wissen. Die Sprache allein, und nicht das stets zweideutige Handeln, erschliesst

dem Menschen ursprünglich den *Massstab*, dem entsprechend er seine Handlungen ordnen und sich selbst prüfen, sich im Leben und in der Natur orientieren kann, auf völlig ungetrübte, von der Möglichkeit der Verwirklichung im Prinzip völlig unabhängige Weise. Von hier aus ist Platons 'Flucht' in die Sprache und seine damit gegebene Lehre von der Transzendenz der Ideen als aus ihrem Ursprung zu verstehen: nur kraft der Sprache weiss der Mensch von der Transzendenz der Tugend"). Cf. Strauss, "Farabi's Plato," 362, 379, and NIPPP, 355.

67. PPH, 142 (GS3, 162).
68. PPH, 151 (GS3, 172).
69. In OMPT,195–96, Strauss traces back such a characteristically modern interest to the spell the idea of providence still exercises on modern "men" (see Svetozar Minkov, "Hobbes as the Founder of Modern Political Though," TNRH, 158) even after their rejection of biblical revelation. For an explicit reference to the presence of "secularized" elements in Hobbes's thought, see PPH, 27–28 (GS3, 41).
70. PPH, 152 (GS3, 173).
71. PPH, 152 (GS3, 173).
72. PPH, 151 (GS3, 172).
73. PPH, 152, including note 2 (GS3, 173, including note 90).
74. PPH, 152–53 (GS3, 173–74).
75. PPH, 153 (GS3, 174, where the penultimate sentence, "Aber aus dieser Einsicht folgt nicht, dass man 'nicht die Worte, sondern die Sachen' zu betrachten habe [*But it does not follow from this perception that one is to consider 'not the words but the things'*]," continues as follows: "sondern im Gegenteil, dass die in der Zweideutigkeit sich zugleich verhüllende und offenbarende Eindeutigkeit der Rede mittels des Durchsprechens offenbar gemacht werden muss und kann [*but, on the contrary, that the unambiguity of speech that hides and reveals itself, at the same time, in ambiguity must and can be brought to light by talking it through*]"). Cf. NRH, 124.
76. PPH, 153–54, my emphasis (GS3, 175). Cf. NIPPP, 355.
77. PPH, 28, 169 (GS3, 41–42, 191).
78. PPH, 162 (GS3, 183).
79. PPH, 163 (GS3, 185).
80. PPH, 163, including note 2 (GS3, 185, including note 119), where Strauss cites Jacob Klein, "Die griechische Logistik und die Entstehung der Algebra," *Quellen und Studien zur Geschichte der Mathematik, Astronomie und Physik*, Abteilung B, III, 66 (where, however, despite its overall phenomenological tone, there is no explicit mention of Husserl). It is worth emphasizing that this "Husserlian" meaning of *natural*, if our indirect attribution is correct, is considered by Strauss to be only qualifiedly valid, as something that may be called natural "with a certain justification" only. This qualification seems to confirm that the meaning par excellence of nature and natural for Strauss is the essentialist one represented by the Platonic concept of idea as he interprets it, i.e., as a synonym

for "fundamental and eternal problem" (WPP, 39). It is also worth underscoring that Strauss's attitude towards the "natural valuations" or common opinions, while being as "paradoxical" as Husserl's "epoché," appears to follow more Socrates's dialectics than twentieth-century phenomenology as such. Cf. LIGPP, 136; NRH, 123–24; and NIPPP, 342–43.

81. PPH, 163–64 (GS3, 185). Regarding the idea of "what is known to all but not understood," cf. LIGPP, 136.

82. PPH, 164 (GS3, 185).

83. PPH, 164 (GS3, 185).

84. PPH, 164 (GS3, 185–86). It is worth noting, at this juncture, that this comparison of Plato's and Hobbes's approaches, with their opposite stance toward the orientation by "natural morals" and speech, may well reflect the kernel of Strauss's own "change of *orientation*" (SCR, 31, my emphasis). Cf., in this regard, his 1931 "Foreword to a Planned book on Hobbes," in HCR, 141 (GS3, 205), with his 1932 "Notes on Carl Schmitt, *The Concept of the Political*," in Heinrich Meier, *Carl Schmitt and Leo Strauss. The Hidden Dialogue* (Chicago: University of Chicago Press, 1995), 118–19 (GS3, 237–38). In the first context Strauss still accepts Hobbes's polemical understanding of the origin of legal order: "Only in view of *unrest* [Unruhe], only *in* unrest, if not indeed in revolts [*Unruhen*] can that understanding of man be gained from which the right created for the satisfaction of man [*das zur Befriedung des Menschen geschaffene Recht*] can be understood: only in this way can it be radically understood that as well as how man needs right; only in this way is *philosophic* understanding of right possible. We thereby approach the view of *Hobbes*, who, 'in relatively *unpeaceful* times [*in relativ* unruhigen *Zeiten*],' in times of civil war, *pacis studio* . . . , and not for the sake of the pure knowledge [*reine Erkenntnis*] of an already present right, carried out a philosophic founding [*Begründung*] of right." In the second context, on the contrary, by criticizing Schmitt's entanglement in the horizon set by liberalism and its founder Hobbes, he begins to embrace a more detached view according to which Schmitt's "entanglement [*Verstrickung*] is no accidental failure but the necessary result of the principle that 'all concepts of the spiritual sphere . . . are to be understood only in terms of concrete political existence' . . . , and that 'all political concepts, ideas, and words' have 'a *polemical* meaning.' *In concreto* Schmitt violates this principle, which itself is entirely bound to liberal presuppositions, by opposing his unpolemical concept of the state of nature to Hobbes's polemical concept of the state of nature; and he fundamentally rejects this principle by expecting to gain the order of human things [*die Ordnung der menschlichen Dinge*] from a '*pure and whole* knowledge [integres *Wissen*].' For a pure and whole knowledge is never, unless by accident, polemical; and a pure and whole knowledge cannot be gained 'from concrete political existence,' from the situation of the age, but only by means of a return to the origin, to 'undamaged, noncorrupt nature [*unversehrte, nicht korrupte Natur*].'" Now, as we have underscored in the body of the text, this "return to the origin [*Rückgang auf den Ursprung*]" is

precisely what in PPH, 164 (GS3, 185) distinguishes Plato's approach from Hobbes's: "Plato *retraces* natural morals and the orientation provided by them *to their origin* [*Platon geht von der natürlichen Moral, von der mit ihr gegebenen Orientierung auf ihren Ursprung zurück*]" (my emphasis). It is also worth reiterating that Strauss traces that origin back to nature understood as idea or essence a few pages before (PPH, 153–54; GS3, 174), thereby coherently following in the wake of the conclusive remarks of his "Notes on Carl Schmitt, *The Concept of the Political*." On this, see chapters I and IV below. Cf. GS3, 394.

85. Cf. GS3, 186 (PPH, 164–65), with GS3, 620.
86. PPH, 164 (GS3, 186).
87. PPH, 164 (GS3, 186). Cf. PL, 135–36, note 2 (GS2, 13–14, note 2).
88. PPH, 164–65 (GS3, 186). As the German original in square brackets shows, note that in this quotation "controversial position" translates the more explicit "polemische [*polemical*] Position."
89. PPH, 165 (GS3, 187).
90. PPH, 165 (GS3, 187).
91. PPH, 165 (GS3, 187). Strauss's prudence in the given context, however significant, seems to concern the view that Hobbes's denial of the existence of a natural standard is "only" the result of his relinquishment of orientation by speech, and not that the latter is a cause of the former. This emerges with greater clarity in the full quote: "That this denial is *only* the result of relinquishing orientation by speech can here only be asserted [*Dass diese Leugnung* nur *die Folge des Verzichtes auf die Orientierung an der Rede ist, kann an dieser Stelle nur behauptet werden*]" (my emphasis).
92. For the attribution of the introduction to Strauss only, see SPPP, 255, under "1963."
93. Homer, *Odyssey*, X, 302–06.
94. HPP, 2.
95. HPP, 2.
96. HPP, 3. Cf. NRH, 123.
97. HPP, 3.
98. HPP, 3.
99. HPP, 3.
100. HPP, 4. Cf. NRH, 120.
101. HPP, 4.
102. HPP, 4.
103. See, in particular, Leo Strauss, "The Spirit of Sparta or the Taste of Xenophon," *Social Research* VI, 4 (November 1939): 502–36, and GS3, 544–87. Cf. GS3, xxxiii; Laurence Lampert, *The Enduring Importance of Leo Strauss* (Chicago: University of Chicago Press, 2013), 7–31; and Alberto Ghibellini, *Al di là della politica. Filosofia e retorica in Leo Strauss* (Genova: Genova University Press, 2012), 23–71.

104. HPP, 4, 5. Cf. NRH, 121–22; Strauss, "Farabi's Plato," 366, 382–84; RCPR, 132–33, 141–42; RR, 146; WPP, 92–94.

105. HPP, 4.

106. HPP, 4–5. Cf. NRH, 124, and NIPPP, 343.

107. PPH, 143 and 163 (GS3, 163 and 185) respectively.

108. PPH, 163 (GS3, 185), my emphasis.

109. PPH, 165 (GS3, 187).

110. PPH, 164 (GS3, 185).

111. PPH, 145 (GS3, 165). See also PPH, 144 (GS3, 164–65).

112. HPP, 5.

113. HPP, 5. Cf. NRH, 122–23, where Strauss, among other things, equates "the nature of a thing" with "its What, its 'shape' or 'form' or 'character,' as distinguished in particular from that out of which it has come into being," to shortly afterwards identify "that to which the question 'What is?' points" with "the *eidos* of a thing, the shape or form or character or 'idea' of a thing."

114. Cf. PPH, 163 (GS3, 185); LIGPP, 136; NIPPP, 343, 355.

115. See, for example, RCPR, 132–33, 142–43; OT, 277.

116. Cf. NRH, 123.

117. Cf. PPH, 153 (GS3, 174).

118. HPP, 7–63.

119. HPP, 26–27. Cf. HPP, 5, and PPH, 143–45 (GS3, 163–65).

120. HPP, 27.

121. HPP, 27.

122. HPP, 27. Cf. Robertson, *Leo Strauss*, 117.

123. HPP, 28. Cf. Strauss, "Farabi's Plato," 364, 371–72, 375, 376, 390–91.

124. HPP, 27. Cf. NIPPP, 355.

125. Cf. HPP, 27, with HPP, 5.

126. HPP, 28.

127. HPP, 28.

128. TM, 13 (my emphasis). Cf. Seth Bernadete, "Leo Strauss's *The City and Man*," *Political Science Reviewer* 8 (1978): 1. On the phenomenological inspiration of this sentence, see Stanley Rosen, "Leo Strauss and the Problem of the Modern," in Steven B. Smith (ed.), *The Cambridge Companion to Leo Strauss* (Cambridge: Cambridge University Press, 2009), 121–22; Daniel Doneson, "Beginning at the Beginning. On the Starting Point of Reflection," in Samuel Fleischacker (ed.), *Heidegger's Jewish Followers. Essays on Arendt, Strauss, Jonas, and Levinas* (Pittsburgh: Duquesne University Press, 2008), 109; and Pierpaolo Ciccarelli, *Leo Strauss tra Husserl e Heidegger* (Pisa: ETS, 2018), 105, including note 28.

129. See chapter III below.

130. PPH, 153 (GS3, 174). Cf. NRH, 123–24.

131. NRH, 123–24. Similarly to what has been observed in note 80 above, in this quote it is worth noticing not only its phenomenological traits (phenomena,

eidos, awareness), but also its conclusion, which heads (back) towards Socratic dialectics. Regarding the key role of "universal doubt" in the genesis, by means of a polemic against the concept of divine omnipotence, of modernity, cf. HCR, 95–99 (GS3, 348–64).

132. See, for example, Strauss, "Farabi's Plato," 365–66, 370, 373, 378, 381, 386, 388; RR, 147. Cf. NIPPP, 342, including note 15.

133. SCR, 29 (cf. PL, 29, 33–34); RR, 148–51, 153. Cf. Meier, *Leo Strauss and the Theologico-Political Problem*, 3–28. On this matter, allow me to refer to Alberto Ghibellini, "Leo Strauss, Gershom Scholem, and the Reason-Revelation Problem," *Interpretation. A Journal of Political Philosophy* XL, no. 1 (2013): 57–78.

134. Robertson correctly insists on the importance of these problems (see, for example, Robertson, *Leo Strauss*, 12, 49, 51, 95, 108, 117, 122, 187, 197). Coherently with his interpretation of Strauss as a radically anti-metaphysical thinker, however, he sometimes forgets to underscore their "permanent" character in Strauss's account (Robertson, *Leo Strauss*, 95). For a milder, more positive stance of Strauss towards metaphysics, see RCPR, 38. Cf. OT, 212; NIPPP, 338–39.

135. Meier, *Leo Strauss and the Theologico-Political Problem*, 11. Cf. Christopher Bruell, "The Question of Nature and the Thought of Leo Strauss," *Klēsis. Revue philosophique*, 19 (2011): 95–96.

136. GS2, 386–87. Cf. 455–56. On this, see chapters IV and VI below.

137. See chapter V below.

138. GS3, 664–65. Cf. GS3, 412–13. On this, see chapter III below.

139. See chapter V below.

140. See GS2, 22 (PL, 33–34), where the emphasis is put on God's omnipotent (*allmächtig*) character, and the resulting possibility of miracles, as an original polemical (defensive) target of modern natural science and its "'unique' 'world-construction' [*einmalige*' *'Weltdeutung*']." Cf., however, GS3, 361–64 (HCR, 107–9), where Strauss explains that Descartes's hypothesis of a *Deus deceptor*, which ultimately rests on God's omnipotence, is accepted by Hobbes only qualifiedly, that is, as a "possible symbolization of the full incomprehensibility of God [*mögliche Symbolisierung der völligen Unbegreifbarkeit Gottes*]," which, however, makes the world "in itself," created by him, "incomprehensible" as well. In either case, science must become subjectivistic (whether according to phenomenalism or artificialism) to "polemically" confront the challenge of the biblical account. On this, see also NIPPP, 338–39.

141. PL, 136 (GS2, 14, note 2).

142. For a resolute emphasis on the influence of phenomenology on Strauss, see the already mentioned books by Robertson and Ciccarelli, as well as Rodrigo Chacon, "Strauss and Husserl," *Idealistic Studies* vol. 44 (2014): 281–96. On the first two, cf. Alberto Ghibellini, "Tre studi su Leo Strauss," *Il Politico* LXXXVII, no. 1 (2022): 133–59.

143. LIGPP, 137. See note 52 on page 139 of the same essay for the explanation of the expression "the sake [i.e., the 'task or subject matter'] of *natural* men."
144. FPP, 12; GS3, 613, 238. Cf. Ciccarelli, *Leo Strauss tra Husserl e Heidegger*, 16.
145. Edmund Husserl, "Die natürliche Einstellung und der 'natürliche Weltbegriff,'" in *Grundprobleme der Phänomenologie 1910/11* (The Hague: Martinus Nijhoff, 1977), 15–42.
146. FPP, 35. Cf. JPCM, 460–61.
147. LIGPP, 134, 137.
148. LIGPP, 135. See also GS3, 108–9 (including note 37), 421–22, and NIPPP, 329–30.
149. Cf. GS3, xix, and Ciccarelli, *Leo Strauss tra Husserl e Heidegger*, 20.
150. GS3, 662. See note 33 above.
151. PAW, 154. Cf. NIPPP, 332.
152. Cf. SPPP, 174, and Strauss, "Farabi's Plato," 377.
153. As far as the influence on Strauss of Heidegger's *Destruktion* is concerned, a pattern for such an attempt can be found in Meier, *Leo Strauss and the Theologico-Political Problem*, 62–64.

Chapter I

1. Leo Strauss, "Anmerkungen zu Carl Schmitt, *Der Begriff des Politischen*" (1932), in GS3, 217–42. There are two available English translations: "Comments on *Der Begriff des Politischen* by Carl Schmitt," by Elsa M. Sinclair, in Leo Strauss, *Spinoza's Critique of Religion* (New York: Schocken Books, 1965), 331–53, and "Notes on Carl Schmitt, *The Concept of the Political*," by J. Harvey Lomax, in Meier, *Carl Schmitt and Leo Strauss. The Hidden Dialogue*, 89–119. In this chapter, and in the continuation of the present book, I have mainly made use of this latter, referring to it as Strauss's "Notes."
2. See Nasser Behnegar, "Carl Schmitt and Strauss's Return to Premodern Philosophy," in R, 127, note 1; SCR, 31.
3. NRH, 81. Cf. JPCM, 111, and GS3, 696.
4. PAW, 155–56. Leo Strauss, "Progress or Return?" in JPCM, 110–11.
5. CM, 11.
6. Strauss, "Notes," 95, 97–98. Cf. SPPP, 147–48.
7. Strauss, "Notes," 92.
8. Strauss, "Notes," 94, 96–97.
9. Strauss, "Notes," 97.
10. Strauss, "Notes," 97.
11. Strauss, "Notes," 104. See also Strauss's letter to Schmitt on September 4, 1932, in Meier, *Carl Schmitt and Leo Strauss*, 125, and Carl Schmitt, *The Concept*

of the Political (Chicago: University of Chicago Press, 2007), 35 ff., 65 ff., 78. Pierpaolo Ciccarelli ("L'écriture réticente, condition de possibilité de la philosophie," in *Archives de Philosophie*, 2023/2, Tome 86: 108) questions my association of Schmitt's concept of destiny with what, in Strauss's terms, is "given by nature." Such association is, however, ultimately Strauss's (cf. his "Notes," 104–5, as well as the just mentioned letter).

12. Strauss, "Notes," 97. See also Leo Strauss, "What Is Liberal Education?" in LAM, 3; cf. CM, 2; SCR, 70–71, 90; and NIPPP, 355.

13. Strauss, "Notes," 97 (Cf. Strauss, *Spinoza's Critique of Religion*, 335, where "Anweisungen" is translated as "indications" rather than "orders"). David Janssens ("A Change of Orientation: Leo Strauss's 'Comments' on Carl Schmitt Revisited," *Interpretation: A Journal of Political Philosophy*, 33, 1, 2005: 96) aptly highlights this passage.

14. The concept of measure or standard (*Massstab*) is recurrent in Strauss's writings and correspondence from the early 1930s. See, for example, his letters to Krüger in GS3, 421, 440, 446, as well as chapters III and IV below. Cf. GS3, 163.

15. On culture interpreted as *cultura animi* see the fit remarks by David Janssens in *Between Athens and Jerusalem. Philosophy, Prophecy and Politics in Leo Strauss's Early Thought* (Albany, NY: State University of New York Press, 2008), 137–38.

16. Strauss, "Notes," 97.

17. Strauss, "Notes," 97–98.

18. Strauss, "Notes," 98. In "Fear, Technology, and the Revival of Hobbes in Weimar and National Socialist Germany" (*Political Theory* 22, no. 4 [November 1994]: 619–52), John P. McCormick overlooks this fundamental distinction. Consequently, he misinterprets Strauss as a follower of Hobbes who aims to turn natural disorder into the order of the state by relying on the passion of fear. This prevents McCormick from discerning Strauss's philosophical attempt to revitalize the question of nature as "exemplary order," and therewith from recognizing the ultimate basis of Strauss's disagreement not only with Hobbes, but also with Schmitt.

19. Strauss, "Notes," 98. Cf. NIPPP, 355.

20. Strauss, "Notes," 99–101. In "Hobbes schmittiano o Schmitt hobbesiano? Sul 'cambio di orientamento' nelle 'Note a Carl Schmitt' di Leo Strauss" (*Bollettino telematico di filosofia politica*, http://archiviomarini.sp.unipi.it/737/, accessed May 30, 2018), Ciccarelli correctly insists on this point. However, I am not convinced by his claim that Strauss's "change of orientation" is unconnected with the concept of "culture of nature" because of Strauss's use of this expression in *Spinoza's Critique of Religion* (see note 12 above). For the concept of "culture of nature," understood as "careful nurture of nature [*sorgfältige Pflege der Natur*]" that rests on a view of nature as "exemplary order [*vorbildliche Ordnung*]," cannot be found in that book, wherein the emphasis, in this respect, is on man's own effort to improve an imperfect original condition. Nor am I persuaded by Ciccarelli's

attempt ("L'écriture réticente, condition de possibilité de la philosophie," 108–10) to see the concept of "exemplary order [*vorbildliche Ordnung*]," against my reading, as implying a view of nature as "authority" as distinct from a mere "standard" (cf. NRH, 91–92, which Ciccarelli himself refers to). For the meaning of *Vorbild* ultimately amounts to the latter.

21. Strauss, "Notes," 98.

22. Thomas Hobbes, *De Cive*, ed. Richard Tuck and Michael Silverthorne (Cambridge: Cambridge University Press, 1998), 21–22; Aristotle, *Politics*, 1253a 2–3; cf. *Nicomachean Ethics*, 1097b 11.

23. Strauss, "Notes," 101–2. See also NRH, 184, for a critical appraisal of Hobbes's view of the state of nature that implicitly underscores the Christian roots of his understanding. Hobbes is in fact the first to identify the natural life of man with a "state of nature" that was alien to previous political philosophy, being instead originally at home in Christian theology that saw it as opposed to the "state of grace." "Hobbes . . . replaced the state of grace by the state of civil society." By doing so, on one hand he rejected the classical view according to which the natural life is the life of human fulfillment (i.e., the life in which the natural end of man is fully accomplished, which, according to the classics, could only happen within civil society); on the other hand, he kept a "polemical" stance, of Christian origin, towards the state of nature, seen as intrinsically defective and in need of being superseded. However, by denying not only a natural end of man, but also sin, Hobbes—no matter how Christian still in his framework—originated a new view, based on the concept of natural right interpreted as an absolute subjective claim. Cf. SPPP, 143.

24. Strauss, "Notes," 102, note 2.

25. In saying *primarily*, I follow Strauss, who notices that Schmitt implicitly accepts Hobbes's view of the conflictual individual relationships when he stresses the role of protection to obtain obligation: *protego ergo obligo*. See Schmitt, *The Concept of the Political*, 52, and Strauss, "Notes," 99–100.

26. Strauss, "Notes," 98, 103–4.

27. Strauss, "Notes," 99. See also his letter to Schmitt in Meier, *Carl Schmitt and Leo Strauss*, 125. On the relationship between natural and extreme, cf. PL, 25, 135–36, note 2. See also Susan Shell, "Taking Evil Seriously: Schmitt's 'Concept of the Political' and Strauss's 'True Politics,'" in Kenneth L. Deutsch, Walter Nicgorski, eds., *Leo Strauss. Political Philosopher and Jewish Thinker* (Lanham: Rowman & Littlefield, 1994), 187–88.

28. Strauss, "Notes," 103, 104. Cf. WPP, 26–27.

29. Strauss, "Notes," 115, 119. See introduction, note 84, above. Heinrich Meier (*Carl Schmitt and Leo Strauss*, 5–6) aptly underscores the polemical character of Schmitt's approach in Strauss's account. Commenting on the antithesis between pure and whole knowledge and polemical stance, however, Meier overlooks nature and insists on a "knowledge" that "can be achieved only by means of pure and whole

questioning" (my emphasis). Meier, in other words, replaces "undamaged, noncorrupt *nature*" with "pure and whole *questioning*," a "radical questioning" that "requires rigorously consistent thought," which, in its turn, is characterized by "*resoluteness* [*Entschiedenheit*]" (my emphasis; for the original German see Heinrich Meier, *Carl Schmitt, Leo Strauss und "Der Begriff des Politischen*," [Dritte Auflage, Stuttgart-Weimar: J. B. Metzler, 2013], 13). But is "undamaged, noncorrupt nature" not the authentic presupposition of that questioning according to Strauss? By omitting reference to nature, as well as emphasizing "resoluteness," Meier appears to be, in Strauss's own terms, still under the influence of the "philosophy of culture," which forgets nature altogether and, ultimately, relies on "decision" or "will" as its foundation.

30. Strauss, "Notes," 117.

31. Strauss, "Notes," 116.

32. Strauss, "Notes," 109. See also SCR, 227–28.

33. See PPH, 13–15, 27–28, 169–70; cf. Michael Oakeshott, "Dr. Leo Strauss on Hobbes" (1937), in *Hobbes on Civil Association* (Indianapolis: Liberty Fund, 2000), 146–47.

34. Cf. HCR, 73–74.

35. Strauss, "Notes," 109–10, 116, 103. See note 23 above.

36. Strauss, "Notes," 110–11. See Meier, *Carl Schmitt and Leo Strauss*, 56–58, who contests Strauss's reading in this instance on the basis of his own interpretation of Schmitt and of the reformulation of the debated point in the 1933 edition of the *Concept of the Political*. It seems, however, likewise possible to maintain that Schmitt emended the text in light of Strauss's critique, which revealed to Schmitt himself its 1932 version's inconsistencies.

37. Strauss, "Notes," 116.

38. Strauss, "Notes," 110.

39. Strauss, "Notes," 109–10. Behnegar ("Carl Schmitt and Strauss's Return to Premodern Philosophy," 126–27) aptly underscores this important point speaking, with Strauss, of "human evil as moral depravity [*Schlechtigkeit*]" (Strauss, *Spinoza's Critique of Religion*, 345). The question arises, however, as to how to interpret such a *Schlechtigkeit*. On this, see the continuation of this chapter and cf. Strauss, "Notes," 115–16 (paragraph 30), as well as GS2, 451 (R, 245).

40. GN, 360. See, however, Meier, *Carl Schmitt and Leo Strauss*, 65, and Carlo Galli, *Janus's Gaze. Essays on Carl Schmitt* (Durham and London: Duke University Press, 2015), 65.

41. Cf. GN, 358.

42. Schmitt, *The Concept of the Political*, 36; Strauss, "Notes," 105.

43. Schmitt, *The Concept of the Political*, 36.

44. Strauss, "Notes," 105.

45. Schmitt, *The Concept of the Political*, 48, quoted by Strauss in "Notes," 105. See Svetozar Y. Minkov, *Leo Strauss on Science* (Albany, NY: State University of New York Press, 2016), 21.

46. Despite his positive stance towards Machiavelli (Schmitt, *The Concept of the Political*, 61, 65–66; cf. Galli, *Janus's Gaze*, 58–77), Schmitt does not acknowledge the fact that the "frauds" of liberalism may be, on the practical level, truly effective tools that, by hiding their "political" features, make themselves more effective. This seems to be implied in the idea of a final war on war, which brings to its highest possible level the polarization between friends and enemies, so that the distinction between enemies and foes becomes almost immaterial. The same kind of polarization characterizes Schmitt's final battle between the "spirit of technicity" and "the opposite spirit and faith which, as it seems, still has no name" (Strauss, "Notes," 118). As Strauss puts it, the positions embodied by these spirits are to be considered, precisely according to Schmitt's innermost view, as "mortal enemies [*Todfeinde*]" (Strauss, "Notes," 117–18; see Meier, *Carl Schmitt and Leo Strauss*, 81–82). It might therefore be that Elsa M. Sinclair's choice, evidently endorsed by Strauss himself, to render *Feind* with foe was not a lapse (see George Schwab's introduction to Schmitt, *The Concept of the Political*, 6, note 9), but a deliberate choice.

47. Strauss, "Notes," 107.

48. Strauss, "Notes," 106.

49. Strauss, "Notes," 107.

50. Strauss, "Notes," 116.

51. Strauss, "Notes," 108–9. See also Meier, *Carl Schmitt and Leo Strauss*, 125.

52. Strauss, "Notes," 109. See Minkov, *Leo Strauss on Science*, 22.

53. Strauss, "Notes," 109.

54. Strauss, "Notes," 111 (GS3, 232), translation slightly modified.

55. Carl Schmitt, *Political Theology. Four Chapters on the Concept of Sovereignty* (Chicago: University of Chicago Press, 2005). Strauss refers to its original German version, published in 1922, in "Notes," 110 and 117.

56. Strauss, "Notes," 110.

57. PPH, 14. Cf. GS3, 27.

58. Strauss, "Notes," 97–98.

59. On this, see Meier (*Carl Schmitt and Leo Strauss*, 72–87) who, however, tends to downplay the role performed by Strauss in revealing, to Schmitt himself, this latter's most profound intention. This, after all, seems to be the meaning of Schmitt's reported utterance according to which Strauss, in his "Notes," had "x-rayed [*durchleuchtet*]" him as "nobody else" had done (Meier, *Carl Schmitt and Leo Strauss*, xvii). He who x-rays someone sees things that the x-rayed couldn't see before. This interpretation is also confirmed by the fact that in 1934 Strauss wrote to Jacob Klein: "Have you seen Carl Schmitt's last pamphlet [*Über die drei Arten des rechtswissenschaftlichen Denkens*]? He is now against the decisionism of Hobbes and for 'thinking in terms of order [*Ordnungsdenken*]' on the basis of the arguments in my review, which of course he does not cite" (Meier, *Carl Schmitt and Leo Strauss*, 130). This means that for Strauss too, in the 1932 edition

of *The Concept of the Political*, Schmitt had embraced, however inconsistently, a kind of Hobbesian decisionism, which only thanks to Strauss's x-ray review he was later able to acknowledge and supersede. Cf. Meier, *Carl Schmitt and Leo Strauss*, 61, note 64.

60. Strauss, "Notes," 112; cf. HCR, 141.

61. Strauss, "Notes," 117.

62. Strauss, "Notes," 115, 118. This purely "negative" destructive function of the affirmation of the political, as well as the explicit reference to the "cultural or social nothing" and "seriousness," aligns Schmitt with the German nihilists whom, almost a decade later, Strauss would evocatively describe in his lecture *German Nihilism* (Schmitt is expressly named in GN, 362. See also GN, 360 and 370). As we shall see, this must be kept in mind also when it comes to interpreting Strauss's reference, in the penultimate paragraph of his "Notes," to the view opposed to "the spirit of technicity," which "as it seems, still has no name" (Strauss, "Notes," 118). Cf. chapter IV below.

63. Strauss, "Notes," 116–17.

64. Strauss, "Notes," 117. Cf. LIGPP, 127–28.

65. Strauss, "Notes," 113.

66. Schmitt, *The Concept of the Political*, 90–91, quoted in Strauss, "Notes," 114.

67. Strauss, "Notes," 114.

68. Strauss, "Notes," 97–98.

69. See Behnegar, "Carl Schmitt and Strauss's Return to Premodern Philosophy," 116 and 128, note 11.

70. Strauss, "Notes," 114. Cf. GS3, 164 (including note 50); PPH, 143 (including note 5).

71. Strauss, "Notes," 114–15. In this quote, Strauss's "essentialist" perspective as to what "being a man" entails should not pass unnoticed.

72. GS3, 399. Krüger's whole letter is unfortunately not extant, but his questions are reported by Strauss in his response on August 19, 1932. On the Strauss-Krüger correspondence, see Susan Meld Shell, ed., *The Strauss-Krüger Correspondence. Returning to Plato through Kant* (New York: Palgrave-MacMillan, 2018). All translations of the correspondence provided in the present book are from this volume, sometimes slightly modified.

73. GS3, 399. Regarding "giving and receiving reason," see Plato, *The Statesman*, 286a 4–5; cf. Plato, *Republic*, 531e.

74. Compared to his more mature position at the end of the "change of orientation," the only element that induces us to speak of "philosophical," and not also of "classical" perspective, is Strauss's reference to probity (*Redlichkeit*) as an equivalent of the "more honest ancient terms." In that respect, his view will change as early as 1935: see PL, 37–38, 137–38 note 13. Cf. SCR, 29–30, and see Jacob Klein's remark in GS3, 539.

75. GS3, 399. Cf. HCR, 140–41. See introduction, note 84, above.

76. Cf. PL, 34; OT, 212; SCR, 29. On the meaning of nature and its relation to reason in Strauss's view, see the introduction to the present volume. For a reading that questions my view of the centrality of nature as exemplary order in Strauss's account, see Isabel Rollandi, "Claude Lafort and Leo Strauss. On a Philosophical Discourse," in Jeffrey A. Bernstein, Jade L. Schiff (eds.), *Leo Strauss and Contemporary Thought. Reading Strauss outside the Lines* (Albany, NY: State University of New York Press, 2021), 95–96, including note 109 on page 107. To this criticism, I however reply: how can one consistently speak of philosophers as "exemplary natures" revealing "an exemplary order" and of "recovery of the permanent problems," as Rollandi herself does, without at least implying the notion of a natural standard? Cf. NRH, vii, 134–35.

77. Strauss, "Notes," 118.

78. Strauss, "Notes," 118.

79. The first interpretation is put forward in Janssens, *Between Athens and Jerusalem*, 145. The second is intimated in Heinrich Meier, *The Lesson of Carl Schmitt: Four Chapters on the Distinction between Political Theology and Political Philosophy* (Chicago: University of Chicago Press, 1998), 148–49, and seems to be confirmed through a comparison of Strauss, "Notes," 111–13, 115, with GN, 362–64. See in particular the similarities between "cultural and social nothing" (Strauss, "Notes," 115) and "fertile nothing" (GN, 363), as well as the definition of Hitler as the "contemptible *tool* of 'History'" and the mention of Schmitt among the "professors and writers who knowingly or ignorantly paved the way for Hitler" in GN, 363 and 362 respectively.

80. See GN, 371. Cf. HCR, 141.

81. Meier, *Carl Schmitt and Leo Strauss*, 81–83.

82. Strauss, "Notes," 119.

83. GS3, 406.

84. Strauss, "Notes," 98. Regarding Strauss's interpretation of nature as a standard, and of classic natural right in particular (an interpretation that leads to the idea of a hierarchy of ends and of the ways of life, but not to an objective moral law), see chapters II and VI below. Cf. PAW, 11, and note 23 above.

85. "You may drive nature out with a pitchfork, but she will keep coming back," Horace, *Epistle*, I, 10, 24, quoted in NRH, 202, and GS3, 663. Cf. SPPP, 183.

86. GS3, 524. The essay by Schmitt that Strauss is referring to by using the expression "Ordnungsdenken" is, as said, *Über die drei Arten des rechtswissenschaftlichen Denkens* (Hamburg: Hanseatische Verlagsanstalt, 1934). Cf. Meier, *Carl Schmitt and Leo Strauss*, 130.

87. See Catherine H. Zuckert, "Leo Strauss: Fascist, Authoritarian, Imperialist?," *Krakowskie Studia Międzynarodowe*, no. 2 (2009): 291.

88. Strauss, "Notes," 119 (my emphasis). See introduction, note 84, above.

89. Strauss, "Notes," 106 (my emphasis).

90. GS3, 421. Cf. GS3, 71–75, 260; Strauss, "Preface," in SCR, 12, 24–25.
91. On this theme, see chapter III below.
92. GS3, 405. Cf. Strauss, "Preface," in SCR, 12, 24–25.

Chapter II

1. On these, see Peter Minowitz, *Straussophobia. Defending Leo Strauss and Straussians against Shadia Drury and Other Accusers* (Lanham, MD: Rowman & Littlefield Publishers, 2009); Catherine H. Zuckert and Michael Zuckert, *The Truth about Leo Strauss. Political Philosophy and American Democracy* (Chicago: University of Chicago Press, 2006), 1–24, 115–54.

2. See Laurence Lampert, *The Enduring Importance of Leo Strauss* (Chicago: University of Chicago Press, 2013). Lampert links Strauss's "enduring importance" to his "rediscovery" of philosophical exotericism in particular. This allows him to downplay the relevance of Strauss's famous contrast between ancients and moderns and to underscore the influence of Nietzsche on his mature philosophical perspective as well. As has already become clear in the previous chapters, and as I will explain in greater details in the following ones, no matter how crucial Strauss's rediscovery of exotericism, I deem both this demotion and promotion not to be wholly adequate. Hence, I here take "enduring importance" in a broader sense, namely, as a way to describe Strauss's stature among the thinkers of the twentieth century more in general. For a periodically updated bibliography of the by now considerable number of books on his thought, let me refer the reader, for the sake of brevity, to https://leostrausscenter.uchicago.edu/on-strausss-thought/. With regard to the critical literature in Italian, see Marco Menon, "Leo Strauss in Italy: The 'Three Waves' of Italian Strauss Studies," *Interpretation. A Journal of Political Philosophy* 46, no. 2 (Spring 2020): 187–227; Pierpaolo Ciccarelli, "Réception italienne de Leo Strauss. De la méfiance à la reconnaissance," *Archives de Philosophie*, 2023/2 (Tome 86): i–vii; as well as Raimondo Cubeddu, "Strauss in Italia," *Il Politico* LXXI, no. I (2006): 46–85.

3. See, for example, Eugene R. Sheppard, *Leo Strauss and the Politics of Exile* (Lebanon, NH: Brandeis University Press, 2006); Anne Norton, *Leo Strauss and the Politics of American Empire* (New Haven: Yale University Press, 2004); Nicholas Xenos, *Cloaked in Virtue: Unveiling Leo Strauss and the Rhetoric of American Foreign Policy* (New York: Routledge, 2008); Shadia B. Drury, *The Political Ideas of Leo Strauss* (New York: Palgrave Macmillan, 2005).

4. See, for example, Allan Bloom, "Foreword," in LAM, v–vi; Thomas L. Pangle, *Leo Strauss. An Introduction to His Thought and Intellectual Legacy* (Baltimore, MD: The Johns Hopkins University Press, 2006); Steven Smith, *Reading Leo Strauss. Politics, Philosophy, Judaism* (Chicago: University of Chicago Press, 2006), 105; Zuckert and Zuckert, *The Truth about Leo Strauss*, 78.

5. See Pangle, *Leo Strauss*, 78, 96–98. Cf. Harvey C. Mansfield and Delba Winthrop, "Editors' Introduction," in Alexis de Tocqueville, *Democracy in America* (Chicago: University of Chicago Press), xvii–lxxxvi.

6. RCPR, 29; cf. LIGPP, 131–38.

7. LAM, 26–64. On Strauss's interpretation of the different kinds of liberalism, see Giovanni Giorgini, "Strauss's Liberalisms," paper presented at the conference "Leo Strauss, Religione e Liberalismo," Rome, May 13–14, 2011, unpublished. By the same author, see also *Liberalismi eretici* (Trieste: Edizioni Goliardiche, 1999), 19–98.

8. Benjamin Constant, "The Liberty of the Ancients Compared with That of the Moderns" (1819), in *The Political Writings of Benjamin Constant*, ed. Biancamaria Fontana (Cambridge: Cambridge University Press: 1988), 309–28.

9. Schmitt, *The Concept of the Political*, 74.

10. Constant, "The Liberty of the Ancients Compared with That of the Moderns," 316, 310–11.

11. Isaiah Berlin, "Two Concepts of Liberty" (1958), in *Liberty*, ed. Henry Hardy (Oxford: Oxford University Press, 2002), 211. Cf. RCPR, 13–17.

12. Constant, "The Liberty of the Ancients Compared with That of the Moderns," 316.

13. On this, see Berlin, "Two Concepts of Liberty," 209–10.

14. NRH, 181–82.

15. Strauss, "Preface," in SCR, 6; cf. LAM, 64.

16. LAM, 15.

17. LAM, 3.

18. Cf. Aristotle, *Nicomachean Ethics*, IV, 1119b 19–1121a 7; 1123a 34–1125a 16.

19. LAM, 28–29. Cf. WPP, 37–38.

20. NRH, 81–82, 86, 90. Cf. GS3, 695.

21. NRH, 92.

22. NRH, 7–8, 162–63. Cf. WPP, 38–40.

23. LAM, 4.

24. See OT, 42, 109 (note 27), 182, 190; XSD, 119, 159–66, 175–77; XS, 49–50, 157–58. Cf. GS3, 567.

25. Plato, *Republic*, 569c. Cf. PAW, 37.

26. Jacob Klein, Leo Strauss, "A Giving of Accounts," in JPCM, 465; Cf. OT, 199–200, SA, 32–33, and XSD, 159–66, Strauss, "Farabi's Plato," 388–89. I have discussed this important matter at greater length in Ghibellini, *Al di là della politica*, 23–71, to which I refer the interested reader for the sake of brevity.

27. JPCM, 463; Cf. RR, 147.

28. NRH, 1, 5–6. Cf. RCPR, 14–15.

29. NRH, 181–84.

30. See, for example, GS3, 667. Strauss however insists on the independence of Hobbes's view of natural right, originally based on moral grounds, from the Galilean revolution in natural science. See, on this topic, PPH, 6–29, in particular.

31. Cf. Strauss, "Farabi's Plato," 370, 378, 381, 386–87, and NIPPP, 342, including note 15.

32. On the difference between liberty and right see chapter V below.

33. NRH, 4. Cf. RCPR, 14–15.

34. On the elusive and problematic character of Strauss's recovery of the classics' natural right, and of their "primordial experience" of moral and political things, see Robert Pippin, "The Unavailability of the Ordinary," *Political Theory* 31, no. 3 (June 2003): 335–58.

35. NRH, 6. Cf. PPH, 164–65 (GS3, 185–86).

36. Cf. NRH, 183; CM, 49; Strauss, "Farabi's Plato," 381.

37. LAM, 64.

38. NRH, 169.

39. Immanuel Kant, *Toward Perpetual Peace and Other Writings on Politics, Peace, and History* (New Haven and London: Yale University Press, 2006), 90. Cf. NRH, 193–94.

40. LAM, 15–16, 18–19, 22.

41. See, for example, NRH, 93; JPCM, 464–66; SA, 33; XS, 158–59. Cf. note 26 above. On this important topic, let me refer the reader, for the sake of brevity, to Ghibellini, *Al di là della politica*, 23–53, 283–98.

42. JPCM, 463; RR, 147.

43. Strauss, "Preface," in SCR, 1, 6. Cf. WPP, 224.

44. See for example Allan Bloom, Foreword to LAM, v–vi, and Pangle, *Leo Strauss*, 98.

45. Cf. LAM, 24, 35. Smith's take on Strauss's "Platonic liberalism" (Smith, *Reading Leo Strauss*, 87–107, 121–22), however insightful, seems not to fully acknowledge this important distinction in Strauss's perspective. In addition, Strauss's "skeptical defense of liberty," in order to be taken as his last word, would need to be entirely reconciled with his remark that "democracy is the only regime *other than the best* in which the philosopher can lead his peculiar way of life without being disturbed" (CM, 131, my emphasis. Cf, Smith, *Reading Leo Strauss*, 224, note 73).

46. Cf. William A. Galston, "Leo Strauss's Qualified Embrace of Liberal Democracy," in Smith (ed.), *The Cambridge Companion to Leo Strauss*, 193, 197.

47. In a letter to Gershom Scholem of September 6, 1972, referring to his admiration for Xenophon, Strauss agrees to define himself "hopeless reactionary [*hoffnungsloser Reaktionär*]." As an amused and by no means astonished Scholem confirms in his reply, this is a definition that coherently fits Strauss. See GS3, 762–63. Cf. Minowitz, *Straussophobia*, 163.

48. For examples of this kind of (mis)reading, see Drury, *The Political Ideas of Leo Strauss*, 170–81; Xenos, *Cloaked in Virtue*, 15–17; William H. F. Altman, *The German Stranger. Leo Strauss and National Socialism* (Lanham, Maryland: Lexington Books, 2011), 403–44.

49. LAM, 24. Cf. RCPR, 31, and Leo Strauss, *On Nietzsche's Thus Spoke Zarathustra*, ed. Richard L. Velkley (Chicago: University of Chicago Press, 2017), 3. On the "waves of modernity," see TWM, 81–98. On the complex issue of Strauss's attitude towards liberal democracy, useful comments can be found in Zuckert and Zuckert, *The Truth about Leo Strauss*, 5–6, 17–22, 54–57, 106–11, 185–86, 199–200, 261–62; Smith, *Reading Leo Strauss*, 87–130; and Smith, *The Cambridge Companion to Leo Strauss*, 13–40, 193–214. Moreover, as regards the adhesion of the young Strauss to Nietzschean and, to some extent, even "fascist" views, see his letters to Löwith of May 19, 1933, and of June 23, 1935, in GS3, 624–25, 648–50. As I show in the continuation of this chapter, as well as in chapters III and IV, there is, however, enough evidence to maintain that those positions, shared by Strauss until the beginning of the 1930s, were later abandoned as a result of his "change of orientation."

50. GN, 353–78. Cf. LIGPP, 115–16.

51. GN, 357.

52. GN, 365.

53. GN, 364–65. See, however, notes 24 and 26 above.

54. GN, 370–71.

55. GN, 371; Strauss, "Preface," in SCR, 29.

56. GN, 371.

57. GN, 369–71. Cf. LIGPP, 127–28.

58. Cf. GN, 368, with GN, 365.

59. GN, 368–69. LIGPP, 115–16. Cf. Strauss, "Notes," 111.

60. In "'To Spare the Vanquished and Crush the Arrogant': Leo Strauss's Lecture on 'German Nihilism,'" in Smith (ed.), *The Cambridge Companion to Leo Strauss*, 171–92, Susan Shell, referring to Sheppard, *Leo Strauss and the Politics of Exile*, 81–100, aptly underscores that "German Nihilism" was delivered in a period when Strauss's "own personal losses" in the war were still to come. As shown, for example, by the letter to Löwith of May 19, 1933 (GS3, 624–25), even before 1941 was it clear to Strauss, however, that Nazism was a mortal enemy for his people.

61. GN, 371. Cf. OT, 209.

62. GN, 370–71.

63. GN, 371–72. Cf. Robert Howse, *Leo Strauss: Man of Peace* (Cambridge: Cambridge University Press, 2014), 31–32. On the polemic affirmation of courage, see also GS3, 415, 620, PPH, 164–65 (GS3, 186), as well as the introduction above.

64. GN, 372. Cf. GN, 370, LIGPP, 125, 131–37, and CM, 11.

65. GN, 373; Cf. Virgil, *Aeneid*, VI, 853.

66. Cf. Leo Strauss, "What Can We Learn from Political Theory?" *The Review of Politics*, 69 (2007): 519–20.

67. Cf. GN, 372, with GN, 371.

68. GN, 372.

69. GN, 371, 372. Cf. GS3, 493. One should not forget, however, that for Strauss Hobbes himself goes against "common sense [*gesunder Menschenverstand*]" in rejecting the traditional view of "human nature" as "given and immutable" (PPH, 167–68; GS3 189–90). Cf. introduction, note 45, above.

70. GN, 372.

71. LAM, 5, 16. Cf. Nathan Tarcov, *Locke's Education for Liberty* (Chicago: University of Chicago Press, 1984).

72. See GN, 363. Cf. GN, 360, 372–73, and GS3, 493, 667. See also Strauss's celebration of Churchill on the day of his death in Catherine H. Zuckert (ed.), *Leo Strauss on Political Philosophy. Responding to the Challenge of Positivism and Historicism* (Chicago: University of Chicago Press, 2018), 123.

73. NRH, 5–6; cf. LAM, 63.

74. Strauss, "Preface," in SCR, 1–2.

75. Cf. GN, 365.

76. LAM, 223, 24–25; JPCM, 314.

77. LAM, 64; cf. LAM, 5.

78. GS3, 625.

79. GS3, 625. The quoted translation can be found in Shell, "'To Spare the Vanquished and Crush the Arrogant': Leo Strauss's Lecture on 'German Nihilism,'" 185–86, to which I refer the reader for thoughtful comments on this and other related matters. On Strauss's letter to Löwith of May 19, 1933, see also Howse, *Leo Strauss: Man of Peace*, 44–47.

80. See chapter IV below.

81. Cf. Hans Jonas, *Erinnerungen* (Frankfurt am Main: Insel Verlag, 2003), 262.

82. GS3, 627 (my translation). Cf. TM, 342, note 181.

83. GS3, 430. Cf. GS3, 433.

84. GS3, 648.

85. PAW, 33–34; CM, 234–35; SA, 49; NIPPP, 357–60; Leo Strauss, "On the Intention of Rousseau," *Social Research* 14, no. 4 (1947): 485. Cf. PPH, 167–68 (GS3, 189–90); WPP, 38; LAM, 63–64; NRH, 134–35; and OT, 199–200, 210–11.

86. NIPPP, 357.

87. LAM, 24. Cf. Smith, *Reading Leo Strauss*, 106–7.

88. CM, 131. Cf. NRH, 143; PAW, 7–8, 17–18; NIPPP, 361.

89. Cf. Strauss, "Farabi's Plato," 384. I have attempted to deal in greater detail with this intricate theme in Ghibellini, *Al di là della politica*, 69–70, note 119, to which I refer the interested reader for the sake of brevity.

90. NRH, 143. Cf. WPP, 92; OT, 194–96.
91. GS3, 668–69; Löwith and Strauss, "Correspondence Concerning Modernity," 113.
92. GS3, 669; Löwith and Strauss, "Correspondence Concerning Modernity," 113.
93. Strauss, "The Spirit of Sparta or the Taste of Xenophon," 502–36.
94. Cf. OT, 193–94.
95. TM, 296. Cf. NIPPP, 354–55.
96. GS3, 662–63; Löwith and Strauss, "Correspondence Concerning Modernity," 107–8. The parenthetical remark, "but today we live precisely . . . was considerably more favourable," occurs in a note in the original.
97. Cf. OT, 208–9. Strauss, "Notes," 111–13.
98. OT, 211. Strauss, "Notes," 114–15.
99. OT, 194; cf. GS3, 662–63.
100. LAM, 5.
101. Löwith and Strauss, "Correspondence Concerning Modernity," 108 (GS3, 663).
102. PAW, 34. See also WPP, 224, and cf. Zuckert and Zuckert, *The Truth about Leo Strauss*, 44.
103. OT, 194. Cf. Strauss, "Farabi's Plato," 384; NIPPP, 357–60.
104. Löwith and Strauss, "Correspondence Concerning Modernity," 108 (GS3, 663). Cf. Horace, *Epistles*, I, 10, 24 and NRH, 202; OT, 203, Strauss, "What Can We Learn from Political Theory?" 528.
105. RCPR, 31; LAM, 63. Cf. LAM, 272; PAW, 34 (note 14), 36–37.
106. LAM, 63. Cf. PAW, 34.
107. LAM, 64. Cf. Strauss, *On Nietzsche's Thus Spoke Zarathustra*, 33. Strauss's quote is from Eric A. Havelock, *The Liberal Temper in Greek Politics* (New Haven: Yale University Press, 1957), 374.
108. WPP, 224–25. Cf. WPP, 222–23.

Chapter III

1. TM, 13.
2. See the introduction above. Cf. NRH, 123–24.
3. TM, 9, 13 (my emphasis).
4. TM, 13.
5. GS2, 14 (note 2), 386–87, 389, 439, 456; Leo Strauss, "How to Study Spinoza's *Theologico-Political Treatise*" (1948), in PAW, 155–56.
6. Richard Rorty, "That Old-Time Philosophy," *The New Republic* (April 4, 1988): 28–32.

7. For the extant correspondence of Strauss and Krüger, including some revealing fragments and drafts by Strauss, see GS3, 377–454. When quoting from this correspondence, in the present book I have mostly availed myself of its translation by Jerome Veith, Anna Schmidt, and Susan Shell, in Shell, ed., *The Strauss-Krüger Correspondence*, 13–88. On the Strauss-Krüger correspondence, see Heinrich Meier, "Vorwort des Herausgebers," in GS3, xxviii–xxx, as well as the interpretive essays included in the above-mentioned volume by Shell.

8. TM, 13. By this quote, however, I do not mean to parallel Strauss's and Machiavelli's thought in their substance, as other interpreters, with various intentions, have done (see, for a recent and eminent example, Heinrich Meier, *Political Philosophy and the Challenge of Revealed Religion* [Chicago: University of Chicago Press, 2017], chap. II). Precisely the topic of the second, unnatural cave, so prominent in the Strauss-Krüger correspondence, seems to me to make this parallel ultimately untenable.

9. See, for example, the following remark by Strauss from January 7, 1930: "However, I cannot yet adopt as my own your fundamental theses regarding the exclusively historical determination of humanity," in GS3, 381.

10. GS3, 387.

11. Leo Strauss, "Review of Julius Ebbinghaus, *On the Progress of Metaphysics*" (1931), in EW, 214–15.

12. EW, 214.

13. Leo Strauss, "Conspectivism" (1929), trans. Anna Schmidt and Martin D. Yaffe, in R, 217–24. The essay, which is a review of Karl Mannheim's *Ideology and Utopia*, was first published, posthumously, in GS2, 365–75.

14. Strauss, "Conspectivism," 220.

15. Leo Strauss, "Religious Situation of the Present" (1930), trans. Anna Schmidt and Martin D. Yaffe, in R, 229. Also this lecture was first published, posthumously, in GS2, 377–91.

16. Strauss, "Religious Situation of the Present," 228.

17. NRH, 24–25.

18. GS3, 396.

19. Strauss, "Religious Situation of the Present," 228. Cf. GS3, 650, 655, 662. On Strauss's interpretation of Heidegger, see Steven Smith, "Destruktion or Recovery? On Strauss's Critique of Heidegger," in Smith, *Reading Leo Strauss*, 108–30, and Richard Velkley, *Heidegger, Strauss, and the Premises of Philosophy: On Original Forgetting* (Chicago: University of Chicago Press, 2011).

20. Leo Strauss, "An Unspoken Prologue to a Public Lecture at St. John's College" (1959), in JPCM, 450.

21. Strauss, "Religious Situation of the Present," 231, 232.

22. Strauss, "Religious Situation of the Present," 232. As usual in Strauss's case, the emphasis in the quote from Maimonides should not be left unnoticed.

23. Strauss, "Religious Situation of the Present," 232–33. Cf. SCR, 181.
24. GS3, 406.
25. Strauss, "Religious Situation of the Present," 234.
26. Strauss, "Religious Situation of the Present," 234.
27. Strauss, "Religious Situation of the Present," 235.
28. EW, 214, 215.
29. EW, 215.
30. GS3, 394–95. Beside Strauss, Krüger, and Ebbinghaus, the fourth person to share this opinion about the present was arguably Strauss's friend Klein, whom he mentions at several junctures in his correspondence with Krüger.
31. GS3, 403. Cf. Leo Strauss, "Outline: The Political Science of Hobbes," in HCR, 151. On Strauss's unpublished manuscript, see HCR, 3–4, 10 (note 27), 11–12 (GS3, ix–x, xvii, note 27, xviii–xix), as well as GS3, 401, 708–9.
32. GS3, 405.
33. GS3, 405. Cf. NIPPP, 330–31, notably note 3.
34. GS3, 405–6.
35. GS3, 406.
36. GS3, 406.
37. GS3, 406.
38. Strauss, "Religious Situation of the Present," 234.
39. Strauss, "Religious Situation of the Present," 233. Cf. Strauss, "Notes," 89–119.
40. GS3, 412.
41. GS3, 412.
42. GS3, 412.
43. GS3, 412.
44. See GS3, 423, where Krüger claims that "Augustine's Platonism . . . is really Platonic: the legitimate repetition of the Platonic problem within the horizon of revelation." Cf. Krüger's remark in GS3, 429: "You know that I take Plato to represent the *greatest relative approximation* of the true way of inquiry" (my emphasis).
45. GS3, 412.
46. GS3, 413. On the influence of twentieth-century phenomenology on Strauss's philosophical approach, see the introduction above.
47. GS3, 413.
48. GS3, 420.
49. GS3, 420.
50. GS3, 420. In a previous draft of the same letter, always referring to Heidegger as its champion, Strauss had expressed the same concept in even a clearer, more straightforward form: "Although Christianity is 'false,' it has brought to light facts concerning human beings that were not adequately known to humanity in antiquity"—facts that make the philosophy that "preserves the 'truth' of Christianity . . . deeper and more radical than Greek philosophy" (GS3, 415–16).

51. GS3, 421. Cf. GS3, 41 (PPH, 28), 259-60.
52. GS3, 421. Cf. GS3, 613-14.
53. GS3, 421. Cf. GS3, 259-60.
54. GS3, 420.
55. GS3, 414.
56. GS3, 421. For a later instance, this time with specific reference to Hobbes, of Strauss's insistence on the key role of *Selbstprüfung* in modernity, which also emphasizes its "Christian Biblical" origin, see PPH, 27-29.
57. GS3, 421. Cf. GS3, 259-60. Regarding the "radical" dimension where only genuine philosophy can take place, one cannot but notice the similarity of Strauss's approach with that characteristic of twentieth-century phenomenology, notably with Husserl's definition of philosophy as "essentially a science of true beginnings, of origins, of *rizomata panton* [the roots of everything]" (Edmund Husserl, "Philosophy as a Rigorous Science," in *Phenomenology and the Crisis of Philosophy* [New York: Harper and Row, 1965], 146). On the latter essay by Husserl, see SPPP, 29-37.
58. In his letter of December 27, 1932, Strauss even hints at the seemingly "romantic" character of this "demand": "Do you remember the first page of Schiller's 'Naïve and Sentimental Poetry'? The naïve human being *is* nature—for the sentimental human being, naturalness is just a *demand*. We moderns are necessarily 'sentimental.' But that means that we must inquire in a 'sentimental' manner—i.e., in a remembering, historical fashion—what the Greeks 'naively' inquired about" (GS3, 421-22; cf. LIGPP, 135, and NIPPP, 329-30).
59. GS3, 421.
60. GS3, 422. For a critique of this attempt, see Robert Pippin, "The Unavailability of the Ordinary. Strauss on the Philosophical Fate of Modernity," *Political Theory* 31, no. 3 (June 2003): 335-58.
61. GS3, 396, 406.
62. Strauss, "Religious Situation of the Present," 234.
63. GS3, 415.
64. GS3, 414-15. Cf. Strauss, "Preface," in SCR, 12.
65. GS3, 415. Cf. GS3, 620, and the introduction above. The same dialectics of *position* and *denial*, this time concerning the concept of *the political*, can also be seen at work in Strauss, "Notes," 99, 101-2, 107-8, 111, 116-17. On this, see chapter I above.
66. GS3, 415.
67. GS3, 409.
68. PL, 136, note 2.
69. GS3, 415. The quote significantly, although somewhat obscurely, goes on as follows: "Nietzsche went back *behind* philosophy, and at the same time avowed it. He fiercely battled 'spirit [*Geist*]' and affirmed it with the utmost passion. This swaying, this fundamental lack of clarity could only be overcome by proceeding to Platonic philosophy." Cf. PL, 136, note 2.

70. See note 68 above.
71. PL, 136.
72. GS3, 423.
73. GS3, 423–24.
74. GS3, 424.
75. GS3, 424.
76. GS3, 425.
77. GS3, 426.
78. GS3, 429.
79. GS3, 429.
80. GS3, 431.
81. GS3, 428–29.
82. GS3, 432–33.
83. GS3, 433.
84. GS3, 433.
85. GS3, 433. Cf. Thomas Hobbes, *Leviathan*, chapter VII.
86. Cf. SCR, 30–31.
87. See GS3, 433, where Strauss, to substantiate the claim that "assuming we *knew* what the right thing was, *this* knowledge would not suffice to *do* the right thing," provides the following "Augustinian example: in order to fulfill the commandment of honoring one's parents, I have to know who my parents are. But I *cannot* actually know this, only believe it. But I also don't just opine it—for what I believe in this case is not an object of serious doubt."
88. See, for example, GS3, 439.
89. GS3, 449.
90. GS3, 422.
91. JPCM, 450. Cf. Velkley, *Heidegger, Strauss, and the Premises of Philosophy*, 6.
92. TM, 14.
93. TM, 13 (my emphasis).
94. TM, 10.

Chapter IV

1. Leo Strauss, "Conspectivism," in R, 217–24; "Religious Situation of the Present," in R, 225–35; "Review of Julius Ebbinghaus, *On the Progress of Metaphysics*," in EW, 214–16.
2. NRH, 24–25. Cf. GS3, 396.
3. Strauss, "Foreword to a Planned Book on Hobbes," in HCR, 137–49. As already observed (see introduction, note 84), this essay was written by Strauss in 1931. However, it was only posthumously published in GS3, 201–15. Cf. GS3, vii–ix.

4. GS3, 396.
5. Strauss, "Foreword to a Planned Book on Hobbes," 148–49.
6. Strauss, "Religious Situation of the Present," 228.
7. On this, see chapter I above.
8. Strauss, "Foreword to a Planned Book on Hobbes," 141.
9. Strauss, "Foreword to a Planned Book on Hobbes," 140, 141. As far as published works are concerned, such a heavily antagonistic perspective on the "*philosophic* understanding" or "founding" of right will be dismissed by Strauss as early as 1932, when he published his "Notes" and started to embrace the unpolemical, yet philosophical approach that characterizes them. This should be borne in mind, in particular, when it comes to explaining the kernel of Strauss's "change of orientation," as we have attempted to do in chapter I and in the introduction (see, for example, its note 84). Concerning Strauss's unpublished works, notably his letters to Krüger, see the continuation of this chapter.
10. GS3, 394.
11. Plato, *Statesman*, 272b 1–3. Cf. HPP, 45–46.
12. Cf. Plato, *Statesman*, 269c 4–d 3.
13. PPH, 23–25; OMPT, 178–79.
14. Plato, *Statesman*, 271e 6–7. Cf. HPP, 50–51.
15. GS3, 440. Cf. PPH, 142–43, NRH, 129–30, PAW, 10–11. See the introduction above, in addition, on the key role of Socratic dialectics, as well as the "orientation by speech" it implies, regarding how this discernment can be achieved, or at least meaningfully sought.
16. Cf. NIPPP, 342, including note 15.
17. GS3, 394.
18. Cf. GS3, 407, 409.
19. See GS3, 441, where Strauss significantly, but somewhat enigmatically, states: "Starting with the analysis of the inverted [*verkehrt*] or indifferent use of reason, of the inverted or indifferent life . . . is that which distinguishes modern morality as such from classical morality. . . . It is the beginning from an inverted state of nature (Hobbes) or indifferent state of nature (Rousseau), from an original freedom, that is only later restricted."
20. GS3, 414.
21. Strauss, "Notes," 89–119.
22. GS3, 399.
23. GS3, 399.
24. GS3, 399.
25. GS3, 399. Regarding "giving and receiving reason," see Plato, *Statesman*, 286a 4–5.
26. GS3, 399.
27. See chapter I, note 20, above.
28. Thomas Hobbes, *Leviathan*, chap. XIV (London: Penguin Books, 1985), 189.

29. PL, 137–38 (note 13), where also Krüger's essay *Philosophie und Moral in der Kantischen Kritik* (Tübingen: Mohr, 1931) is mentioned. On the still open and problematic character of the Socratic-Platonic inquiry into the "right way of life," see, for example, GS3, 417.

30. GS3, 399. On the meaning of these quotes, see also chapter I above. Cf. HCR, 141.

31. Meier, *Carl Schmitt and Leo Strauss*, 130.

32. Strauss, "Notes," 117.

33. My emphasis.

34. PPH, 16; NRH, 249–50.

35. GS3, 402.

36. GS3, 404.

37. GS3, 442. See PL, 21–22, including note 1 on the "irrationalistic" character of modern rationalism. Cf. GS3, 162–63 (PPH, 142–43), and the introduction above. As early as 1946, in his critique of Wild's *Plato's Theory of Man* (NIPPP, 335 ff.), Strauss seems to embrace a different view of that matter in that he now warns against the "temptation to identify modern philosophy with sophistry"—a temptation he defines as "considerable" and to which "Wild is not the first to succumb" since it ultimately characterized the interpretation of the Enlightenment advanced by German idealism (to which Strauss, apparently, assimilates his previous views, at least implicitly). It is worth underscoring, however, that Strauss here is not making specific reference to Hobbes's modern rationalism, but to modern philosophy more generally. In addition, a close reading of Strauss's argument shows that what he finds particularly debatable in the given context is Wild's identification of sophistry with modern idealism as distinct from English empiricism (NIPPP, 335–38). This comes up clearly in note 6 on pages 335–36, where Strauss defends German idealism—whose boundaries he interprets so broadly as to include Husserl and Heidegger with their insistence on "intentionality"—by the following revealing words: "A man who claims to be a Platonist is under an obligation to stress the fact that German idealism attempted to restore important elements of Plato's and Aristotle's teaching in opposition to western (English and French) philosophy, if on the basis of a foundation laid by western philosophy."

38. Cf. Plato, *Protagoras*, 321c 5–6, with Hobbes, *Leviathan*, chap. XIII, 186.

39. GS3, 426. These two utterances are interspersed with the following remark: "In a world that arises without plan or order, everything human is in order (Socrates can be glad to live among Athenians and not among the wild), whereas in truth it is the case that, in a world produced through planning, the human realm is precisely *not* in order." By saying so, Strauss seems to be underlining the "revolutionary" effect of natural right understood as a standard on the established political order, which always falls short of it. See, on this matter, the introduction above and cf. NRH, 13–14.

40. GS3, 424.

41. GS3, 426. Cf. PPH, 142–43 (GS3, 162–63). See introduction, pp. 11–12, above.

42. GS3, 424.

43. Plato, *Phaedo*, 99c 5.

44. Plato, *Phaedo*, 99e 5.

45. Cf. PPH, 142–43, 153 (GS3, 162–63, 174).

46. GS3, 399.

47. Cf. Jean-Jacques Rousseau, "Discourse on the Arts and Sciences," in *The First and Second Discourses*, ed. Roger D. Masters (New York: St. Martin's Press, 1964), 38.

48. GS3, 435. Cf. Meier, *Carl Schmitt and Leo Strauss*, 129–31.

49. GS3, 430.

50. On this blunder, I refer the reader to Ghibellini, *Al di là della politica*, 21 (note 4) and 188 (note 34).

51. GS3, 625. As previously, I am following the translation Susan Shell provides in "'To Spare the Vanquished and Crush the Arrogant': Leo Strauss's Lecture on 'German Nihilism,'" in Smith, ed., *The Cambridge Companion to Leo Strauss*, 171–92 (trans. quoted on pages 185–86). On this matter, see also GS2, 299–306.

52. GS3, 625. The full quotation from Virgil's *Aeneid* (VI, 851–53) reads as follows: "Tu regere imperio populos, Romane, memento (hae tibi erunt artes) pacisque imponere morem, parcere subiectis et debellare superbos" (You, Roman, remember to rule the peoples with your empire—these will be your arts—and to impose the custom of peace, to spare the subjects and crush the arrogant).

53. GS3, 627.

54. GS3, 433. See chapter III, p. 85, above.

55. There is in fact no encyclopedia article "on the state" in Mussolini's opera.

56. *Inter alia*: "Fascism wants man active and committed to action with all his energy . . . It conceives of life as a fight, thinking that it is up to man to conquer that life which is really worthy of him by creating, first of all in himself, the tool (material, moral, intellectual) to build it. . . . Hence, the high worth of culture in all its forms (art, religion, science) and the utmost importance of education. Hence, the essential worth of labor as well, by which man conquers [*vince*] nature and creates the human world (economic, political, moral, intellectual)," *Scritti e discorsi di Benito Mussolini*, vol. VIII (Milano: Ulrico Hoepli, 1934), 69. On the importance of labor in this modern, distinctly Hegelian sense, cf. NRH, 250; OT, 208.

57. GS3, 433.

58. GS3, 432.

59. Strauss, "Religious Situation of the Present," 234, and GS3, 406, 414–15. See also the introduction above.

60. GS3, 415. Cf. LIGPP, 137–38.

61. LAM, 24. Cf. RCPR, 31, TWM, 98, and Strauss, *On Nietzsche's* Thus Spoke Zarathustra, 3.
62. WPP, 172. See also chapter V below.
63. Strauss, "Notes," 98. Cf. chapter I above.
64. GS3, 396.
65. GS3, 405. See chapter I, p. 47, and chapter III, p. 76, above. Cf. NIPPP, 354–55.
66. Strauss, "Review of Julius Ebbinghaus," 215; GS3, 422. See chapter III, pp. 79–80 and 86–87, above.
67. GS3, 440. On the standard as available "in speech" only, see the introduction to the present book. Cf. chapter I, note 20, above.
68. In GS3, 417, Strauss even stresses the "problematic" character of that assumption from a Platonic perspective as he understands it: "For every other philosophy presupposes in one way or another that the βιος θεωρητικος is the right βιος [*sic*]—for Socrates-Plato, however, it is precisely this presupposition that is problematic." See also NRH, 163.
69. GS3, 451.
70. GS3, 451. Cf. NIPPP, 354–55.
71. Aristotle, *Politics*, 1277a 20–23.
72. Cf. JPCM, 463; Cf. RR, 147.

Chapter V

1. Cf. Daniel Tanguay, *Leo Strauss. Une biographie intellectuelle* (Paris: Éditions Grasset & Fasquelle, 2003), 269.
2. Strauss, "Progress or Return?," in JPCM, 116.
3. GS3, 393 (English trans., in Shell, ed., *The Strauss-Krüger Correspondence*, 28).
4. WPP, 81, 90.
5. NRH, 34.
6. Strauss, "What Can We Learn from Political Theory?" 515. Interestingly, by contrasting such a purely theoretical approach with political philosophy, Strauss interprets it as intrinsically action-oriented: "A purely theoretical, detached knowledge of things political is the safest guide for political action, just as a purely theoretical, detached knowledge of things physical is the safest guide toward conquest of nature: this is the view underlying the very term political theory." Cf. WPP, 88–89.
7. NRH, 34. Cf. GS3, 404.
8. WPP, 80–81, 84, 86, 91–92, 94. Cf. Leo Strauss, "The Spirit of Sparta and the Taste of Xenophon," *Social Research* VI, 4 (1939): 502–36.

9. WPP, 90–92. Cf. GS3, 404, and NIPPP, 342–43. On the "orientation by speech" characteristic of Socrates's dialectics, see the introduction above.

10. OMPT, 163–96. This essay was first brought to my attention by Daniel Tanguay, who makes extensive reference to, and thoughtfully comments on it in "*Natural Right and History* in Preparation: Leo Strauss's Critique of Secularization," a paper, still unpublished, he presented at the conference "Leo Strauss, Religione e Liberalismo," Rome, May 13–14, 2011.

11. Nathan Tarcov, "Introduction to Two Unpublished Lectures by Leo Strauss," *The Review of Politics*, 69 (2007): 513. Tarcov refers to "What Can We Learn from Political Theory?" and "The Re-education of Axis Countries Concerning the Jews" (*The Review of Politics*, 69 (2007): 515–29 and 530–38 respectively), but his comment applies well to all the papers Strauss left unpublished. See also, in this regard, Svetozar Minkov, "Hobbes as the Founder of Modern Political Philosophy," in TNRH, 155.

12. Strauss, "Notes," 116. See chapter I above.

13. OMPT, 186–87. Cf. PPH, viii–ix.

14. Strauss, "Preface," in SCR, 29; cf. PL, 36–37.

15. OMPT, 194. Cf. NRH, 279–80.

16. OMPT, 195.

17. OMPT, 195–96. Cf. GS3, 259–60. On this matter, useful remarks can be found in Minkov, "Hobbes as the Founder of Modern Political Philosophy," 157–58.

18. NRH, 60–61, note 22; GS3, 661, 667–68; Leo Strauss, "Natural Right (1946)," in TNRH, 236. Cf. FPP, 74–76; TWM, 82–83.

19. Tanguay, "*Natural Right and History* in Preparation: Leo Strauss's Critique of Secularization," towards the end.

20. PAW, 97–98; NRH, 157–58, 163–64.

21. Strauss, "Preface to Isaac Husik, *Philosophical Essays*," in JPCM, 252. Cf. NIPPP, 327–28.

22. WPP, 44. See, however, Meier, *Political Philosophy and the Challenge of Revealed Religion*, 37 (including footnote 26), where the author—presumably relying on WPP, 9–10, but, in my view, without sufficient evidence—contests the relevance of that expression with regard to Strauss's "esoteric" interpretation of Machiavelli, consequently downplaying as "exoteric" Strauss's whole treatment of Machiavelli in the above-mentioned work.

23. Georg W. F. Hegel, *The Phenomenology of Mind*, trans. J. B. Baillie (London: George Allen & Unwin; New York: Humanities Press, 1966), 164: "To supersede [*aufheben*] is at once to negate and to preserve." Cf. TWM, 95; OT, 207; PPH, 57–58, 96 (cf. GS3, 115); SCR, 92 (cf. GS3, 135); and NIPPP, 358.

24. OMPT, 171.

25. OMPT, 171.

26. OMPT, 171.

27. OMPT, 171–72.
28. OMPT, 172.
29. OMPT, 172.
30. OMPT, 172.
31. RCPR, 31. Cf. LAM, 266–67.
32. OMPT, 172–73.
33. OMPT, 173.
34. OMPT, 173.
35. OMPT, 173.
36. OMPT, 173.
37. OMPT, 173–74, my emphasis. Cf. NIPPP, 328, including note 2.
38. OMPT, 175.
39. OMPT, 175.
40. OMPT, 175.
41. OMPT, 171.
42. OMPT, 179.
43. OMPT, 178.
44. OMPT, 178–79.
45. OMPT, 176.
46. OMPT, 176.
47. OMPT, 179.
48. OMPT, 179.
49. OMPT, 179–80.
50. OMPT, 179. Cf. Hobbes, *Leviathan*, ch. XV (Cambridge: Cambridge University Press, 1935), 109.
51. OMPT, 178. Cf. Hobbes, *Elements of Law*, part I, ch. XVII, sect. 12.
52. OMPT, 180.
53. OMPT, 180. Among that "number of medieval thinkers," Suarez unsurprisingly gives prominence to William of Occam. See Suarez, *Tractatus de legibus ac Deo Legislatore*, Lib. I, c. V.8, and, particularly, Lib. II, c. VI.4.
54. Strauss, "Progress or Return?" in JPCM, 110–11, 119.
55. OMPT, 180 (my emphasis). For an analogous statement by Strauss, see OMPT, 186: ". . . he [Hobbes] was *too sensible not to see that there is* a fundamental difference between human appetite as such and . . . right or good human appetite" (my emphasis; in the typewritten original, as well as in the text edited by Colen and Minkov we are presently following, an additional "between" occurs in lieu of the second ellipsis, which, however, seems to me to be out of place).
56. OMPT, 180.
57. OMPT, 180.
58. OMPT, 180–81.
59. OMPT, 181. Cf. Thomas Hobbes, "An Answer to Bishop Bramhall," *The English Works of Thomas Hobbes* (London: John Bohn, 1840; reprint: Aalen: Scientia Verlag, 1966), vol. IV, 285.

60. PPH, 23–25.

61. OMPT, 177. *Ineffective*, rather than *invalid*, might seem to be a better term to use here. Nonetheless, this is what Strauss literally states in the wake of Hobbes, *De cive*, ch. XIV, art. 21: "Thus, the obligation to civil obedience, the obligation to which all civil laws owe their *validity*, is prior to any civil law" (OMPT, 177; my emphasis).

62. OMPT, 176. Cf. Hobbes, *Leviathan*, ch. XV, 98.

63. Cf. NRH, 181.

64. OMPT, 183.

65. OMPT, 183. Cf. Hobbes, *Leviathan*, ch. XIV, 95–96, and SCR, 95.

66. JPCM, 252. Cf. LIGPP, 124–25; GS3, 41 (PPH, 27–28).

67. OMPT, 173.

68. See OMPT, 173, note a.

69. OMPT, 173.

70. OMPT, 174 (ellipsis in Strauss's original). Cf. Hobbes, *Leviathan*, ch. XLVI, 503–4.

71. OMPT, 174 (second ellipsis in Strauss's original). Cf. Hobbes, *Leviathan*, ch. XLVI, 504.

72. OMPT, 174–75. Cf. Hobbes, *Leviathan*, ch. XL, 349, 352, and ch. XLVI, 495; *De cive*, ch. 11, art. 4.

73. OMPT, 174 (my emphasis).

74. OMPT, 174. Cf. Hobbes, *Leviathan*, ch. XXX, 244–45.

75. OMPT, 174, note b.

76. GS3, 769. Cf. Ghibellini, "Leo Strauss, Gershom Scholem, and the Reason-Revelation Problem," 69.

77. OMPT, 173–74.

78. OMPT, 174.

79. OMPT, 174.

80. OMPT, 195.

81. OMPT, 195 (my emphasis).

82. OMPT, 195.

83. If this reading is plausible and one had to speculate, a suitable time could be when "Athens and Jerusalem" came into contact for the first time. Arguably, this event can be traced back at least to the Septuagint translation of the Hebrew Bible into Greek, which happened as early as the third century BC. As regards political history, a prominent event may be seen in Alexander the Great's seizure of Jerusalem in 332 BC.

84. OMPT, 195.

85. OMPT, 195.

86. Cf. Leo Strauss, "1962 Autumn Quarter Course on Natural Right," ed. Svetozar Minkov, lecture of November 19, 1962, University of Chicago: https://wslamp70.s3.amazonaws.com/leostrauss/s3fs-public/pdf/transcript/Natural_Right_1962.pdf, 270.

87. See chapter I, note 23, above.

88. NRH, 184. See also NRH, 184–85, footnote 23, and cf. CM, 42–44.

89. Strauss, "Notes," 119. See chapter I above.

90. PPH, 23. As is well known, the book was first published in English translation in 1936, but the German manuscript had already been completed by Strauss the previous year. See GS3, 7; OT, 230.

91. Leo Strauss, "Paul de Lagarde" (1924), in EW, 90–101 (GS2, 323–31).

92. EW, 98. Cf. Leo Strauss, "A Note on the Discussion on 'Zionism and Anti-Semitism'" (1923), in EW, 79. On Paul de Lagarde, see the biographical note in EW, 97–99. On the young Strauss, see the editor's introduction in EW, 3–49; Eugene Sheppard, *Leo Strauss and the Politics of Exile: The Making of a Political Philosopher* (Lebanon, NH: University Press of New England—Brandeis University Press, 2006); Steven B. Smith, "Leo Strauss: The Outlines of a Life," in Smith (ed.), *The Cambridge Companion to Leo Strauss*, 13–18; David Janssens, *Between Athens and Jerusalem: Philosophy, Prophecy, and Politics in Leo Strauss's Early Thought* (Albany, NY: State University of New York Press, 2008); and Carlo Altini, *Philosophy as Stranger Wisdom. A Leo Strauss Intellectual Biography* (Albany, NY: State University of New York Press, 2022), 11–112.

93. "No sooner do they almost touch than they move apart—the radical moralism of the German hailing from Fichte, and the radical moralism of the Zionist writers and politicians who stand under entirely different influences" (EW, 97).

94. EW, 96. Cf. GS3, 391.

95. GS3, 430. Cf. GS3, 625. On this, see chapters II and IV above.

96. On this point, see Michael Zank's fit remarks in EW, 35.

97. EW, 94 (my emphasis). Cf. LAM, 268; GS3, 516–17.

98. EW, 94.

99. EW, 94 (GS2, 327). On "culturedness," which reflects a purely artificial attitude towards culture and education, see EW, 101, note 15. Cf. LAM, 266.

100. EW, 100, note 12.

101. EW, 93–94. Cf., however, LAM, 268, where Strauss (although about four decades later) endorses the rejection of "the common Christian notion of Jewish 'pharisaism.'"

102. EW, 92–93.

103. EW, 94 (GS2, 327–28).

104. EW, 92–93. Cf. LAM, 267.

105. EW, 94.

106. EW, 94 (GS2, 328). Cf. LAM, 268; GS3, 516–17.

107. EW, 94 (GS2, 328).

108. Cf. EW, 90.

109. EW, 94 (GS2, 328).

110. See note 96 above.

111. EW, 94 (GS2, 238). Cf. GS3, 516–17. Although it can also be inferred from the context, Strauss's ultimate agreement seems to me to be implicit, at least,

in his acceptance of the view that "only through a kind of 'Jewification' of the German spirit was [the assimilation of the Jews] possible" (see note 109 above). For this sentence directly matches (even from a syntactic standpoint in German) Lagarde's previous remark that, as Strauss summarizes it, "only thus"—namely, by way of liberalism as "secularized Judaism"—"have the Jews been able to gain influence over the Germans, without rebirth in the German spirit." In addition, it is worth noting that Strauss emphasized the role of liberalism in the legal and political emancipation of the Jews in Germany throughout his life (cf. PAW, 3-6).

112. Cf. EW, 220-21.
113. EW, 94. Cf. EW, 108.
114. EW, 94. On Gumpelino, the character of Heinrich Heine's *Die Bäder von Lucca*, see Zank's note 15 in EW, 101.
115. Cf. GS3, 516-17.
116. NRH, 177. Cf. PPH, xv-xvi; TWM, 84.
117. NRH, 181-82. Cf. Strauss, "Notes," 100.
118. Minkov, "Hobbes as the Founder of Modern Political Philosophy," 157-58.
119. GS3, 524.
120. SCR, 29.
121. PPH, 23.
122. See chapter III above.
123. Cf. EW, 93.
124. As Strauss himself underscores, unlike Moses who is "the greatest example of an armed prophet," Jesus is "the greatest example of an unarmed prophet" (WPP, 44; cf. LAM, 268).
125. EW, 94.
126. Cf. EW, 93.
127. Cf. GS3, 632.
128. Leo Strauss, "Perspective on Good Society," in LAM, 260-72.
129. LAM, 268; cf. TWM, 95.
130. RCPR, 31.
131. SCR, 29; cf. PL, 36-37.
132. OMPT, 194-96.
133. OMPT, 187-88, 193.
134. OMPT, 194 (my emphasis). Cf. CM, 42; NRH, 279.
135. OMPT, 194. Cf. Leo Strauss, "Notes on Lucretius," in LAM, 94: according to Lucretius, "nothing is more alien to wisdom than that with which wisdom is above everything else concerned: the atoms and the void. The first things are in no way a model for man." Yet "reason alone, the study of nature, can give man tranquility of mind. Nature and the study of nature are the sole sources of happiness."
136. Hobbes, *Leviathan*, ch. XI, 63. Cf. LAM, 131, 133.
137. Cf. LAM, 95.

138. OMPT, 194. Cf. LAM, 93–94, 107, 112, 126. See also how coherently this approach is matched by a realistic epistemological stance in LAM, 114–16.
139. OMPT, 194. Cf. Machiavelli, *Discourses on Livy*, I.6.4.
140. OMPT, 194. Cf. LAM, 122, and CM, 42–43.
141. OMPT, 191.
142. OMPT, 194.
143. Strauss, "Notes," 110. Cf. NRH, 271; TWM, 85, 87, 90.
144. OMPT, 194. Cf. NRH, 279; Strauss, "Notes on Lucretius," in LAM, 77, 93–94, 96, 99, 122, 123, 130, 131, 132–33; CM, 42.
145. OMPT, 194. Cf. RR, 145–46; TWM, 85–86.
146. OMPT, 180.
147. PAW, 107–8. See also JPCM, 110, and cf. Ghibellini, *Al di là della politica*, 156–57.
148. See RCPR, 46.
149. OMPT, 195.
150. PL, 32–34; RR, 176–77; NIPPP, 338–39; CM, 42–44; HCR, 94–109; cf. HCR, ix–xi, including footnote 4.
151. JPCM, 110–11, 119; NIPPP, 338.
152. NRH, 81; JPCM, 110–11; GS3, 696; HPP, 2–3. Cf. SPPP, 153, 167, 186, 195.
153. WPP, 172. Cf. Leo Strauss, "Preface to the 7th Impression," in NRH, vii, and GS3, 8. See Meier, *Political Philosophy and the Challenge of Revealed Religion*, 33, note 20.
154. WPP, 172. Cf. GS3, 620, and the introduction above.
155. Tanguay, "*Natural Right and History* in Preparation: Leo Strauss's Critique of Secularization," towards the end.
156. Löwith and Strauss, "Correspondence Concerning Modernity," 112 (GS3, 668).
157. Löwith and Strauss, "Correspondence Concerning Modernity," 112 (trans. modified) (GS3, 667). The seminar paper Strauss alludes to appears to be Leo Strauss, "Natural Right (1946)," in TNRH, 221–48, which Strauss first delivered on January 9, 1946 (that is, in the previous academic year) in the General Seminar at the New School for Social Research. I am grateful to Svetozar Minkov for this suggestion.
158. Löwith and Strauss, "Correspondence Concerning Modernity," 112 (trans. modified) (GS3, 667). Cf. GS3, 41 (PPH, 28).
159. Strauss, "Preface to Isaac Husik, *Philosophical Essays*," in JPCM, 252. Cf. NIPPP, 327–28.
160. Strauss, "Natural Right (1946)," 234–36.
161. Strauss, "Natural Right (1946)," 236.
162. See note 11 above.
163. Löwith and Strauss, "Correspondence Concerning Modernity," 112 (trans. modified) (GS3, 667). Cf. GS3, 41 (PPH, 28).

164. GS3, 544-87. Cf. Lampert, *The Enduring Importance of Leo Strauss*, 7-32; Ghibellini, *Al di là della politica*, 23-71.

165. Leo Strauss, "1954 Winter Quarter Course on Natural Right," ed. Jerry Weinberger, lecture of February 15, 1954, University of Chicago: https://wslamp70.s3.amazonaws.com/leostrauss/pdf/Natural+Right+(1954).1.pdf, 181. I take "sublimation" to refer to the concept of *Aufhebung*. It should also be emphasized that Strauss starts his remarks about secularization by stressing their "only conversational" character, begging his audience not to quote them.

166. Strauss, "1954 Winter Quarter Course on Natural Right," 182. It is worth noting, however, that after categorically affirming the impossibility to understand Machiavelli's attempt to conquer chance as the secularization of the biblical teaching, and after emphasizing the similarities between his doctrine and modern science, Strauss observes: "If this is so, and if the later thinkers like Hobbes presuppose that modern natural science, the question would be this: If we want to understand modern political thought as a secularized version of the Biblical thought, we would have to trace modern natural science in its specific character to the Bible." In this context, Strauss proves to regard attempts in that direction as "not convincing." But those familiar with him will recall that the main thesis of his 1935 book on Hobbes was precisely that his political philosophy was ultimately independent from the new natural science, and that in the introduction to *Philosophy and Law* (PL, 33-34) he clearly hints at the relationship between the biblical concept of God's omnipotence and modern natural science to explain the latter's "idealistic" character. On this, see also HCR, 94-109 (GS3, 348-64).

167. Strauss, "1962 Autumn Quarter Course on Natural Right," 262.

168. Strauss, "1962 Autumn Quarter Course on Natural Right," 266-67. Cf. NRH, 184, and chapter I, note 23, above.

169. Strauss, "1962 Autumn Quarter Course on Natural Right," 270. Cf. PPH, 27-28 (GS3, 41), and the introduction above.

170. Strauss, "1962 Autumn Quarter Course on Natural Right," 264. Cf. PL, 33-34, and HCR, 94-109 (GS3, 348-64), where Hobbes is, however, described by Strauss as less radical than Descartes in his skepticism about the existence of an external world. Hobbes in fact confronts the "possibility that the world is the incomprehensible work of a simply incomprehensible God" (HCR, 109) rather than that of a *Deus deceptor* in particular.

Chapter VI

1. See Bruno Leoni, "Giudizi di valore e scienza politica (risposta al professor Strauss)," *Il Politico* XXII, 1 (1957): 86-94; Arnaldo Momigliano, "Ermeneutica e pensiero politico classico in Leo Strauss" (1967-1977), in *Pagine ebraiche* (Torino: Einaudi, 1987), 189-99.

2. Guido Alpa, "Prefazione," in Leo Strauss, *Diritto naturale e storia* (Genova: il melangolo, 2009), 7–27. For a detailed analysis of Strauss's reception in Italy until recent times, see also Marco Menon, "Leo Strauss in Italy: The 'Three Waves' of Italian Strauss Studies," *Interpretation. A Journal of Political Philosophy* 46, no. 2 (Spring 2020): 187–227, and Raimondo Cubeddu, "Strauss in Italia," *Il Politico* LXXI (2006): 46–85.

3. Guido Fassò, "Diritto naturale e storicismo," *Il Mulino* IV (Aprile 1958): 239–47, and "Oggettività e soggettività nel diritto naturale," *Rivista di diritto civile* I (1958): 264–71.

4. Cf. Alpa, "Prefazione," 15–17.

5. Leoni, "Giudizi di valore e scienza politica (risposta al professor Strauss)," 87.

6. On Strauss and Weber, see Nasser Behnegar, *Leo Strauss, Max Weber, and the Scientific Study of Politics* (Chicago: University of Chicago Press, 2003).

7. Ramin Jahanbegloo, *Conversations with Isaiah Berlin* (London: Peter Halban Publishers, 1992), 32.

8. Cf. Strauss, "Preface to the 7th Impression," in NRH, vii. For Strauss's critique of Berlin's "relativism," see RCPR, 13–26.

9. PAW, 158.

10. Jahanbegloo, *Conversations with Isaiah Berlin*, 32.

11. PAW, 158.

12. Cf. PAW, 155, with PL, 136.

13. PL, 136.

14. NRH, 6. Cf. Robert Pippin, "The Unavailability of the Ordinary, Strauss on the Philosophical Fate of Modernity," *Political Theory* 31, no. 3 (June 2003): 335–58.

15. LAM, 24.

16. GS3, 624–25.

17. GS2, 299–306; EW, 64–75.

18. GS2, 300; EW, 65. For more details about the "Breslau" movement and Moses, see EW, 4–6, 64–65.

19. GN, 373. On this, see Shell, "To Spare the Vanquished and Crush the Arrogant," 185–90, and chapter II above.

20. Cf. Minowitz, *Straussophobia*, 83–86, 154–63.

21. See, for example, Drury, *The Political Ideas of Leo Strauss*; Xenos, *Cloaked in Virtue*; William Altman, *The German Stranger*. For a critique of these authors, I refer the reader to Ghibellini, *Al di là della politica*, 21 (note 4), 42–43, 51, 63–64 (note 54), 68 (note 87), 188 (note 34), 300 (note 18), 303–4 (note 46), and 307–8 (note 76).

22. Zuckert, "Leo Strauss: Fascist, Authoritarian, Imperialist?," 291. For Strauss's 1952 letter to Scholem, see GS3, 728.

23. On this point, I refer the reader, for the sake of brevity, to Ghibellini, *Al di là della politica*, 34 (including note 49), 214–16 (note 224), 218–20 (note 241).

24. GS3, 536; Leo Strauss, "Letter to Helmut Kuhn," *Independent Journal of Philosophy* 2 (1978): 24.

25. GS3, 625. Cf. Shell, "To Spare the Vanquished and Crush the Arrogant," 185–86.

26. JPCM, 463; WPP, 32.

27. PAW, 10–11.

28. PAW, 11.

29. PAW, 11.

30. NRH, 164. Cf. NIPPP, 347, note 24.

31. PAW, 97–98.

32. PAW, 95.

33. SPPP, 137–38.

34. NRH, 154; cf. SPPP, 140–41.

35. NRH, 155.

36. "Nothing that I have learned has shaken my inclination to prefer 'natural right,' especially in its classic form, to the reigning relativism, positivist or historicist" (NRH, vii).

37. Strauss, "Letter to Helmut Kuhn," 23–26.

38. Strauss, "Letter to Helmut Kuhn," 24.

39. Strauss, "Letter to Helmut Kuhn," 23.

40. PPH, viii–ix. OMPT, 183–85. On this, see chapter V above.

41. OMPT, 184: "The distinction, made by Hobbes, is, to some extent, identical with the distinction, made in German jurisprudence, between right in the subjective sense ('Right') and right in the objective sense ('Law')."

42. PPH, ix. See chapter V, above.

43. Strauss, "Letter to Helmut Kuhn," 24; cf. PAW, 95 (note 1).

44. Cf. GS3, 440.

45. NRH, 162–63.

46. NRH, 144.

47. NRH, 139.

48. Cf. Ghibellini, *Al di là della politica*, 321. Cf. chapter II above.

49. NRH, 134–35. This quote too is a good example in which the different use of *right* mentioned above—as a countable noun when referred to the modern interpretation, and as an uncountable when referred to the classical perspective—can be fully appreciated.

50. NRH, 7–8 (my emphasis). Cf. NIPPP, 339.

51. NRH, 33.

52. GN, 357. See chapter II, above.

53. NRH, 4, note 2.

54. NRH, 42.
55. NRH, 42–43.
56. NRH, 35–36; 74–76. Cf. Behnegar, "Strauss and Social Science," 231–32.
57. Strauss, "Foreword to a Planned Book on Hobbes" (1931), in HCR, 137–49 (GS3, 201–15). Cf. GS3, 396, 394.
58. Strauss, "Foreword to a Planned Book on Hobbes," 137 (GS3, 201).
59. Strauss, "Foreword to a Planned Book on Hobbes," 141 (GS3, 205). For a broader interpretation of this quote, which underscores its provisional character concerning Strauss's attempt to recover a "natural" kind of philosophizing, see introduction, note 84, and chapter IV above, as well as the following paragraph.
60. Strauss, "Foreword to a Planned Book on Hobbes," 145 (GS3, 210).
61. Strauss, "Foreword to a Planned Book on Hobbes," 141 (GS3, 205).
62. NRH, 169.
63. NRH, 108.
64. PL, 36. In light of this materialistic perspective, modern hedonism, however *political* if compared to its classical counterpart due to its devaluation of the theoretic life, still retains an unpolitical tendency in terms of its final goal. See, on this, Strauss, "Notes," 100–102, including note 2, and CM, 32–34, 49.
65. Strauss, "Preface," in SCR, 1–3, 6–7. Cf. LAM, 5, and CM, 193–94. See, on this, chapter II above.
66. GS3, 524. Cf. NIPPP, 355.
67. Strauss, "Notes," 117.
68. Strauss, "Foreword to a Planned Book on Hobbes," 137 (GS3, 201).
69. NRH, 36. Cf. NRH, 92.
70. TM, 296.
71. NRH, 139.
72. Strauss, "Farabi's Plato," 384. Cf. chapter II above.
73. NRH, 35–36.
74. NRH, 35, 89–90; OT, 212; GS2, 447, 451. Cf. Bruell, "The Question of Nature and the Thought of Leo Strauss," 97–98.
75. GS2, 379. Cf. Nathan Tarcov, "Philosophy as the Right Way of Life in *Natural Right and History*," in Pawel Armada and Arkadiusz Górnisiewicz (eds.), *Modernity and What Has Been Lost. Considerations on the Legacy of Leo Strauss* (South Bend, IN: St. Augustine's Press, 2011), 43–52.
76. TM, 296. Cf. NIPPP, 354–55.
77. TM, 296. Cf. JPCM, 463, and RR, 147. On this, see Mauro Farnesi Camellone, "The City and Stranger," in Antonio Lastra and Josep Monserrat-Molas (eds.), *Leo Strauss, Philosopher. European Vistas* (Albany, NY: State University of New York Press, 2016), 81–100.
78. I have dealt with such a theme in Ghibellini, *Al di là della politica*, 235–318, to which I refer the interested reader.
79. See chapter III above. Cf. NIPPP, 354–55.

80. PAW, 155, and PL, 136, respectively.
81. GS3, 405.
82. PL, 136; GS2, 14 (note 2).
83. PAW, 155.
84. Leo Strauss, "Conspectivism," in R, 217–24 (GS2, 365–75).
85. EW, 214–16 (GS2, 437–39).
86. Strauss, "Religious Situation of the Present," in R, 227 (GS2, 379–80).
87. Strauss, "Religious Situation of the Present," 228 (GS2, 380–81). Cf. NRH, 33.
88. Strauss, "Religious Situation of the Present," 231; cf. Strauss, "Conspectivism," 223, and SPPP, 147.
89. Strauss, "Religious Situation of the Present," 231 (GS2, 384).
90. See, for example, GS3, 613–14. Cf. GS3, 656, 692.
91. Strauss, "Religious Situation of the Present," 231 (GS2, 385).
92. Strauss, "Religious Situation of the Present," 232 (GS2, 386).
93. Strauss, "Conspectivism," 223 (GS2, 372).
94. Strauss, "Religious Situation of the Present," 232 (GS2, 386–87).
95. Cf. Strauss, "Religious Situation of the Present," 232 (GS2, 386–87), with Leo Strauss, "The Intellectual Situation of the Present," in R, 248 (GS2, 455–56).
96. Strauss, "Religious Situation of the Present," 232–33 (GS2, 387). Cf. SCR, 181.
97. Strauss, "Religious Situation of the Present," 233 (GS2, 387). Cf. chapter III above.
98. Cf. PL, 58, 139 (note 10), and R, 249.
99. Strauss, "Religious Situation of the Present," 233 (GS2, 387).
100. Cf. OMPT, 194–96. See, on this, chapter V above.
101. Strauss, "Religious Situation of the Present," 233 (GS2, 388).
102. NRH, 81. Cf. JPCM, 111, 381; GS3, 696; HPP, 2–3. Cf. SPPP, 153, 167, 186, 195. In light of what we have observed in the previous chapter, the fact that Strauss singles out the *Old* Testament becomes even more noteworthy.
103. JPCM, 119; cf. JPCM, 111.
104. JPCM, 110.
105. JPCM, 119.
106. JPCM, 110.
107. PL, 33–34.
108. Strauss, "Religious Situation of the Present," 233 (GS2, 388).
109. Strauss, "Religious Situation of the Present," 233 (GS2, 388).
110. Strauss, "Religious Situation of the Present," 233 (GS2, 388).
111. Cf. PL, 33–34, and HCR, 94–109.
112. Strauss, "Notes," 109–10; WPP, 43. Cf. PL, 135, note 2.
113. Strauss, "Religious Situation of the Present," 234 (GS2, 388).
114. NRH, 29–31.

115. Strauss, "Religious Situation of the Present," 234 (GS2, 388).
116. Strauss, "Religious Situation of the Present," 234 (GS2, 389).
117. Strauss, "Religious Situation of the Present," 234–35 (GS2, 389).
118. Strauss, "Religious Situation of the Present," 234 (GS2, 389).
119. Cf. Strauss's letter to Löwith of June 23, 1935, where Strauss states that Nietzsche "so dominated and bewitched me between my 22nd and 30th years, that I literally believed everything . . . that I understood of him" (GS3, 648). It is worth noting that "Religious Situation of the Present" was "to be delivered on December 21, 1930" (GS2, 377), namely, after Strauss had turned thirty-one. In this regard, see also the reference, towards the end of the lecture, to "the *factual ignorance* of the origins," which Strauss exemplifies by referring to the difference between the classical "μεγαλοψυχία" and "nobility [*Vornehmheit*]." This latter concept may well be an implicit reference to Nietzsche. On this, see the final paragraph of Strauss, "Note on the Plan of Nietzsche's *Beyond Good and Evil*," in SPPP, 190–91, which ends with the remark "Die vornehme Natur ersetzt die göttliche Natur" (SPPP, 191): a polemical view of nature, now regarded as "noble" in opposition to its biblical demotion, replaces the classical understanding of nature as the truly divine. Cf. GN, 356, 372; GS3, 414–15, 613–14, and see, on this matter, Giovanni Giorgini, "Leo Strauss, Platone e Nietzsche: che cos'è aristocratico?," in Antonio Masala, Marco Menon, and Flavia Monceri (eds.), *La passione della libertà. Saggi in onore di Raimondo Cubeddu* (Torino: IBL Libri, 2021), 263–76.
120. Strauss, "The Intellectual Situation of the Present," in R, 249 (GS2, 456). The only real difference (Cf. Strauss, "Religious Situation of the Present," 232; GS2, 387) is that "historical difficulty [*geschichtliche Schwierigkeit*]" replaces "artificial difficulty [*künstliche Erschwerung*]" (literally: "artificial complication"). It is also worth noting that the identification of natural philosophizing with Greek philosophy becomes, significantly, even more explicit.
121. Cf. Strauss, "The Intellectual Situation of the Present," 248 (GS2, 455–56), with Strauss, "Religious Situation of the Present," 232 (GS2, 386).
122. Strauss, "The Intellectual Situation of the Present," 248 (GS2, 456).
123. Strauss, "The Intellectual Situation of the Present," 253 (GS2, 462).
124. See Strauss, "Religious Situation of the Present," 234–35 (GS2, 388–89).
125. Strauss, "The Intellectual Situation of the Present," 246 (GS2, 453).
126. JPCM, 252.
127. Strauss, "The Intellectual Situation of the Present," 246 (GS2, 452).
128. EW, 215 (GS2, 438).
129. Cf. the "Plan of the Lecture in Draft," where Strauss explicitly speaks of "division of historical consciousness" and of the need to "overcome [*aufheben*]" historical consciousness "*insofar as it means: it itself constitutes as such a superior manner of knowing*" (Strauss, "The Intellectual Situation of the Present," 252; GS2, 460).

130. Strauss, "The Intellectual Situation of the Present," 246–47 (GS2, 453–54).
131. Strauss, "The Intellectual Situation of the Present," 246 (GS2, 453).
132. Strauss, "The Intellectual Situation of the Present," 247 (GS2, 453).
133. Strauss, "The Intellectual Situation of the Present," 247 (GS2, 454).
134. Strauss, "The Intellectual Situation of the Present," 247 (GS2, 454).
135. Strauss, "The Intellectual Situation of the Present," 247, trans. modified (GS2, 454).
136. Strauss, "The Intellectual Situation of the Present," 252 (GS2, 460–61). Cf. PL, 135–36.
137. Strauss, "The Intellectual Situation of the Present," 247 (GS2, 454).
138. Strauss, "The Intellectual Situation of the Present," 247 (GS2, 454–55). Cf. SCR, 178.
139. See the following paragraph. Cf. PL, 135 (GS2, 13, note 2): "The Enlightenment's aim was the rehabilitation of the natural through the denial (or limitation) of the supernatural, but what it accomplished [*ihre Leistung*] was the discovery of a new 'natural' which, so far from being natural, is rather the residue, as it were, of the 'supernatural.'"
140. Strauss, "The Intellectual Situation of the Present," 248 (GS2, 455–56).
141. Strauss, "The Intellectual Situation of the Present," 248–49 (GS2, 455–56).
142. Strauss, "The Intellectual Situation of the Present," 247–48 (GS2, 455), trans. slightly modified.
143. Strauss, "The Intellectual Situation of the Present," 250 (GS2, 458–59).
144. Strauss, "The Intellectual Situation of the Present," 250 (GS2, 459).
145. Strauss, "The Intellectual Situation of the Present," 241 (GS2, 445).
146. Strauss, "The Intellectual Situation of the Present," 244 (GS2, 450).
147. Strauss, "The Intellectual Situation of the Present," 245 (GS2, 450).
148. Strauss, "The Intellectual Situation of the Present," 245 (GS2, 451).
149. Strauss, "The Intellectual Situation of the Present," 245 (GS2, 451).
150. Strauss, "The Intellectual Situation of the Present," 245 (GS2, 451).
151. Strauss, "The Intellectual Situation of the Present," 245 (GS2, 451).
152. Strauss, "The Intellectual Situation of the Present," 245 (GS2, 451).
153. Strauss, "The Intellectual Situation of the Present," 245 (GS2, 451). Cf. Strauss, "Notes," 114–15.
154. Strauss, "The Intellectual Situation of the Present," 245 (GS2, 452).
155. Strauss, "The Intellectual Situation of the Present," 249 (GS2, 456). Both the emphases in the final quote are mine.
156. PL, 38 (GS2, 26–27).
157. PL, 38 (GS2, 26–27).
158. PL, 21 (GS2, 9). Strauss's use of the term *prejudice* (*Vorurteil*) in this circumstance does not seem to impair our previous remarks on the prejudices of biblical origin that the Enlightenment tried to free itself from, while remaining

entrapped in them. For, as becomes clear at the end of the introduction (PL, 38–39; GS2, 27), he is here attempting to find a way out of the conundrum of modernity. Against the latter's "prejudices" strictly understood, which are ultimately of biblical origin (Strauss, "The Intellectual Situation of the Present," 248–49; GS2, 456), he can only raise a counter-prejudice, as it were. On the tentative nature of Strauss's effort in this regard, see, for example, Klein's letter to Strauss of May 6, 1935 (GS3, 538).

159. PL, 22 (GS2, 9–10).

160. With regard to modern rationalism as "sophistry," see also PL, 135, note 1 (GS2, 9, note 1), and GS3, 404, 442. Cf. chapter IV, notably note 37, above.

161. PL, 22 (GS2, 10).

162. Tanguay, *Leo Strauss. Une biographie intellectuelle*, 280–81.

163. PL, 24 (GS2, 11).

164. PL, 24.

165. PL, 24 (GS2, 12).

166. PL, 25 (GS2, 12).

167. PL, 25 (GS2, 13).

168. PL, 135 (GS2, 13, note 2).

169. See the previous paragraph.

170. PL, 135 (GS2, 13, note 2).

171. PL, 135 (GS2, 13, note 2). Cf. note 139 above.

172. PL, 136 (GS2, 14, note 2).

173. PL, 136 (GS2, 14, note 2).

174. PL, 33–34. Cf. chapter V above.

175. PL, 30 (GS2, 19).

176. PL, 30–31 (GS2, 19).

177. PL, 31 (GS2, 19). Note, in that respect, the incidental remark "to say the least." Cf. PL, 32.

178. PL, 31 (GS2, 19). Cf. PAW, 104–8.

179. PL, 31 (GS2, 19).

180. PL, 32 (GS2, 20).

181. PL, 32 (GS2, 20–21).

182. PL, 34 (GS2, 22).

183. PL, 34 (GS2, 22). If so, the question arises whether the view that philosophy is the best possible life is wholly meaningful under that premise (cf. Nasser Behnegar, "Strauss and Social Science," in Smith, *The Cambridge Companion to Leo Strauss*, 231–32) or whether it does not rather need a different understanding of nature from that of modern science to be so, irrespective of any possible elenctic justification by refuting revelation (cf. Meier, *Leo Strauss and the Theologico-political Problem*, 24–28).

184. Friedrich Nietzsche, *Beyond Good and Evil*, trans. W. Kaufmann (New York: Vintage Books, 1989), 16. Cf. SPPP, 176–77. On "preferences," see NRH, 4–5, 47–49, 72.

185. PL, 33–34. Cf. Strauss, "1962 Autumn Quarter Course on Natural Right," 264.
186. Strauss, "Religious Situation of the Present," 233 (GS2, 388).
187. PL, 33, including note 11 on page 137 (GS2, 21).
188. PL, 33–34 (GS2, 22).
189. See RR, 147. Cf. NRH, 74–75.
190. PL, 35 (GS2, 23).
191. PL, 35 (GS2, 23).
192. Strauss, "Notes," 97–98 (GS3, 222). See chapter I above.
193. PL, 33–34 (GS2, 22). See also PPH, 28, and cf. GS3, 41.
194. PL, 36 (GS2, 24). It is worth noting that the use of the term *foreground* (*Vordergrund*) conceptually implies the presence of a "background [*Hintergrund*]," which could well be, in light of what we have seen before and what we shall see now, the biblical view. On this, I refer the reader to Alberto Ghibellini, "Da 'cauto e riservato' ad 'audace e attivo': l'ateismo moderno secondo Leo Strauss," *Cahiers di Scienze Sociali* Anno VIII, no. 18 (Dicembre 2021): 132–46.
195. PL, 36 (GS2, 24).
196. PL, 36 (GS2, 24).
197. PL, 36 (GS2, 24). Cf. Strauss, "Preface," in SCR, 29.
198. Joel Kraemer, "The Medieval Arabic Enlightenment," in Smith, *The Cambridge Companion to Leo Strauss*, 145, including note 32.
199. As Kraemer suggests in the previously mentioned note 32, "to cultivate his garden" could also be a citation from Voltaire's *Candide*: "il faut cultiver notre Jardin" (chapter XXX, *in fine*). If so, and if one can trust Pangloss (but also some additional textual evidence in Voltaire's novel), the latter garden, rather than to Epicurus's, could be metaphorically compared to the Garden of Eden, where man "was put *ut operaretur eum*, in order for him to work" (chapter XXX, *in fine*). See, on this, Ghibellini, "Da 'cauto e riservato' ad 'audace e attivo': l'ateismo moderno secondo Leo Strauss," 140–41. Cf., however, GS2, 612.
200. *Genesis*, I.26 ff. ("Then God said, 'Let us make mankind in our image, in our likeness, so that they may rule over the fish in the sea and the birds in the sky, over the livestock and all the wild animals, and over all the creatures that move along the ground'"; "Be fruitful and increase in number; fill the earth and subdue it. Rule over the fish in the sea and the birds in the sky and over every living creature that moves on the ground"; "I give you every seed-bearing plant on the face of the whole earth and every tree that has fruit with seed in it. They will be yours for food"). Cf. *Genesis*, II.8 ("Now the Lord God had planted a garden in the east, in Eden; and there he put the man he had formed"), and II.15 ("The Lord God took the man and put him in the Garden of Eden to work it and take care of it").
201. PL, 31–32, my emphasis (GS2, 20).
202. *Genesis* III.5–7; III.16–19.

203. Strauss, "Notes on Lucretius," in LAM, 122: ". . . nature abounds in defects . . . The largest part of the world is unfit for human life and habitation. That part which is useful for man would be covered by nature with thorns if man did not resist nature with his sweat and toil . . ." Another suitable reference of Strauss's remarks may be Hobbes, who speaks of the awakening effect of "damnorum experientia" in *De Cive*, "Praefatio ad Lectores" (cf. GS3, 259). This, however, could also be an implicit reference to the biblical background, in light of Hobbes's entanglement, by way of "polemical" opposition, in that tradition (GS3, 259–60).

204. PL, 35–36 (GS2, 24). Cf. NRH, 175.
205. Strauss, "The Intellectual Situation of the Present," 247 (GS2, 455).
206. PL, 38 (GS2, 26).
207. PL, 57–58 (GS2, 45).
208. PAW, 155.
209. PAW, 154.
210. PAW, 153.
211. PAW, 153.
212. PAW, 153.
213. PAW, 154–55.
214. PAW, 155.
215. PAW, 155. Cf. NIPPP, 330, note 3.
216. PAW, 155–56. Cf. EW, 215; GS3, 421.
217. PAW, 157.
218. PAW, 158.
219. PAW, 158.
220. See PAW, 156.
221. SCR, 15.
222. SCR, 15.
223. SCR, 16.
224. SCR, 16. Cf. FPP, 61.
225. SCR, 16. Cf. Spinoza, *Ethics*, IV, Pref.
226. SCR, 16.
227. Strauss, "The Intellectual Situation of the Present," 253 (GS2, 462).

Conclusion

1. Strauss, "The Intellectual Situation of the Present," in R, 249 (GS2, 456), my emphasis.
2. NRH, 73. Cf. R, 242–43, 251 (GS3, 447–48, 460).
3. See, respectively, PL, 22, 135 (note 1), and GS3, 424. Cf. NRH, 78.
4. Cf. Robertson, *Leo Strauss*, 104–8.
5. RCPR, 38. Cf. OT, 212; NIPPP, 338–39.

6. PAW, 157.
7. OT, 212. Cf. NIPPP, 338–39.
8. PPH, 142–43 (GS3, 162–63); GS3, 426. Cf. Velkley, *Heidegger, Strauss, and the Premises of Philosophy*, 3.
9. Cf. NIPPP, 354–55.
10. PAW, 153.
11. TM, 13.
12. SCR, 31, my emphasis.
13. PL, 21, my emphasis. Cf. chapter VI, note 158, above.
14. See, for example, CM, 11; RCPR, 29; PAW, 153.
15. Stanley Rosen, *The Elusiveness of the Ordinary* (New Haven, CT: Yale University Press, 2002), 157.
16. See Löwith and Strauss, "Correspondence Concerning Modernity," 107 (GS3, 662), and PPH, 153 (GS3, 174), respectively.

Works Cited

Works by Leo Strauss

The Argument and the Action of Plato's Laws. Chicago: University of Chicago Press, 1975.
The City and Man. Chicago: University of Chicago Press, 1978.
"Correspondence Concerning Modernity: Karl Löwith and Leo Strauss." *Independent Journal of Philosophy* 4 (1983): 105–19.
"Correspondence: Karl Löwith and Leo Strauss." *Independent Journal of Philosophy* 5/6 (1988): 177–92.
The Early Writings (1921–1932). Edited by Michael Zank. Albany, NY: State University of New York Press, 2002.
Faith and Political Philosophy: The Correspondence between Leo Strauss and Eric Voegelin, 1934–1964. Edited by Peter Emberley and Barry Cooper. Columbia, MO: University of Missouri Press, 2004.
"Farabi's Plato." In *Louis Ginzberg Jubilee Volume*, 357–93. New York: The American Academy for Jewish Research, 1945.
"German Nihilism." *Interpretation. A Journal of Political Philosophy*, 26 (1999): 352–78.
Gesammelte Schriften, Band 1. Dritte Auflage. Hrsg. von Heinrich Meier. Stuttgart–Weimar: Verlag J. B. Metzler, 2008.
Gesammelte Schriften, Band 2. Zweite Auflage. Hrsg. von Heinrich Meier. Stuttgart–Weimar: Verlag J. B. Metzler, 2013.
Gesammelte Schriften, Band 3. Zweite Auflage. Hrsg. von Heinrich und Wiebke Meier. Stuttgart–Weimar: Verlag J. B. Metzler, 2008.
Hobbes's Critique of Religion and Related Writings. Edited by Gabriel Bartlett and Svetozar Minkov. Chicago: University of Chicago Press, 2011.
History of Political Philosophy. Edited by Leo Strauss and Joseph Cropsey. Chicago: Rand McNally, 1972.
Jewish Philosophy and the Crisis of Modernity. Edited by Kenneth Hart Green. Albany, NY: State University of New York Press, 1997.

Leo Strauss on Political Philosophy. Responding to the Challenge of Positivism and Historicism. Edited by Catherine H. Zuckert. Chicago: University of Chicago Press, 2018.
"Letter to Helmut Kuhn." *Independent Journal of Philosophy* 2 (1978): 23–26.
Liberalism Ancient and Modern. Chicago: University of Chicago Press, 1995.
"The Living Issues of German Postwar Philosophy." In *Leo Strauss and the Theologico-Political Problem* by Heinrich Meier, 115–39. Cambridge: Cambridge University Press, 2006.
Natural Right and History. Chicago: University of Chicago Press, 1953; 7th impression, 1971.
"1954 Winter Quarter Course on Natural Right." Edited by Jerry Weinberger. Lecture of February 15, 1954. University of Chicago: https://wslamp70.s3.amazonaws.com/leostrauss/pdf/Natural+Right+(1954).1.pdf.
"1962 Autumn Quarter Course on Natural Right." Edited by Svetozar Minkov. Lecture of November 19, 1962. University of Chicago: https://wslamp70.s3.amazonaws.com/leostrauss/s3fs-public/pdf/transcript/Natural_Right_1962.pdf.
"Notes on Carl Schmitt, *The Concept of the Political.*" Translated by J. Harvey Lomax. In *Carl Schmitt and Leo Strauss. The Hidden Dialogue* by Heinrich Meier, 89–119. Chicago: University of Chicago Press, 1995.
"On a New Interpretation of Plato's Political Philosophy." *Social Research* XIII, no. 3 (1946): 326–67.
On Nietzsche's Thus Spoke Zarathustra. Edited by Richard L. Velkley. Chicago: University of Chicago Press, 2017.
"On the Intention of Rousseau." *Social Research* 14, no. 4 (1947): 455–87.
On Tyranny. Including the Strauss-Kojève Correspondence, Revised and Expanded Edition. Edited by Victor Gourevitch and Michael S. Roth. Chicago: University of Chicago Press, 2000.
"The Origin of Modern Political Thought." In *Toward Natural Right and History. Lectures and Essays by Leo Strauss, 1937–1946*, edited by J. A. Colen and Svetozar Minkov, 163–206. Chicago: University of Chicago Press, 2018.
Persecution and the Art of Writing. Chicago: University of Chicago Press, 1988.
Philosophy and Law. Contributions to the Understanding of Maimonides and His Predecessors. Translated by Eve Adler. Albany, NY: State University of New York Press, 1995.
The Political Philosophy of Hobbes. Its Basis and Its Genesis. Translated by Elsa M. Sinclair. Chicago: University of Chicago Press, 1963.
"Reason and Revelation." In *Leo Strauss and the Theologico-Political Problem* by Heinrich Meier, 141–80. Cambridge: Cambridge University Press, 2006.
The Rebirth of Classical Political Rationalism. Edited by Thomas Pangle. Chicago: University of Chicago Press, 1989.
"The Re-education of Axis Countries Concerning the Jews." *The Review of Politics* 69 (2007): 530–38.

Reorientation: Leo Strauss in the 1930s. Edited by Martin D. Yaffe and Richard S. Ruderman. New York: Palgrave Macmillan, 2014.
Socrates and Aristophanes. Chicago: University of Chicago Press, 1980.
Spinoza's Critique of Religion. Translated by Elsa M. Sinclair. New York: Schocken Books, 1965.
Spinoza's Critique of Religion. Translated by Elsa M. Sinclair. Chicago: University of Chicago Press, 1997.
"The Spirit of Sparta or the Taste of Xenophon." *Social Research* VI, no. 4 (November 1939): 502–36.
Studies in Platonic Political Philosophy. Edited by Thomas Pangle. Chicago: University of Chicago Press, 1983.
Thoughts on Machiavelli. Chicago: University of Chicago Press, 1978.
"The Three Waves of Modernity." In *An Introduction to Political Philosophy: Ten Essays by Leo Strauss*, edited by Hilail Gildin, 81–98. Detroit, MI: Wayne State University Press, 1989.
Toward Natural Right and History. *Lectures and Essays by Leo Strauss, 1937–1946*. Edited by J. A. Colen and Svetozar Minkov. Chicago: University of Chicago Press, 2018.
"What Can We Learn from Political Theory?" *The Review of Politics*, 69 (2007): 515–29.
What Is Political Philosophy? And Other Studies. Chicago: University of Chicago Press, 1988.
Xenophon's Socrates. South Bend, IN: St. Augustin's Press, 1998.
Xenophon's Socratic Discourse. An Interpretation of the Oeconomicus. South Bend, IN: St. Augustin's Press, 1998.

Other Works

Alpa, Guido. "Prefazione." In *Diritto naturale e storia* by Leo Strauss, 7–27. Genova: il melangolo, 2009.
Altini, Carlo. *Una filosofia in esilio. Vita e pensiero di Leo Strauss*. Roma: Carocci, 2021.
Altini, Carlo. *Philosophy as Stranger Wisdom. A Leo Strauss Intellectual Biography*. Albany, NY: State University of New York Press, 2022.
Altman, William H. F. *The German Stranger. Leo Strauss and National Socialism*. Lanham, MD: Lexington Books, 2011.
Behnegar, Nasser. "Carl Schmitt and Strauss's Return to Premodern Philosophy." In *Reorientation: Leo Strauss in the 1930s*, edited by Martin D. Yaffe and Richard S. Ruderman, 115–29. New York: Palgrave Macmillan, 2014.
Behnegar, Nasser. *Leo Strauss, Max Weber, and the Scientific Study of Politics*. Chicago: University of Chicago Press, 2003.

Behnegar, Nasser. "Strauss and Social Science." In *The Cambridge Companion to Leo Strauss*, edited by Steven B. Smith, 215–40. Cambridge: Cambridge University Press, 2009.

Berlin, Isaiah. "Two Concepts of Liberty." In *Liberty*, edited by Henry Hardy, 166–217. Oxford: Oxford University Press, 2002.

Bernadete, Seth. "Leo Strauss's *The City and Man*." *Political Science Reviewer* 8 (1978): 1–20.

Bloom, Allan. "Foreword." In *Liberalism Ancient and Modern* by Leo Strauss, v–vi. Chicago: University of Chicago Press, 1995.

Bruell, Christopher. "The Question of Nature and the Thought of Leo Strauss." *Klēsis. Revue philosophique*, 19 (2011): 92–101.

Chacon, Rodrigo. "Strauss and Husserl." *Idealistic Studies* 44 (2014): 281–96.

Ciccarelli, Pierpaolo. "Hobbes schmittiano o Schmitt hobbesiano? Sul 'cambio di orientamento' nelle 'Note a Carl Schmitt' di Leo Strauss." *Bollettino telematico di filosofia politica*, http://archiviomarini.sp.unipi.it/737/.

Ciccarelli, Pierpaolo. "L'écriture réticente, condition de possibilité de la philosophie." *Archives de Philosophie* Tome 86, no. 2 (2023): 91–119.

Ciccarelli, Pierpaolo. *Leo Strauss tra Husserl e Heidegger*. Pisa: ETS, 2018.

Ciccarelli, Pierpaolo. "Réception italienne de Leo Strauss. De la méfiance à la reconnaissance," *Archives de Philosophie* Tome 86, no. 2 (2023): i–vii.

Constant, Benjamin. "The Liberty of the Ancients Compared with That of the Moderns." In *The Political Writings of Benjamin Constant*, edited by Biancamaria Fontana, 309–28. Cambridge: Cambridge University Press, 1988.

Cubeddu, Raimondo. "Strauss in Italia." *Il Politico* LXXI, no. I (2006): 46–85.

Doneson, Daniel. "Beginning at the Beginning. On the Starting Point of Reflection." In *Heidegger's Jewish Followers. Essays on Arendt, Strauss, Jonas, and Levinas*, edited by Samuel Fleischacker, 106–30. Pittsburgh, PA: Duquesne University Press, 2008.

Drury, Shadia B. *The Political Ideas of Leo Strauss*. New York: Palgrave Macmillan, 2005.

Farnesi Camellone, Mauro. "The City and Stranger." In *Leo Strauss, Philosopher. European Vistas*, edited by Antonio Lastra and Josep Monserrat-Molas, 81–100. Albany, NY: State University of New York Press, 2016.

Fassò, Guido. "Diritto naturale e storicismo." *Il Mulino* IV (Aprile 1958): 239–47.

Fassò, Guido. "Oggettività e soggettività nel diritto naturale." *Rivista di diritto civile* I (1958): 264–71.

Galli, Carlo. *Janus's Gaze. Essays on Carl Schmitt*. Durham and London: Duke University Press, 2015.

Galston, William A. "Leo Strauss's Qualified Embrace of Liberal Democracy." In *The Cambridge Companion to Leo Strauss*, edited by Steven B. Smith, 193–214. Cambridge: Cambridge University Press, 2009.

Ghibellini, Alberto. *Al di là della politica. Filosofia e retorica in Leo Strauss*. Genova: Genova University Press, 2012.

Ghibellini, Alberto. "Da 'cauto e riservato' ad 'audace e attivo': l'ateismo moderno secondo Leo Strauss." *Cahiers di Scienze Sociali* Anno VIII, no. 18 (Dicembre 2021): 132–46.

Ghibellini, Alberto. "Leo Strauss, Gershom Scholem, and the Reason-Revelation Problem." *Interpretation. A Journal of Political Philosophy* XL, no. 1 (2013): 57–78.

Ghibellini, Alberto. "Tre studi su Leo Strauss." *Il Politico* LXXXVII, no. 1 (2022): 133–59.

Giorgini, Giovanni. "Leo Strauss, Platone e Nietzsche: che cos'è aristocratico?" In *La passione della libertà. Saggi in onore di Raimondo Cubeddu*, edited by Antonio Masala, Marco Menon, and Flavia Monceri, 263–76. Torino: IBL Libri, 2021.

Giorgini, Giovanni. *Liberalismi eretici*. Trieste: Edizioni Goliardiche, 1999.

Giorgini, Giovanni. "Strauss's Liberalisms." Paper presented at the conference "Leo Strauss, Religione e Liberalismo," Rome, May 13–14, 2011.

Havelock, Eric A. *The Liberal Temper in Greek Politics*. New Haven, CT: Yale University Press, 1957.

Hegel, Georg W. F. *The Phenomenology of Mind*. Translated by J. B. Baillie. London: George Allen & Unwin; New York: Humanities Press, 1966.

Hobbes, Thomas. "An Answer to Bishop Bramhall." In *The English Works of Thomas Hobbes*, Vol. IV, edited by William Molesworth, 279–384. London: John Bohn, 1840; reprint: Aalen: Scientia Verlag, 1966.

Hobbes, Thomas. *De Cive*. Edited by Richard Tuck and Michael Silverthorne. Cambridge: Cambridge University Press, 1998.

Hobbes, Thomas. *Leviathan*. Edited by A. R. Waller. Cambridge: Cambridge University Press, 1935.

Hobbes, Thomas. *Leviathan*. Edited by C. B. Macpherson. London: Penguin Books, 1985.

Howse, Robert. *Leo Strauss: Man of Peace*. Cambridge: Cambridge University Press, 2014.

Husserl, Edmund. "Die natürliche Einstellung und der 'natürliche Weltbegriff.'" In *Grundprobleme der Phänomenologie 1910/11*, edited by I. Kern, 15–42. The Hague: Martinus Nijhoff, 1977.

Husserl, Edmund. *Ideas Pertaining to a Pure Phenomenology and to a Phenomenological Philosophy. First Book: General Introduction to a Pure Phenomenology*. Translated by F. Kersten. The Hague: Martinus Nijhoff, 1982.

Husserl, Edmund. "Philosophy as a Rigorous Science." In *Phenomenology and the Crisis of Philosophy*, edited by Q. Lauer, 71–148. New York: Harper and Row, 1965.

Jahanbegloo, Ramin. *Conversations with Isaiah Berlin*. London: Peter Halban Publishers, 1992.

Janssens, David. *Between Athens and Jerusalem. Philosophy, Prophecy and Politics in Leo Strauss's Early Thought*. Albany, NY: State University of New York Press, 2008.

Janssens, David. "A Change of Orientation: Leo Strauss's 'Comments' on Carl Schmitt Revisited." *Interpretation: A Journal of Political Philosophy* 33, no. 1 (2005): 93–104.

Jonas, Hans. *Erinnerungen*. Frankfurt am Main: Insel Verlag, 2003.

Kant, Immanuel. *Toward Perpetual Peace and Other Writings on Politics, Peace, and History*. Edited by Pauline Kleingeld. New Haven and London: Yale University Press, 2006.

Klein, Jacob. "Die griechische Logistik und die Entstehung der Algebra." *Quellen und Studien zur Geschichte der Mathematik, Astronomie und Physik*, Abteilung B, *Studien* 3, no. 1 (Berlin 1934): 18–105.

Kraemer, Joel. "The Medieval Arabic Enlightenment." In *The Cambridge Companion to Leo Strauss*, edited by Steven B. Smith, 137–70. Cambridge: Cambridge University Press, 2009.

Krüger, Gerhard. *Philosophie und Moral in der Kantischen Kritik*. Tübingen: Mohr, 1931.

Lampert, Laurence. *The Enduring Importance of Leo Strauss*. Chicago: University of Chicago Press, 2013.

Leoni, Bruno. "Giudizi di valore e scienza politica (risposta al professor Strauss)." *Il Politico* XXII, no. 1 (1957): 86–94.

Löwith, Karl. "Kierkegaard und Nietzsche." *Deutsche Vierteljahresschrift für Literaturwissenschaft und Geistesgeschichte* XI (1933): 43–66.

Mansfield, Harvey C., and Delba Winthrop. "Editors' Introduction." In *Democracy in America* by Alexis de Tocqueville, xvii–lxxxix. Chicago: University of Chicago Press, 2000.

McCormick, John P. "Fear, Technology, and the Revival of Hobbes in Weimar and National Socialist Germany." *Political Theory* 22, no. 4 (November 1994): 619–52.

Meier, Heinrich. *Carl Schmitt, Leo Strauss und "Der Begriff des Politischen,"* Dritte Auflage. Stuttgart–Weimar: J. B. Metzler, 2013.

Meier, Heinrich. *Leo Strauss and the Theologico-Political Problem*. Translated by Marcus Brainard. Cambridge: Cambridge University Press, 2006.

Meier, Heinrich. *The Lesson of Carl Schmitt: Four Chapters on the Distinction between Political Theology and Political Philosophy*. Translated by Marcus Brainard. Chicago: University of Chicago Press, 1998.

Meier, Heinrich. *Political Philosophy and the Challenge of Revealed Religion*. Translated by Robert Berman. Chicago: University of Chicago Press, 2017.

Meier, Heinrich. "Vorwort des Herausgebers." In *Gesammelte Schriften, Band 3*, Zweite Auflage, by Leo Strauss, vii–xxxviii. Stuttgart–Weimar: Verlag J. B. Metzler, 2008.

Menon, Marco. "Leo Strauss in Italy: The 'Three Waves' of Italian Strauss Studies." *Interpretation. A Journal of Political Philosophy* 46, no. 2 (Spring 2020): 187–227.

Minkov, Svetozar Y. "Hobbes as the Founder of Modern Political Thought." In *Toward* Natural Right and History. *Lectures and Essays by Leo Strauss, 1937–1946*, edited by J. A. Colen and Svetozar Minkov, 155–62. Chicago: University of Chicago Press, 2018.

Minkov, Svetozar Y. *Leo Strauss on Science*. Albany, NY: State University of New York Press, 2016.

Minowitz, Peter. *Straussophobia. Defending Leo Strauss and Straussians against Shadia Drury and Other Accusers*. Lanham, MD: Rowman & Littlefield Publishers, 2009.

Momigliano, Arnaldo. "Ermeneutica e pensiero politico classico in Leo Strauss." In *Pagine ebraiche*, 189–99. Torino: Einaudi, 1987.

Mussolini, Benito. *Scritti e discorsi di Benito Mussolini*, vol. VIII. Milano: Ulrico Hoepli, 1934.

Nietzsche, Friedrich. *Beyond Good and Evil*. Translated by W. Kaufmann. New York: Vintage Books, 1989.

Norton, Anne. *Leo Strauss and the Politics of American Empire*. New Haven, CT: Yale University Press, 2004.

Oakeshott, Michael. "Dr. Leo Strauss on Hobbes." In *Hobbes on Civil Association*, 141–58. Indianapolis, IN: Liberty Fund, 2000.

Pangle, Thomas L. *Leo Strauss. An Introduction to His Thought and Intellectual Legacy*. Baltimore, MD: Johns Hopkins University Press, 2006.

Pippin, Robert. "The Unavailability of the Ordinary." *Political Theory* 31, no. 3 (June 2003): 335–58.

Robertson, Neil G. *Leo Strauss. An Introduction*. Cambridge: Polity Press, 2021.

Rollandi, Isabel. "Claude Lafort and Leo Strauss. On a Philosophical Discourse." In *Leo Strauss and Contemporary Thought. Reading Strauss outside the Lines*, edited by Jeffrey A. Bernstein, and Jade L. Schiff, 75–107. Albany, NY: State University of New York Press, 2021.

Rorty, Richard. "That Old-Time Philosophy." *The New Republic* (April 4, 1988): 28–32.

Rosen, Stanley. *The Elusiveness of the Ordinary*. New Haven, CT: Yale University Press, 2002.

Rosen, Stanley. "Leo Strauss and the Problem of the Modern." In *The Cambridge Companion to Leo Strauss*, edited by Steven B. Smith, 119–36. Cambridge: Cambridge University Press, 2009.

Rousseau, Jean-Jacques. "Discourse on the Arts and Sciences." In *The First and Second Discourses*, edited by Roger D. Masters, 30–74. New York: St. Martin's Press, 1964.

Schmitt, Carl. *The Concept of the Political*. Translated by George Schwab. Chicago: University of Chicago Press, 2007.

Schmitt, Carl. *Political Theology. Four Chapters on the Concept of Sovereignty*. Translated by George Schwab. Chicago: University of Chicago Press, 2005.

Schmitt, Carl. *Über die drei Arten des rechtswissenschaftlichen Denkens*. Hamburg: Hanseatische Verlagsanstalt, 1934.

Schwab, George. "Introduction." In *The Concept of the Political* by Carl Schmitt, 3–16. Chicago: University of Chicago Press, 2007.

Shell, Susan, ed. *The Strauss-Krüger Correspondence. Returning to Plato through Kant*. New York: Palgrave Macmillan, 2018.

Shell, Susan. "Taking Evil Seriously: Schmitt's 'Concept of the Political' and Strauss's 'True Politics.'" In *Leo Strauss. Political Philosopher and Jewish Thinker*, edited by Kenneth L. Deutsch and Walter Nicgorski, 175–93. Lanham: Rowman & Littlefield, 1994.

Shell, Susan. "'To Spare the Vanquished and Crush the Arrogant': Leo Strauss's Lecture on 'German Nihilism.'" In *The Cambridge Companion to Leo Strauss*, edited by Steven B. Smith, 171–92. Cambridge: Cambridge University Press, 2009.

Sheppard, Eugene R. *Leo Strauss and the Politics of Exile*. Lebanon, NH: Brandeis University Press, 2006.

Smith, Steven B., ed. *The Cambridge Companion to Leo Strauss*. Cambridge: Cambridge University Press, 2009.

Smith, Steven B. *Reading Leo Strauss. Politics, Philosophy, Judaism*. Chicago: University of Chicago Press, 2006.

Tanguay, Daniel. *Leo Strauss. Une biographie intellectuelle*. Paris: Éditions Grasset & Fasquelle, 2003.

Tanguay, Daniel. "*Natural Right and History* in Preparation: Leo Strauss's Critique of Secularization." Paper presented at the conference "Leo Strauss, Religione e Liberalismo," Rome, May 13–14, 2011.

Tarcov, Nathan. "Introduction to Two Unpublished Lectures by Leo Strauss." *The Review of Politics*, 69 (2007): 513–14.

Tarcov, Nathan. *Locke's Education for Liberty*. Chicago: University of Chicago Press, 1984.

Tarcov, Nathan. "Philosophy as the Right Way of Life in *Natural Right and History*." In *Modernity and What Has Been Lost. Considerations on the Legacy of Leo Strauss*, edited by Pawel Armada and Arkadiusz Górnisiewicz, 43–52. South Bend, IN: St. Augustine's Press, 2011.

Velkley, Richard. *Heidegger, Strauss, and the Premises of Philosophy: On Original Forgetting*. Chicago: University of Chicago Press, 2011.

Wild, John. *Plato's Theory of Man. An Introduction to the Realistic Philosophy of Culture*. Cambridge, MA: Harvard University Press, 1946.
Xenos, Nicholas. *Cloaked in Virtue: Unveiling Leo Strauss and the Rhetoric of American Foreign Policy*. New York: Routledge, 2008.
Zuckert, Catherine H. "Leo Strauss: Fascist, Authoritarian, Imperialist?" *Krakowskie Studia Międzynarodowe*, no. 2 (2009): 277–91.
Zuckert, Catherine H., and Michael Zuckert. *The Truth about Leo Strauss. Political Philosophy and American Democracy*. Chicago: University of Chicago Press, 2006.

Index of Names

Abraham, 128
Adeimantos, 22, 23
Adler, Eve, viii, 238
Alexander the Great, 66, 221n83
Alpa, Guido, 226n2, 226n4, 239
Altini, Carlo, xv, 191n45, 222n92, 239
Altman, William H. F., 208n48, 226n21, 239
Anaxagoras, 11
Aquinas, Thomas, 142, 146
Aristotle, 9, 10, 11, 12, 15, 16, 28, 35, 50, 54, 55, 58, 65, 66, 67, 103, 107, 113, 116, 122, 142, 144, 148, 153, 160, 164, 165, 192n57, 200n22, 206n18, 216n37, 218n71
Armada, Pawel, 228n75, 244
Augustine, 70, 78, 83, 86, 212n44,

Bacon, Francis, 34, 60
Baillie, J. B., 219n23, 241
Bartlett, Gabriel, vii, 237
Behnegar, Nasser, xv, 198n2, 201n39, 203n69, 226n6, 228n56, 232n183, 239, 240
Benda, Julien, 107
Berlin, Isaiah, 51, 142, 185, 206n11, 206n13, 226n8, 240
Berman, Robert, 242
Bernadete, Seth, 24, 196n128, 240
Bernstein, Jeffrey A., 204n76, 243

Bloom, Allan, 205n4, 207n44, 240
Bobbio, Norberto, 141
Bodin, Jean, 112, 113
Brainard, Marcus, 242
Brown, Montgomery, xiv
Bruell, Christopher, 197n135, 228n74, 240

Caesar, Gaius Julius, 62, 63, 81
Calvin, John, 106, 122
Chacon, Rodrigo, 197n142, 240
Charybdis, 148
Churchill, Winston, 61, 144, 209n72
Ciccarelli, Pierpaolo, 196n128, 197n142, 198n144, 198n149, 199n11, 199n20, 200n20, 205n2, 240
Cicero, Marcus Tullius, 116, 147
Cohen, Arthur A., 131
Colen, J. A., ix, 220n55, 238, 239, 243
Constant de Rebecque, Benjamin Henri, 50, 51, 52, 57, 206n8, 206n10, 206n12, 240
Cooper, Barry, vii, 237
Costa, Vincenzo, xv
Cronus, 92
Cropsey, Joseph, viii, 18, 237
Cubeddu, Raimondo, xv, 205n2, 226n2, 240

247

De Ligio, Giulio, xv
Democritus, 18, 165
Descartes, René, 10, 139, 171, 197n140, 225n170
Deutsch, Kenneth L., 200n27, 244
Dilthey, Wilhelm, 75, 76
Doneson, Daniel, xv, 196n128, 240
Drury, Shadia B., 205n3, 208n48, 226n21, 240

Ebbinghaus, Julius, 71, 72, 73, 75, 79, 80, 212n30
Emberley, Peter, vii, 237
Epicurus, 165, 177, 233n199
Euclid, 11, 13

Farnesi Camellone, Mauro, xv, 228n77, 240
Fassò, Guido, 141, 226n3, 240
Faulkner, Robert, xv
Fichte, Johann Gottlieb, 59, 222n93
Fleischacker, Samuel, 240
Fontana, Biancamaria, 206n8, 240

Galilei, Galileo, 13
Galli, Carlo, 201n40, 202n46, 240
Galston, William A., 207n46, 240
Garsten, Bryan, xiv
Gentile, Giovanni, 100, 101
Ghibellini, Alberto, 195n103, 197n133, 197n142, 206n26, 207n41, 209n89, 217n50, 221n76, 224n147, 225n164, 226n21, 227n23, 227n48, 228n78, 233n194, 233n199, 241
Gildin, Hilail, ix, 239
Giorgini, Giovanni, xv, 206n7, 230n119, 241
Glaukon, 22
Górnisiewicz, Arkadiusz, 228n75, 244
Gourevitch, Victor, viii, 238
Green, Kenneth Hart, viii, 237
Gumpelino, 129, 223n114

Guslandi, Silvia, xv

Hansen, Peter, xv
Hardy, Henry, 206n11, 240
Havelock, Eric A., 210n107, 241
Hegel, Georg Wilhelm Friedrich, 3, 17, 59, 112, 164, 219n23, 241
Heidegger, Martin, 3, 6, 8, 28, 73, 76, 77, 78, 79, 87, 135, 184, 190n15, 191n33, 192n65, 198n153, 211n19, 212n50, 216n37,
Heine, Heinrich, 223n114
Hermes, 18
Hesiod, 64
Hitler, Adolf, 60, 144, 151, 204n79
Hobbes, Thomas, xi, 5, 10, 11, 12, 13, 14, 15, 16, 17, 20, 24, 26, 34, 35, 37, 38, 40, 41, 45, 47, 52, 55, 59, 60, 75, 91, 92, 93, 94, 95, 96, 97, 98, 101, 108, 109, 110, 112, 113, 114, 115, 116, 117, 118, 119, 120, 121, 122, 123, 124, 126, 129, 130, 131, 132, 133, 134, 135, 136, 138, 139, 147, 153, 154, 166, 171, 173, 176, 184, 193n69, 194n84, 195n84, 195n91, 197n140, 199n18, 200n22, 200n23, 200n25, 202n59, 207n30, 209n69, 213n56, 214n85, 215n19, 215n28, 216n37, 216n38, 220n50, 220n51, 220n55, 220n59, 221n61, 221n62, 221n65, 221n70, 221n71, 221n72, 221n74, 223n136, 225n166, 225n170, 227n41, 234n203, 241
Homer, 18, 81, 160, 195n93
Hooker, Richard, 117, 118
Horace, 45, 67, 204n85, 210n104
Howse, Robert, 208n63, 209n79, 241
Hume, David, 60
Husserl, Edmund, 16, 24, 28, 190n13, 190n15, 191n49, 192n49, 193n80, 194n80, 198n145, 213n57, 216n37, 241

Jaeger, Werner, 28
Jahanbegloo, Ramin, 226n7, 226n10, 242
Janssens, David, 199n13, 199n15, 204n79, 222n92, 242
Jaspers, Karl, 2
Jesus Christ, 78, 79, 128, 223n124,
Job, 125
Jonas, Hans, 209n81, 242
Joshua, 122

Kant, Immanuel, 50, 56, 71, 83, 126, 130, 207n39, 242
Kaufmann, Walter, 232n184, 243
Kelsen, Hans, 92, 151, 152
Kern, I., 241
Kersten, F., 241
Kierkegaard, Soren, 3
Klein, Jacob, 16, 20, 24, 28, 79, 86, 87, 154, 193n80, 202n59, 203n74, 206n26, 212n30, 232n158, 242
Klein, Susanne, 189n5
Kleingeld, Pauline, 242
Kraemer, Joel, 233n198, 233n199, 242
Krüger, Gerhard, xii, xv, 5, 43, 46, 63, 70, 71, 72, 73, 74, 75, 77, 78, 79, 80, 81, 82, 83, 84, 85, 86, 87, 89, 90, 92, 94, 95, 97, 98, 99, 100, 101, 102, 106, 130, 184, 187, 199n14, 203n72, 211n7, 211n8, 212n30, 212n44, 215n9, 216n29, 242
Kuhn, Helmut, 147, 148

Lagarde, Paul de, 126, 127, 128, 129, 130, 131, 222n92, 223n111
Lampert, Laurence, 195n103, 205n2, 225n164, 242
Lapini, Walter, xv
Lastra, Antonio, 228n77, 240
Lauer, Q., 241
Leoni, Bruno, 141, 142, 225n1, 226n5, 242

Lerner, Ralph, xv
Locke, John, 50, 55, 59, 60, 153
Lomax, J. Harvey, 198n1, 238
Löwith, Karl, xi, 2, 3, 4, 5, 6, 7, 8, 9, 10, 17, 26, 27, 28, 62, 63, 65, 67, 81, 98, 99, 100, 136, 137, 138, 143, 184, 187, 189n5, 189n6, 189n9, 190n10, 190n15, 190n27, 190n28, 191n29, 191n30, 191n31, 191n32, 191n33, 191n42, 191n45, 191n46, 191n47, 192n50, 192n51, 192n52, 192n53, 192n63, 208n49, 208n60, 209n79, 210n91, 210n92, 210n96, 210n101, 210n104, 224n156, 224n157, 224n158, 224n163, 230n119, 235n16, 242
Lucretius, 223n135,

Mably, Gabriel Bonnot de, 51
Machiavelli, Niccolò, 25, 69, 88, 129, 138, 202n46, 211n8, 219n22, 224n139, 225n166
Macpherson, C. B., 241
Maimonides, 73, 78, 142, 158, 160, 163, 165, 166, 170, 177, 179, 187, 211n22
Mannheim, Karl, 86, 211n13
Mansfield, Harvey C., xiv, xv, 206n5, 242
Masala, Antonio, 230n119, 241
Masters, Roger D., 217n47, 244
McCormick, John P., 199n18, 242
McKeen, Gayle, xiv
Meier, Heinrich, vii, viii, ix, 189n2, 194n84, 197n133, 197n135, 198n153, 198n1, 198n11, 200n27, 200n29, 201n29, 201n36, 201n40, 202n46, 202n51, 202n59, 203n59, 204n79, 204n81, 204n86, 211n7, 211n8, 216n31, 217n48, 219n22, 224n153, 232n183, 237, 238, 242, 243

250 / Index of Names

Meier, Wiebke, vii, 237
Meld Shell, Susan, xii, xiv, xv, 200n27, 203n72, 208n60, 209n79, 211n7, 217n51, 218n1, 226n19, 227n25, 244
Menon, Marco, xv, 205n2, 226n2, 230n119, 241, 243
Mess, Derek, xv
Minkov, Svetozar, vii, ix, xv, 193n69, 201n45, 202n52, 219n11, 219n17, 220n55, 221n86, 223n118, 224n157, 237, 238, 239, 243
Minowitz, Peter, 205n1, 207n47, 226n20, 243
Molesworth, William, 241
Momigliano, Arnaldo, 141, 225n1, 243
Mommsen, Theodor, 127
Monceri, Flavia, 230n119, 241
Monserrat-Molas, Josep, 228n77, 240
Moses, 123, 223n124
Moses, Walter, 144, 226n18
Mussolini, Benito, 63, 100, 101, 217n55, 243

Nah, Darren, xv
Nicgorski, Walter, 200n27, 244
Nietzsche, Friedrich, xii, 3, 4, 5, 7, 9, 17, 27, 28, 38, 58, 59, 60, 63, 76, 77, 81, 82, 101, 106, 127, 135, 136, 153, 162, 172, 174, 190n15, 205n2, 213n69, 230n119, 232n184, 243
Norton, Anne, 205n3, 243

Oakeshott, Michael, 201n33, 243
Occam, William of, 220n53
Odysseus, 18
Orwin, Alexander, xv
Orwin, Clifford, xv

Pangle, Thomas L., viii, ix, 205n4, 206n5, 207n44, 238, 239, 243

Pangloss, 233n199
Paul of Tarsus, 127
Phalen, Lynn, xv
Pericles, 81
Pippin, Robert, xiv, 207n34, 213n60, 226n14, 243
Plato, xii, 5, 6, 9, 10, 11, 12, 13, 14, 15, 16, 17, 20, 22, 24, 26, 28, 32, 42, 43, 44, 47, 50, 54, 55, 57, 58, 64, 65, 66, 67, 69, 70, 71, 73, 74, 75, 76, 78, 81, 82, 83, 84, 87, 92, 93, 95, 97, 98, 102, 113, 116, 142, 143, 144, 148, 153, 158, 162, 163, 165, 172, 192n54, 193n66, 194n84, 195n84, 203n73, 206n25, 212n44, 215n11, 215n12, 215n14, 215n25, 216n37, 216n38, 217n43, 217n44, 218n68

Rice Martini, Martha, xiv
Robertson, Neil G., 191n34, 196n122, 197n134, 197n142, 234n4, 243
Rollandi, Isabel, 204n76, 243
Rorty, Richard, 210n6, 243
Roth, Michael S., viii, 238
Rosen, Stanley, 187, 196n128, 235n15, 243
Rousseau, Jean-Jacques, 17, 51, 52, 113, 166, 215n19, 217n47, 244
Ruderman, Richard S., viii, 239,

Saul, 122, 123
Schacter, Rory, xv
Schelling, Friedrich Wilhelm Joseph, 59
Schiff, Jade L., 204n76, 243
Schiller, Friedrich, 28, 213n58
Schmidt, Anna, xv, 211n7, 211n13, 211n15
Schmitt, Carl, 31, 32, 33, 35, 36, 37, 38, 39, 40, 41, 42, 43, 44, 45, 46, 47, 50, 92, 95, 96, 99, 101, 130, 152,

153, 154, 194n84, 198n11, 199n11, 199n18, 200n25, 200n27, 200n29, 201n36, 201n42, 201n43, 201n45, 202n46, 202n55, 202n59, 203n59, 203n62, 203n66, 204n79, 204n86, 206n9, 244
Scholem, Gershom, 144, 207n47, 226n22
Schwab, George, 202n46, 244
Scylla, 148
Sensen, Kathryn, xv
Sheppard, Eugene R., 205n3, 208n60, 222n92, 244
Sieber-Gasser, Charlotte, xv
Silverthorne, Michael, 200n22, 241
Sinclair, Elsa M., viii, ix, 198n1, 202n46, 238, 239
Smith, Steven B., xiv, 196n128, 205n4, 207n45, 207n46, 208n49, 208n60, 209n87, 211n19, 217n51, 222n92, 232n183, 233n198, 240, 242, 243, 244
Socrates, xii, 6, 10, 11, 14, 19, 20, 21, 22, 24, 25, 28, 47, 75, 76, 81, 82, 102, 162, 192n65, 194n80, 216n39, 218n68, 219n9
Spinoza, Baruch, 15, 37, 178, 179, 180, 181, 189n1, 234n225
Suarez, Francisco, 118, 220n53

Tanguay, Daniel, xiv, 111, 113, 114, 121, 136, 218n1, 219n10, 219n19, 224n155, 232n162, 244
Tarcov, Nathan, xiv, 209n71, 219n11, 228n75, 244

Thucydides, 164
Tocqueville, Alexis de, 50, 206n5, 242
Trout, Bernhardt, xiv, xv
Tuck, Richard, 200n22, 241
Tucker, George E., 189n5

Veith, Jerome, 211n7
Velkley, Richard L., 208n49, 211n19, 214n91, 235n8, 238, 244
Virgil, 60, 62, 63, 99, 208n65, 217n52
Voltaire, 233n199

Waller, A. R., 241
Weber, Max, 141, 151, 168, 226n6
Weinberger, Jerry, 225n165, 238
Wellhausen, Julius, 127
Wild, John, 7, 191n43, 216n37, 245
Wingo, Ajume, xiv
Winthrop, Delba, 206n5, 242

Xenophon, 54, 58, 185, 207n47
Xenos, Nicholas, 205n3, 208n48, 226n21, 245

Yaffe, Martin D., viii, 211n13, 211n15, 239

Zank, Michael, vii, 222n96, 223n114, 237
Zeus, 93
Zuckert, Catherine H., 144, 145, 204n87, 205n1, 205n4, 208n49, 209n72, 210n102, 226n22, 238, 245
Zuckert, Michael, 205n1, 205n4, 208n49, 210n102, 245

www.ingramcontent.com/pod-product-compliance
Ingram Content Group UK Ltd.
Pitfield, Milton Keynes, MK11 3LW, UK
UKHW041934140426
5217IPUK00014B/468